INTRODUCTORY MACROECONOMICS
A TEXTBOOK FOR CLASS XII
(CBSE)

ZAHIDA JABEEN

M.A, M.Phil. (Gold Medallist) B.Ed.NET(UGC) Qualified for lectureship (Economics), Ex- Headmistress.

A Senior Secondary Teacher (PGT)

International Indian School, Riyadh K.S.A

INDIA · SINGAPORE · MALAYSIA

PREFACE

I would like to thank The Almighty for granting me knowledge, experience, and capacity to write a text book of Economics. I am indebted to the Almighty without whose blessing I would have not been able to write this book.

This book is written as per syllabus of grade XII CBSE. It is an attempt to explain concepts of macroeconomics in simple and easy way with the help of various examples, graphs, pictures and tables.

I would like to express my sincere gratitude to my parents, husband, children, students and all near and dear who have directly or indirectly helped me grow as a professional.

It is a small effort to make macroeconomics easily understandable to the young readers. This book is as per latest pattern of CBSE, practice question and answer has been added after each lesson which would be helpful for the students to prepare for Board Examination. Some extra information is also provided for the students to have better knowledge about the subject.

I am highly thankful to Notion Publication for their effort in printing this book.

ZAHIDA JABEEN
M. A, M.Phil. B. Ed. NET qualified. Gold Medallist (more than 25 years of teaching experience).

ECONOMICS (CODE NO. 030)

Units		Marks	Periods
Part A	**Introductory Macroeconomics**		
1	National Income and Related Aggregates	10	30
2	Money and Banking	06	15
3	Determination of Income and Employment	12	30
4	Government Budget and the Economy	06	17
5	Balance of Payments	06	18
		40	
Part B	**Indian Economic Development**		
6	Development Experience (1947-90) and Economic Reforms since 1991	12	28
7	Current Challenges facing Indian Economy	20	50
8	Development Experience of India – A Comparison with Neighbours	08	12
	Theory Paper (40 + 40 = 80 Marks)	**40**	
			200
Part C	**Project Work**	**20**	**20**

Project: 20 Marks

Part A: Introductory Macroeconomics

Unit 1: National Income and Related Aggregates   30 Periods

What is Macroeconomics?

Basic concepts in macroeconomics: consumption goods, capital goods, final goods, intermediate goods; stocks and flows; gross investment and depreciation.

Circular flow of income (two sector model); Methods of calculating National Income - Value Added or Product method, Expenditure method, Income method.

Circular flow of income (two sector model); Methods of calculating National Income - Value Added or Product method, Expenditure method, Income method.

Unit 2: Money and Banking   15 Periods

Money – meaning and functions, supply of money - Currency held by the public and net demand deposits held by commercial banks.

Money creation by the commercial banking system.

Central bank and its functions (example of the Reserve Bank of India): Bank of issue, Govt. Bank, Banker's Bank, Control of Credit through Bank Rate, Cash Reserve Ratio (CRR), Statutory Liquidity Ratio (SLR), Repo Rate and Reverse Repo Rate, Open Market Operations, Margin requirement.

Unit 3: Determination of Income and Employment   30 Periods

Aggregate demand and its components.

Propensity to consume and propensity to save (average and marginal). Short-run equilibrium output; investment multiplier and its mechanism. Meaning of full employment and involuntary unemployment.

Problems of excess demand and deficient demand; measures to correct them - changes in government spending, taxes and money supply.

Unit4: Government Budget   17 marks

Government budget - meaning, objectives and components.

Classification of receipts - revenue receipts and capital receipts. Classification of expenditure – revenue expenditure and capital expenditure.

Balanced, Surplus and Deficit Budget – measures of government deficit.

Unit 5: Balance of Payments

18 Periods Balance of payments account - meaning and components; Balance of payments – Surplus and Deficit Foreign exchange rate - meaning of fixed and flexible rates and managed floating. Determination of exchange rate in a free market, Merits and demerits of flexible and fixed exchange rate. Managed Floating exchange rate system.

CONTENTS

UNIT: 1 National Income Accounting and its Aggregates 12

1.1 National Income Accounting and Related Aggregates 12

1.2 Difference between Microeconomics and Macroeconomics 12

1.3 Primary and Secondary Inputs 13

1.4 Factor Payment &Transfer Payment 13

1.5 Important Concept of National Income 14

1.6 Difference between Current Transfer and Capital Transfer 15

1.7 Consumption Goods and Capital Goods 15

1.8 Difference between Intermediate Goods and Final Goods 15

1.9 Difference between Final Goods and Intermediate Goods on the Basis of
End Use of Goods and Services 16

1.10 Difference between Intermediate Expenditure and Final Expenditure 16

1.11 Economic Territory or Domestic Territory 17

1.12 Real and Nominal National Income 17

1.13 Who is a Normal Resident of a Country? 18

1.14 Distinguish between Stock and Flow Variables 18

1.15 Circular Flow of Income in Two Sector 19

1.16 Circular Flow of Income in Two Sector with Capital Market 20

1.17 Circular Flow of Income in Three Sector (Not in syllabus) 20

1.18 Concepts Related to Calculation Of National Income 21

1.19 Factor Cost and Market Price 22

1.20 Tax and Subsidy 23

1.21 Net Factor Income from Abroad 23

1.21 Basic Concept of Formulas Related to NNP_{fc} 24

1.22 Distinguish between the Following 25

1.23 Value of Output vs. Value Added 25

1.24 Value Added Approach Eliminates Double Counting 27

1.25 Numerical of Value Added Method 29

1.26 Income Method 32

1.27 Numericals of Income Method 35

1.28 Expenditure Method 38

1.30   Numerical of Expenditure Method.. 40

1.31   Net National Disposable income(NNDI) and Gross National Disposable Income(GNDI)......................... 43

1.32   Domestic Income can be divided into two parts 43

1.31   Conversion of Nominal GNP into Real GNP 43

1.32   Is GDP or GNP a correct Index of welfare?... 44

1.33   Green GNP.. 45

1.34   Items Include in Domestic Income and National Income... 45

1.35   Items which are not included in Calculation of Domestic Income and National Income...................... 46

1.36   Main Uses of National Income Accounting... 47

1.37   Important Formulae 47

1.38   Terms to Remember: [Understanding terms having same meaning].. 48

1.39   Revision of Key Points 49

1.40   Practice Question-Answers 50

UNIT: 2 Money and Banking.. **87**

2.1   Evolution of Money 87

2.2   Important Concept 88

2.3   Drawbacks of Barter System 90

2.4   Functions of Money: "Money is a Matter of Function Four, A Medium, A Measure,
A Standard, A Store" 91

2.5   Qualities of Good Money.. 91

2.6   Classification of Money 92

2.7   Definition of Money 93

2.8   Money Supply and its Components 94

2.9   Demand for Money... 94

2.10   Banking.. 95

2.11   Functions of Commercial Bank 96

2.12   Central Bank 98

2.13   Distinguish between Commercial Bank and Central Bank 100

2.14   Some Schemes of Government 100

UNIT: 3 Determination of Income and Employment... **116**

3.1   Approaches of Macro Economics 116

3.2   Keynesian Theory of Income and Employment 117

3.3   Components of Aggregate Demand 117

3.4   Aggregate Supply (AS) 119

3.5   Consumption Function 119

3.5   Keynesian Psychological Law of Consumption 120

3.6   Propensity to consume are of two types: APC & MPC 120

3.7   Features of Average Propensity to Consume 120

3.8   Marginal Propensity to Consume (MPC) 121

3.9   Features of MPC 121

3.10 Distinguish Between APC and MPC 121

3.11 Saving Function (Propensity to Save) 122

3.12 Break-Even Point 122

3.13 Relation between Income and saving 122

3.14 Average Propensity to Save and Marginal Propensity to Save (APS & MPS) 123

3.15 Marginal Propensity to Save (MPS) 123

3.16 Features of MPS 124

3.17 Difference Between APS and MPS 124

3.18 Relationship Between APC and APS, MPC and MPS 124

3.19 Numericals 125

3.20 Derivation of Saving Function from Consumption Function with the help Diagram ... 128

3.21 Derive Consumption Function from Saving Function 128

3.22 Investment Function 129

3.23 Investment is of Two Types 129

3.24 Planned Savings (Ex-ante Savings) and Planned Investment (Ex-ante Investment) ... 130

3.25 Actual Savings (Ex-post Savings) and Actual Investment (Ex-post Investment) 130

3.26 Equilibrium of an Economy 130

3.27 Determination of Equilibrium Level of Income (S = I) 131

3.28 Adjustment in Output to Achieve Equilibrium 131

3.29 Determination of National Income Equilibrium through AD and AS Approach 131

3.30 Short Run Equilibrium Level of Output 132

3.31 Effective Demand 132

3.32 Paradox of Thrift 132

3.33 Deriving the Value of Equilibrium Output and Aggregate Demand at Fixed Price and Rate of Interest 133

3.34 Numerical on Equilibrium Level of Income, Consumption and Investment 133

3.35 Investment Multiplier (K) 136

3.36 Graphic Presentation of Investment Multiplier 137

3.37   Relationship between Multiplier and MPC 137

3.38   Relationship between Multiplier and MPS 137

3.39   Minimum and Maximum Value of Multiplier 138

3.40   Numerical on Investment Multiplier 138

3.41   Voluntary Unemployment/Full Employment/Involuntary Unemployment 140

3.42   Full Employment Equilibrium and Under-Employment Equilibrium 140

3.43   Deficient Demand and Deflationary Gap 141

3.44   Excess Demand and Inflationary Gap 143

3.45   NOTE: Bank Rate / Marginal Standing Facility 144

3.46   Distinguish Between Inflationary Gap and Deflationary Gap 145

3.47   Points to remember 145

3.48   Important Formulae and Concepts 146

3.49   Practice Question Answer 147

UNIT: 4   Government Budget and the Economy 164

4.1   Government Budget 164

4.2   Element of Budget 164

4.3   Objectives of Government Budget 164

4.4   Importance of Budget 165

4.5   Types of Budget 165

4.6   Components of Budget 166

4.7   Debt Creating and Non-Debt Creating Capital Receipt 168

4.8   Difference Between Direct and Indirect Tax 168

4.9   Difference Between Revenue and Capital Receipt 168

4.10   Distinguish between Tax and Non-Tax Revenue 169

4.12   Budget Expenditure 169

4.13   Revenue Expenditure 169

4.14   Capital Expenditure 170

4.15   Distinguish between Revenue Expenditure and Capital Expenditure 170

4.16   Balanced Budget: Surplus Budget: Deficit Budget 170

4.17   Surplus Budget 171

4.18   Deficit Budget 171

4.19   Types of Deficit Budget 172

4.20   Revenue Deficit 172

4.21   Fiscal Deficit 173

4.22   Primary Deficit 174

4.23   Goods and Service Tax 174

4.24   Practice Question Answer 175

4.25   Question-Answers (Multiple-Choice) 176

UNIT: 5   Balance of Payment and Foreign Exchange 191

5.1   Balance of Payment 191

5.2   Structure of BOP 191

5.3   Components of Balance of Payment Accounts 191

5.4   Components of Capital Account of BOP 192

5.5   Official Reserve Account 192

5.6   Difference Between Visible and Invisible Items of BOP 192

5.7   Current Account of BOP 193

5.8   Capital Account of BOP 193

5.9   Difference between Current Account of BOP and Capital Account of BOP 193

5.10   Difference Between Balance of Current Account and Balance of Trade 193

5.11   Distinguish between Balance of Trade and Balance of Payment 194

5.12   Differentiate Between Current Account of BOP and Balance of Payment 194

5.13   Difference Between Autonomous Items and Accommodating Items of BOP ... 194

5.14   Causes of Disequilibrium in Balance of Payment 195

5.15   Methods to Correct Disequilibrium in BOP 195

5.16   Relationship between National Income and BOP 196

5.17   Foreign Exchange 196

5.18   Foreign Exchange Rate 196

5.19   Foreign Exchange Market 196

5.20   Two Types of Foreign Exchange Market 197

5.21   Difference Between Spot Market and Forward Market 197

5.22   Nominal and Real Exchange Rate 197

5.23   Functions of a Foreign Exchange Market 197

5.24   Sources of Demand for Foreign Exchange 197

5.25   Reasons or 'Rise in Demand' for Foreign Exchange 198

5.26   Demand Curve of Foreign Exchange is Downward Sloping 198

5.27   Sources of Supply of Foreign Exchange 199

5.28 Relationship Between Rate of Foreign Exchange and Supply 199

5.29 Reason for Increase in Supply When Rate of Foreign Exchange Rises 199

5.30 Determination of Foreign Exchange Rate 199

5.31 Fixed and Flexible Exchange Rate 200

5.32 Difference Between Fixed Exchange Rate and Flexible Exchange Rate 201

5.33 Managed Floating Exchange Rate 201

5.34 Crawling Peg System 202

5.35 Central Bank and Foreign Exchange Rate 202

5.36 Appreciation and Revaluation of Currency 202

5.37 Depreciation and Devaluation 203

5.38 Points to Remember 203

5.39 Practice Question Answer 204

Practice Paper – 1 .... *221*

Answers of Practice Paper – 1 .... *227*

Practice Paper – 2 .... *231*

Answers of Practice Paper – 2 .... *237*

Practice Paper – 3 .... *240*

Answers of Practice Paper – 3 .... *245*

UNIT: 1

NATIONAL INCOME ACCOUNTING AND ITS AGGREGATES

1.1 National Income Accounting and Related Aggregates

Macroeconomics is the study of economy as a whole and its aggregates. Such as National Income, aggregate saving and investment, general price level, total employment, poverty etc.

Fig 1.1

Prof. J.M. Keynes

The famous book of J.M. Keynes "General Theory of Employment, Interest and Money" was published in 1936 which brought revolution in economic thoughts called the **Keynesian Revolution**. He gave theory to control Business cycle with the background of Great Depression of 1929 to 1933. He is known as father of Modern Macro Economics.

Importance of Macroeconomics

- It helps to determine National income and employment of complicated modern economy.
- It helps to achieve the goal of economic growth, higher level of GDP and higher level of employment.
- It explains how Balance of Payment is determined. It helps to know the causes of deficit balance of payment and measures to control.
- It helps to solve the economic problems like poverty, unemployment, business cycle etc.
- It helps to formulate economic policies and International policies.
- It helps in bringing stability in price and methods to control Inflation and deflation.

Macroeconomics mainly deals with determination of income and employment therefore it is also known as "THEORY OF INCOME AND EMPLOYMENT".

1.2 Difference between Microeconomics and Macroeconomics

Micro Economics (Price theory)	Macro Economics (Theory of Income and Employment)
It is study of individual economic unit of an economy.	It is study of economy as a whole and it's aggregate.
Demand and supply are the main tools.	Aggregate demand and aggregate supply are the main tool.
Its central problem is price determination and allocation of resources.	It determines level of Income and employment
It studies about consumers equilibrium and producers equilibrium.	It determines economy's equilibrium level of income, employment and output.
Deals with individual Income, individual price and output of individual firm or unit.	Deals with national income, aggregate output, and general price level.
Price is the main determinant	Income is the main determinant
Solves central problem of what to produce, how to produce and for whom to Produce.	Solve the central problem of full employment of resources in the economy.

1.3 Primary and Secondary Inputs

Economic Growth: The process of sustainable increase in real income over a period of time.

Per Capita Income: $\dfrac{National\ Income}{Mid\ Year\ Population}$ 

Factors of Production: Land, Labour, Capital, Entrepreneur

Primary Inputs (Factor Inputs): It renders services (provides factor services). Example: Land, labour, Capital, Enterprise

Secondary Inputs (Non-Factor Inputs): These inputs get merged in the process of production: Example: raw materials, Seed, water, fertilizers etc.

FACTORS OF PRODUCTION:

Land: All natural resources which are free gift of nature. Land includes soil, rivers, water, forests, desert, sea etc.

Labour: The person who provides physical and mental effort for producing goods and services in an economy. It provides expertise, manpower and services to add value to the raw material or to convert inputs into output.

Capital: It is the assets used in the process of producing goods and services. It includes buildings, machine, tools, equipment etc.

Entrepreneur: An individual who starts a business by assembling all the factors of production. He is risk taker. He gets profit for his efforts.

1.4 Factor Payment &Transfer Payment

Factor Payment/Factor Income	Transfer Payment/Transfer Income
It includes rent, wages, profit and interest, retirement pension etc.	It includes gift, subsidy, donation, scholarship, old age pension etc.
It is earned income.	It is unearned income.
It is bilateral.	It is unilateral.
Money is received after providing services.	Money is received without providing any service.
It is Included in calculating National Income and Domestic Income	It is not included while calculating National Income and domestic income.

1.5 Important Concept of National Income

Economy: A system by which people get their earning.

Or

Economy is the collection of producing units located within a geographical area or a country.

That is why it is called Indian Economy, Russian Economy, British Economy, Chinese Economy etc.

Three parts of an Economy:

1. Production – An activity which produces material goods and services.

OR

Which increases value of commodities already produced (adds value to existing commodity).

Example: Production of wheat, rice, cloth, furniture, bread. Services of Doctors, Teachers, Bankers, Managers etc.

2. Consumption – The process of using up goods and services for direct satisfaction of individuals or for collective satisfaction of society.

e.g,-food, clothes, house, fridge, furniture, TV, services of doctors, teachers, bankers etc.

3. Capital Formation – Net addition to capital stock of an economy during a given period. In an economy production in a year is not consumed fully so that production which is not consumed in the same year and kept for future consumption is called Investment or Capital formation e.g- Machine, factories, transport equipment's etc.

1.6 Difference between Current Transfer and Capital Transfer

Current Transfer	Capital Transfer
Transfer from current income of the payer added to the current income of the recipient.	Transfer in cash or kind for the purpose of investment or saving to the donor.
Recurring or regular in nature	Non-recurring or irregular in nature
Scholarship, Old age Pension, subsidy	Investment, Grants, War Damages, Capital gain

1.7 Consumption Goods and Capital Goods

Consumption Goods or consumer goods: Goods which are used by ultimate consumers or which meet the immediate needs of the consumers directly.

Example: Furniture, food, cars milk, chair fruits etc.

It is further classified as Durable, Non-durable and semi durable.

Durable Goods-Goods which are used again and again. House, Car, Furniture, Fridge

Semi-Durable Goods –Goods used for some years or months like shoes, books, dresses etc.

Non-Durable Goods (Perishable Goods)-Goods of single use like milk, fruits, bread coal etc.

Capital Goods: The goods which are used for producing other goods.

Example: Machine, tools, Building, equipment etc.

These goods make production possible.

They undergo wear and tear and need repair and replacement.

They are backbone of production.

1.8 Difference between Intermediate Goods and Final Goods

Intermediate Goods	Final Goods
The goods which are used as raw material for production or for resale in the same year or the goods which get consumed up during the process of production.	The goods which are meant for consumption by households or investment by entrepreneurs or individuals.

They are used up during the process of production. They undergo transformation during the process of production.	They do not undergo further transformation. They remain as it is.
They are not included in calculation of national Income and domestic income.	They are included in calculation of national Income and domestic income.
E.g. Sugar, milk and flour for Making biscuit. Expenditure on maintenance of office building. Chalk, duster, markers purchased by a school. Services of a lawyer for a firm.	E.g. Milk, Bread bought by household, Furniture, computer purchased by a firm (investment). Machine purchased by a firm. Car purchased by a taxi owner.

1.9 Difference between Final Goods and Intermediate Goods on the Basis of End Use of Goods and Services

Goods	Final Goods		Intermediate Goods
	Consumption Goods	**Capital Goods(investment)**	
Vehicle (Car/Jeep/Truck, motorcycle)	Purchased by household for personal use.	Purchased by Taxi-Driver to use as a taxi	Purchased by a dealer for re-sale. Purchased by a firm for transportation.
Sewing Machine/Fridge/ Mixer grinder/Food Processor	Purchased by household for personal use.	Purchased by a tailor/ shopkeeper/restaurant owner for business use.	Purchased by a dealer for resale. Purchased by the government/firm for using in production.
Wheat/Rice/Millets/ Sugar/Milk	Purchased by household for personal use.	Unsold with the Shopkeeper at the end of the year.	Purchased for resale by shopkeepers. Purchased for making some dish to sell by the restaurant.
Pen/ Pencil/ Chalk/ Marker	Purchased by household or students for personal use.	Unsold with the shopkeeper till the end of year.	Purchased by the school/ College / University for teaching purpose.

1.10 Difference between Intermediate Expenditure and Final Expenditure

Intermediate Expenditure (consumption)	**Final Expenditure (consumption)**
Expenditure done by firm on purchase of raw materials or goods for resale in the same year.	Expenditure done on purchase of goods and services meant for final consumption or investment.
Not included in calculating National Income or Domestic Income	Included while estimating National Income or Domestic income

1.11 Economic Territory or Domestic Territory

The geographical area ruled by a government within which people, goods and capital can move freely.

Items included in Domestic Territory

1. Area lying within the geographical and political boundary.

2. Ships, Aircrafts owned and operated by the residents between two or more countries.

3. Fishing vessels, oil and natural gas rigs and floating platforms operated by the residents of a country in the International water.

4. Embassies, Consulates and military establishments of the country located abroad. Example: Indian Embassy located in Japan, USA, UK, Russia is a part of domestic territory of India. Military establishment of USA in Saudi Arabia is a part of domestic territory USA.

Items Not Included In Domestic Territory

- Foreign Embassies located in a country. Example: Russian Embassy in India or British Embassy and Consulate in India. They are called Territorial enclaves.

- International organizations like, Red Cross, UNICEF, WHO etc. located in India are not a part of Domestic territory of India.

1.12 Real and Nominal National Income

Real National Income (National Income at constant Price)

- If goods and services produced in a country in a year are evaluated on base year price, it is called National Income at constant prices or Real National Income.

- It is affected only by change in output only because price is constant (base year price).

- It reflects actual development of the economy.

- It helps to make International comparison.

- It helps to make year to year comparison of the output.

Year	Output	Price	National Income(Price X Output)
2000	1000	₹ 5	₹ 5000
2005	2000	₹ 5	₹ 10,000
2010	500	₹ 5	₹ 2500

NOMINAL NATIONAL INCOME (National Income at current Prices)

- ➢ If goods and services produced in a country in a year are evaluated at current year prices, it is called Nominal National Income.

- ➢ It is affected by two factors change in price and change in output.

- ➢ Nominal national income can be deceptive as it may increase due to increase in price even when production has decreased as in the year 2010 in the example given below.

- ➢ National income in money term may increase because of increase in price. (Current price)

Year	Output	Price	National income
2000	1000	₹ 5	₹ 5000
2005	1000	₹ 8	₹ 8000
2010	500	₹ 20	₹ 10000

1.13 Who is a Normal Resident of a Country?

- A person or an institution who resides in a country for more than a year and whose economic interest lies in that country.
- Period of stay should be at least one year or more but not applied to students studying abroad or medical patients being treated abroad even though they continue to stay more than a year.
- Normal resident can be Individual or Institution.
- It includes both citizens and non-citizens residing in the country for more than a year.
- Local employees in foreign embassies located in their countries.

Example: Indians working in British Embassy.

- International bodies like WHO, Red Cross etc. are not resident of the country in which these organizations operate but are treated as residents of International Territory.
- Workers from across the border who cross border in the morning to work in the other country and return home in the evening are not residents of the country where they work.

Example: Indian working in Bhutan/Nepal and coming home at night to India.

1.14 Distinguish between Stock and Flow Variables

Flow Variable:

A quantity which is measured over a period of time.

It has time dimension like hours, days, weeks.

It is dynamic concept.

Example: National Income, Interest, Savings, Investment, Change in stock, Expenditure, change in inventory, Capital formation, Domestic Income, Government Revenue, Exports and imports, etc.

It is like a **video** taken by a camera which shows picture of a specific duration.

Stock Variable:

A quantity which is measured at a point of time.

It has no time dimension like 1st January 5 pm 2020.

It is static concept.

Example: Capital, Wealth, Money supply, Foreign Debt, stock, inventory, Labour force, Total employment

It is like a **still photo** taken by a camera which shows picture of a particular moment.

Note: Wealth (accumulated savings) is a stock variable but whereas saving is flow.

1.15 Circular Flow of Income in Two Sector

Circular flow of income refers to the continuous flow of goods, services and money between different sectors in cyclic way. It is circular in nature because the movement of goods, services and money is in a circle coming back to the starting point again.

There are four sectors between which goods, services and money circulates; they are -Producing sector, Consuming sector, Government and Rest of the World(Abroad).

Here we are studying in context to two sector (closed economy) where there is no government and no exports and imports

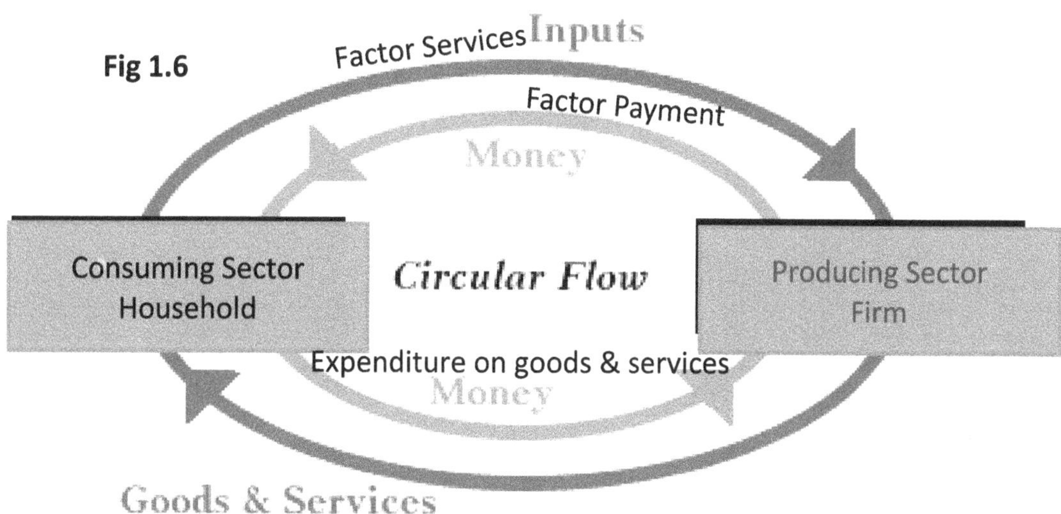

Let us assume that in an economy there is only two sector the producing sector that is **FIRM** and consuming sector that is **HOUSEHOLD.** We assume that it is a closed economy (no export and import) no government, no saving and no investment.

The firm hires factors of production i.e, land, labour, capital and enterprise for producing goods and services from the households. Goods are produced in the **FIRM**. In return of their factor services, they are paid factor payment in the form of rent, wages, interest and profit to the household. Money moves from the firm to the household.

Household needs goods and services for consumption which they purchase from the firm by paying money. Thus, the money which was with households goes back to the Firm (as expenditure on goods and services).

Again, goods and services are produced in the firm with the help of factors of production and money is paid to them for their services. Hence money will move from the firm to the households again.

Again households need goods and services which they will purchase from the firm, so money goes back to firm again. This process continues and it is called Circular flow of income in two sectors.

Outer two arrows in the diagram shows real flow (goods & services) and inner two arrow shows money flow.

Money Flow (Nominal Flow) –This refers to the flow of money in the form of factor payment like rent, wages, interest, profit and consumption expenditure on goods and services.

Real Flow (Physical Flow)- This refers to the flow of goods and services in the form of land, labour, capital and enterprise from household to firm and goods and services from firm to household.

1.16 Circular Flow of Income in Two Sector with Capital Market

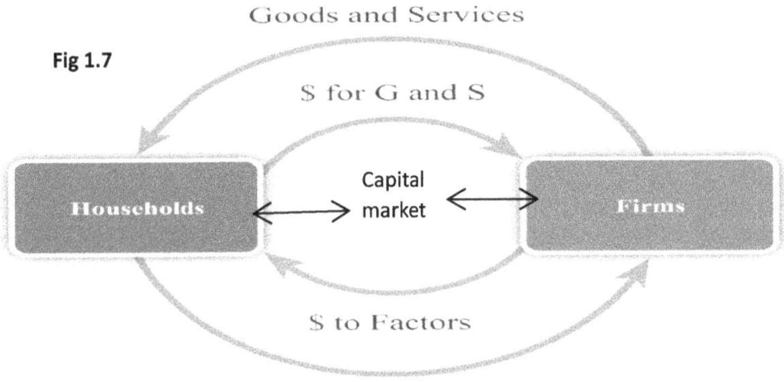

Let us assume that there are only two sectors in an economy, the producing sector i.e., Firm and the consuming sector i.e., household.

❖ All saving and borrowings are channeled through Capital Market or Financial Institution.

❖ All money earned is not spend but a part is saved in Capital market, firm saves with the aim to meet depreciation cost or expansion and diversifying its product. Household saves to meet future needs.

❖ Firm or household sometime borrows from financial market.

❖ Household provides services to the firm and gets factor payment i.e., rent. wages. Interest etc. money moves from firm to household.

❖ Goods are purchased by household, so the goods move to households and money moves to the firm.

❖ This is continuous process of movement of money from firm to household and household to firm.

❖ But some amount is saved in the capital market that is leakage from circular flow of income.

Leakage and Injections

Leakage: It is the amount of money which is withdrawn from the circular flow of income. E.g.-saving, taxes and spending on imports.

Injections: It is the amount of money which is added in the flow of income. E.g., investment earning, government earning and export earnings.

1.17 Circular Flow of Income in Three Sector (Not in syllabus)

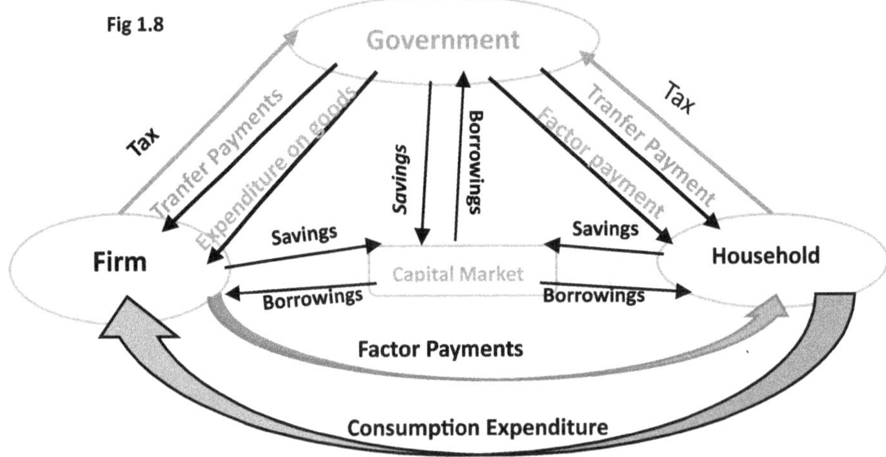

Let us assume that in an economy there are three sector the producing sector that is **FIRM** and consuming sector that is **HOUSEHOLD and the Government.** We assume that it is a closed economy so there is no export and imports.

The firm hires factors of production i.e, land, labour, capital and enterprise for producing goods and services from the households. Goods are produced in the **FIRM**. In return of their factor services, they are paid factor payment in the form of rent, wages, interest and profit to the household. Money moves from the firm to the household. People work in government sector so they get payment in return of their services from government. Government gives transfer payment to household in the form old age pension, subsidies etc. Household pays tax, fees, fines etc. to government. Firm also pay tax and fee to the government. Government gives subsidies to firm. Government purchase goods and services from the firm and make payment for it. Government, firm and household they all save money in capital market and when required they take loan from the capital market.

Household needs goods and services for consumption which they purchase from the firm by paying money. Thus, the money which was with households goes back to the Firm (as expenditure on goods and services).

Hence money will move between the firm, the households and the government. again.

This process continues and it is called Circular flow of income in three sectors.

1.18 Concepts Related to Calculation Of National Income

Investment-Addition to the stock of capital goods is called investment. Example; buildings, equipment. Inventory adds to the future productive capacity of the economy.

Gross **Investment: Investment + Depreciation cost.**

Net Investment = Gross Investment – Depreciation

It is addition to the capital which also includes replacement cost for wear and tear that undergoes over a period of time. It includes depreciation.

Fixed Investment and Inventory investment:

Fixed Investment (Fixed Capital Formation): It refers to increase in stock of fixed assets by a producers during an accounting year. Purchase of machine, plants, equipment is called fixed assets.

Fixed Investment = Stock of fixed assets at the end of the year- Stock of fixed assets in the beginning of the year.

For example: A tailoring shop has 4 sewing machine in the beginning of the year, then owner purchased 2 new sewing machine. The fixed investment will be increase in stock = 2 sewing machine.

Inventory investment: At a point time, producers hold stock of finished goods which are not sold, semi-finished goods which are under the process of production and raw materials. The stock keeps on changing throughout the year.

Inventory investment = Closing Stock-Opening stock.

Depreciation: Loss in the value of fixed asset (building, machinery) due to its normal wear & tear, passage of time or expected obsolescence in the process of production. It is also called **Consumption of fixed capital or Current replacement cost or replacement cost of fixed capital or capital consumption allowance.**

Depreciation of assets can be due to following reasons:

    i. **Normal wear and tear**: Continuous use of fixed asset in the production process will lead to wear and tear of machine, plants and buildings.

ii. **Time period**: Fixed assets loses its value with the passage of time even if it is not used. It becomes old asset and natural factor like wind, rain etc. contribute to fall in its value.

iii. **Expected obsolescence**: It is expected that after certain period technology will become outdated due to invention of new technology, machine and assets lose its value.

Planned Inventory Accumulation is called change in stock.

Unplanned Inventory Accumulation is change in stock of inventories occurring in unplanned way.

Capital Loss: Fall in the value of fixed capital due to natural calamities (like flood, fire, earthquakes) and unforeseen factors like war, thefts etc. is called capital loss.

Depreciation provision: Provision of funds made by enterprise for replacement of worn out fixed capital over its expected life is called depreciation provision.

Net Product = Gross Product-Depreciation

Net Value Added = Gross Value Added –Depreciation

Net Domestic Capital formation = Gross domestic Capital Formation –Depreciation.

1.19 Factor Cost and Market Price

Money value of final goods can be estimated by two ways- factor cost and market price. The difference between them is **Net Indirect Tax.**

- **MP = FC-NIT**

- **Net Indirect tax = (Indirect Tax-Subsidies)**

  Factor Cost: Payment made by a firm to the factors of production for rendering their services. It is cost to the producer in the form **of rent, wages, interest, profit.**

  Market Price The price at which a commodity is sold or purchased in the market.

- It includes indirect taxes added to factor cost. Market price will increase (**MP>FC**).

- Government gives subsidies to certain commodity (like sugar, fertilizer, LPG cylinder) which is subtracted from the factor cost. Here market price will be less than factor cost.

  MP = FC + NIT

  MP-FC = NIT

1.20 Tax and Subsidy

TAX-*It is legally a compulsory transfer payment to the government.*

Indirect Taxes: Tax levied by government on production and sale of commodities. e.g.: **excise duty, sales tax, custom duty, octroi, etc.**

Subsidies: These are cash grant given to the producers to encourage production of certain commodities. Subsidies lowers the price of the commodity to benefit of consumers.

Taxes are of two types

Direct Tax	Indirect Tax
Such taxes where liability to pay the tax and burden of the tax falls on the same person.	Such taxes where the liability to pay the tax falls on one person but burden can be shifted on others.
It is generally **progressive** in nature.	It is **regressive** in nature.
Burden of tax cannot be transferred on others.	Burden of tax can be transferred on others.
It is generally imposed on individual and Institutions.	It is imposed on commodities or services.
Example: Income Tax, Wealth tax, Gift tax, corporate tax, estate duty, Fringe Benefit Tax (*This is tax on the facilities other than salary like gym charges, education allowance etc.*) Dependent Tax (*it is a type of tax which is imposed on family members of the workers living in Saudi Arabia*)etc.	Example: Sales tax, excise Duty, custom Duty, entertainment Tax, Octroi (Toll Tax)GST,VAT, Service Tax etc.

1.21 Net Factor Income from Abroad

Factor income received from abroad –Factor income paid to abroad.

NFIA = (FIFA-FITA)

The difference between National Income and Domestic Income is Net Factor Income from Abroad(NFIA).

National Income = Domestic Income + Net factor income from Abroad

$\{\text{NNP}_{fc} = \text{NDP}_{fc} + \text{NFIA}\}$

Domestic Income = National Income –Net factor Income from Abroad

$\{\text{NDP}_{fc} = \text{NNP}_{fc} - \text{NFIA}\}$

Components of NFIA:

i. **Net compensation of employees**: The difference between income from work received by a resident worker who is living or employed abroad (less than a year)] **and** Payment done to non-resident workers living or employed in the country (less than a year)]. [Wages and salaries of residents received from abroad- wages and salary paid to non- residents abroad]

ii. **Net income from property & entrepreneurship (Rent, Interest, Profit):** It the difference between Income from property and entrepreneurship received by the residents of the country **and** similar payment done to non-residents.

iii. **Net retained earnings of resident companies abroad**: It is the difference between the retained earnings of the resident companies located abroad **and** retained earnings of the non-resident companies located within the domestic territory of the country.

NFIA can be Positive, Negative or Zero:

1. **Positive NFIA:** When income earned from abroad is more than payment done abroad.

2. **Negative NFIA:** When Payment done abroad is more than income earned from abroad by the residents.

3. **Zero NFIA:** When income earned from abroad is equal to payment done abroad.

1.21 Basic Concept of Formulas Related to NNP_{fc}

- **Gross** = Net + Depreciation

- **Net** = Gross-Depreciation

- **Depreciation = Gross-Net**

- **National Income** = Domestic Income + Net Factor Income from abroad ($NNPfc = NDP_{fc} + NFIA$)

- **Domestic Income** = National Income-Net Factor Income from abroad. ($NDP_{fc} = NNPfc-NFIA$)

- **Net Factor Income from Abroad** = National Income-Domestic income ($NFIA = NNP_{fc}-NDP_{fc}$)

- **Market price** = Factor cost + Net Indirect Tax ($MP = FC + NIT$)

- **Factor Price** = Market Price-Net Indirect Tax ($FC = MP-NIT$)

- **Net Indirect Tax** = Market Price-Factor cost($NIT = MP-FC$)

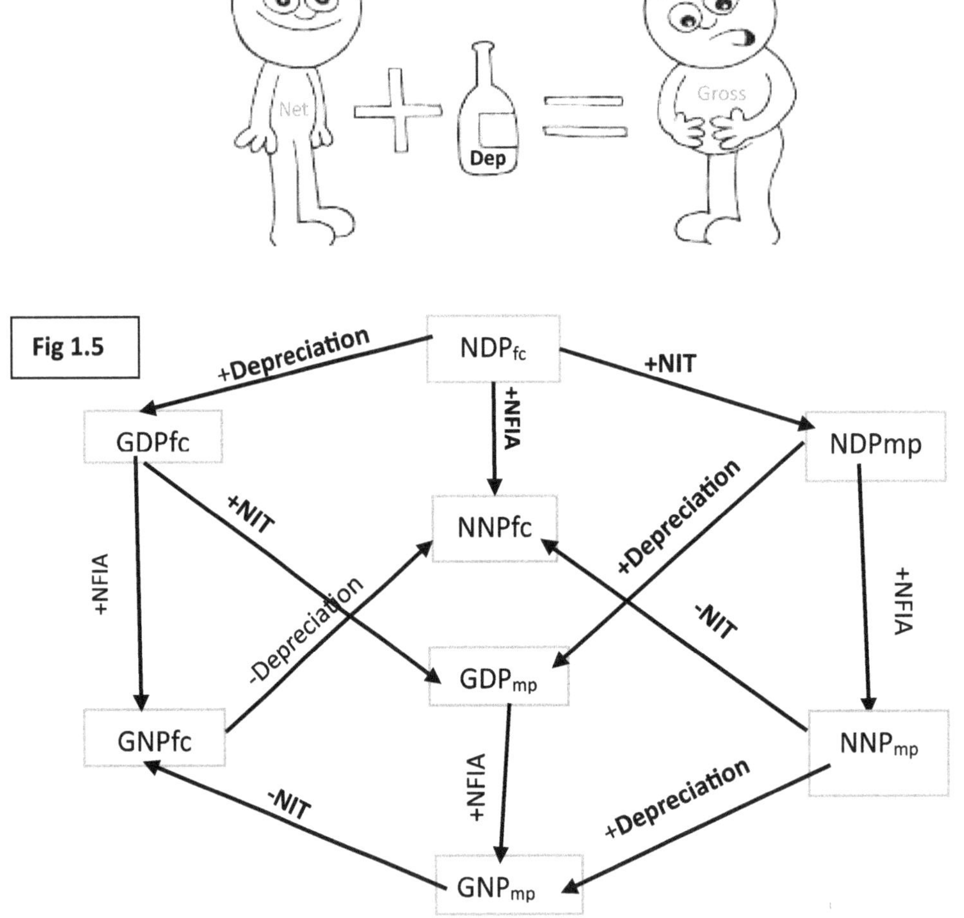

Examples

1.22 Distinguish between the Following

1. GDP and GNP

2. NNP and GDP

3. GDP_{mp} and NNP_{mp}

4. NNP_{mp} and GDP_{fc}

5. GNPfc and NDPfc

6. NDPfc and GNP_{mp}

7. NDP_{MP} and GNP_{fc}

8. NNPfc and GDPmp

9. NDPfc and GNPMP

10. Can Domestic Income be greater than National Income? Explain.

11. When is NFIA negative?

12. Is capital loss a part of depreciation?

Solution

1. GDP = GNP-NFIA

2. NNP = GDP- Dep + NFIA

3. GDPmp = NNPmp + Dep - NFIA

4. NNPmp = GDPfc- Dep + NFIA + NIT

5. GNPfc = NDPfc + Dep + NFIA

6. NDP_{fc} = GNP_{mp} –Dep- NFIA –NIT

7. NDP_{MP} = GNP_{fc} -Dep –NFIA + NIT

8. NNPfc = GDPmp-Dep + NFIA –NIT

9. NDPfc = GNPmp-Dep –NFIA -NIT

10. Domestic Income can be greater than National Income if NFIA is negative. This is condition when Factor income to abroad is more than factor income from abroad.

11. NFIA is negative when factor income from abroad is less than factor income to abroad.

12. No, capital loss is not a part of depreciation as it unforeseen loss in the value of assets.

1.23 Value of Output vs. Value Added

VALUE OF OUTPUT:

The goods and services produced by a firm in a year is called **Output or Gross output**.

Market value of goods and services produced by an enterprise during a year is called **Value of Output** (GVO). It is Gross Value of Output at *Market Price*.

Value of output = Quantity produced X Price

Value of Output = Sales + Change in Stock

In short Value of output is money value of gross output calculated at market price.

Value Added: The addition of value to the raw material by a firm during the process of production so as to made the commodity useful for consumer is called Value Added.

Value Added = Value of Output –Intermediate Consumption. [GVA = GVO-IC]

Note: The contribution of a firm to National Income is Value added by it not the Value of output because value of output includes value of intermediate inputs.

Example-1: A carpenter manufactures furniture's like sofa Bedroom set, chairs, tables, wardrobe etc. The carpenter purchase wood, sun mica sheets, nails, varnish, adhesive etc. of 10,000 and sells its output (Sofa) at ₹ 15,000.

Value Added = Value of output – Value of Inputs

Value Added = 15,000-10,000 = ₹ 5000. Whereas Value of output is ₹15,000

The difference between Value of Output and Value added is intermediate consumption (Value of Inputs).

Intermediate consumption means expenditure incurred on secondary inputs like raw materials, wood, sun mica, varnish, paints, nails, Glue, cloth etc. used for production.

Example:2: Let us assume that there are three producing units, a farmer, a miller and a baker

Farmer produces 100 kg of wheat with zero cost of input and sells it at ₹10 per kg to miller.

Miller grinds 100 kg wheat which he purchased at ₹1000 (cost of input) into flour and sells it the baker at ₹12 per kg.

The baker purchase100 kg flour at ₹ 1200 and prepares bread and sells it at ₹15 per kg.

Value of Output = Output X Price

By Farmer = 100 kg of wheat X ₹ 10per kg = ₹ 1000

By Miller = 100 kg of flour X ₹12 per kg = ₹ 1200

By Baker = 100 kg of Bread X ₹15 per kg = ₹ 1500

Total value of output = 1000 + 1200 + 1500 = ₹3700

Total value of inputs = 0 + 1000 + 1200 = 2200 [Value Added = 3700-2200 = 1500]

Value Added = Value of Output –Intermediate Consumption

By Farmer = 1000-0 = 1000

By Miller = 1200-1000 = 200

By Baker = 1500-1200 = 300

Total Value Added = 1000 + 200 + 300 = ₹1500

The producer has generated an income of ₹1500 not ₹3700.

1.24 Value Added Approach Eliminates Double Counting

What do you mean by Double Counting?

Counting the value of same product more than once is called double counting.

While calculating National income with output method (Final Product Method) value of only final goods should be taken in account. Value of intermediate goods should not be taken into calculation. But when a producer sells his commodity he treats it as final product irrespective whether it is used as final or intermediate product.

Example: A supermarket sells Pepsi as final good but that Pepsi was purchased by a Canteen owner and he sells in his canteen. Here the sale of Pepsi by supermarket was not final sale it was intermediate product. Sales by Canteen owner will be final sale but the supermarket treats it final sale. It will lead to double counting. Thus there will be overestimation of National Income.

This is called problem of double counting.

How to avoid problem of double counting?

There are two ways to avoid problem of double counting

- Final Product approach
- Value Added Approach

In actual practice double counting occurs unintentionally in Final Product approach because each seller treats his sale as Final Product although the same might have been used by the buyer as intermediate product.

Problem of double counting is perfectly solved by using **Value Added Method** because in this method value added by each firm at each stage of production is included in accounting National Income.

Methods of Measurement of National Income

There are three methods of calculating National Income

1. **Production (Value Added) Method**
2. **Income Method**
3. **Expenditure Method**

Value Added Method

Steps of Value added method

- Identify all the producing units in the domestic economy as primary, secondary and tertiary sector.
- Estimate NVA_{fc} by adding value added by all the sectors.
- Value Added (GVA) = Value of Output -Value of Input i.e., (GVA = GVO-IC)

- NVA_{fc} (Domestic Income NDP_{fc}) = Value of output –IC-Dep-NIT

- NNP_{fc} (National Income) = GVO-IC-Dep-NIT + NFIA

Precautions of Value Added Method

Items Included

- Imputed rent of owner occupied house.

- Imputed goods for self-consumption.

- Only value added not value of output by producing units should be included.

- Brokerage or commission paid to the broker or agent for their services (both for first hand or second hand goods).

Items Not Included:

- Sale of second hand goods because they are not current year production.

- Sale and purchase of bonds and shares because they are merely financial transactions

- Imputed services like, Services of the housewives are not included as it is difficult to estimate its market value.

- Income from illegal activities are not included like smuggling, gambling, black marketing etc.

- Income from lottery and windfall gain is not included as no new goods or services are produced.

Formulas of Value added Method

Briefly:

- ➢ **Value of Output (GVO) = Sales + Change in Stock**

- ➢ *Sales = Price X Quantity*

- ➢ **GVO** = Price X Quantity

- ➢ **Gross Value Added at MP = Value of output(GVO)-Value of Inputs(IC)**

- ➢ GVA_{MP} **= GVO-IC**

- ➢ GVA_{MP} **= Sales + Change in Stock-IC**

- ➢ **Change in Stock** = {Closing stock –Opening stock}

- ➢ GVA_{mp} **means** GDP_{mp}

- ➢ **NVAmp** = GVAmp-Depreciation

- ➢ **NVAFc** = GVAmp-Depreciation-Net indirect tax

- ➢ NVA_{fc} = Sales + change in stock –IC-Dep-NIT

- NNP_{fc} = Sales + Change in Stock-IC-Dep-NIT + NFIA

- NVA_{fc} or NDP_{fc} is called **Domestic Income**

- NNF_{fc} is called **National Income**

- NVA_{fc} = NVA_{mp} - NIT

- *Net value added at FC = Sum of factor income*

NOTE: *Sales = Domestic sales + Exports + goods used for self-consumptions.*

Value of Output = *Price X Output (Quantity)* **if entire output is sold.**

Value of Output = *Price X Quantity sold X Change in Stock* **(if partial output is sold).**

- **Intermediate cost or Intermediate consumption** = *Cost of raw material + Electricity charge + Transport cost +* **Imports**

- **Sales includes exports.**

- **Intermediate Consumption includes imports**

Intermediate Consumption does not include: -*Purchase of Building, machinery, Plants, buildings etc.* **These are investments** *which are used for production again and again.*

Intermediate Consumption Includes	Value of Output includes

Purchase
1) Domestic Purchase
   • From Government
   • From Firm
   • From Household
2) External Purchase(Imports)
	1) Sale
	a) Domestic Sales
	   • From Government
	   • From Firm
	   • From Household
	b) External sales (Exports)
	2) Change in stock
	3) Goods used for self-consumption

Fig 1.2

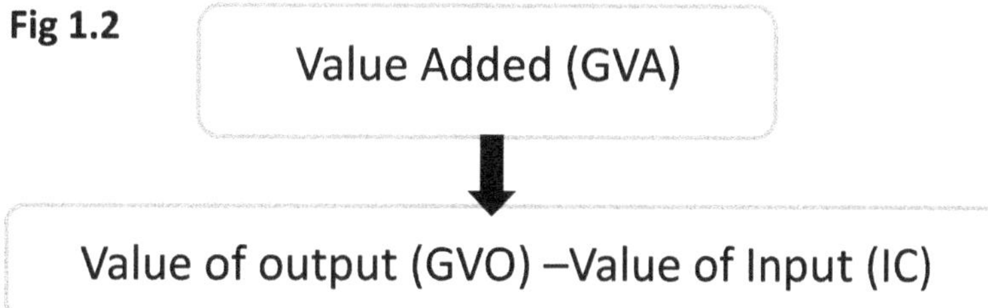

Fig 1.3

1.25 Numerical of Value Added Method

1. Calculate: (a) NNP at FC and (b) NDP at FC

Items	₹ in crores
Depreciation	2400
Indirect Tax	3600
Subsidies	300
GNP at MP	17,450
Net factor Income from abroad	1600

Solution:1

    a. NNPfc = GNPmp-Dep-NIT

        = 17450-2400-(3600-300) = **₹ 11, 750 crores**

    b. NDPfc = NNPfc –NFIA

        = 11,750-1600 = **₹ 10, 150 crores**

2. Calculate GNP at factor cost

Items	₹ in Crores
NDP mp	24000
Depreciation	4000
Indirect Taxes	120
Subsidies	30
Factor income from abroad	400
Factor income to rest of the world	600

Solution: 2 GNPfc = NDPmp + Dep + NFIA –NIT

= 24,000 + 4000 + (400-600) - (120-30)

= 24,000 + 4,000 + (-200) – (90)

GNPfc = **₹ 27, 710 crores**

3. Calculate **Value of Output:**

Net Value added at factor cost	₹ 100 lakhs
Intermediate Cost	75 lakhs
Excise Duty	20 lakhs
Subsidy	5 lakhs
Depreciation	10 lakhs

Solution: 3 NVAfc = Sales + Change in stock –IC –Dep –NIT

NVAfc = Value of Output –IC –Dep –NIT

100 = GVO -75 -10 – (20-5)

100 = GVO – 100

100 + 100 = GVO

Value of Output = ₹ 200 lakhs

4. Calculate(i) Value Added by firm A and Firm B (ii) Gross Domestic Product at factor cost :

Sales by firm A	₹ 300 lakhs
Purchases from firm B by firm A	₹120 lakhs
Purchases from firm A by firm B	₹ 180 lakhs
Sales by firm B	₹600lakhs
Closing stock by firm A	₹60 lakhs
Closing stock by firm B	₹105
Opening stock by firm A	₹75

| Opening stock by firm B | ₹135 |
| Indirect tax by both the firm | ₹90 |

Solution: 4— (a) Value Added by Firm A(GVA) = Sales by firm A + (Closing stock of firm A- Opening Stock of firm A)- Purchases from firm B by firm A

GVA of A = 300 + (60-75)-120 = **₹165 lakhs**

Value Added by Firm B (GVA) = Sales by firm b + (Closing stock of firm B- Opening Stock of firm B)- Purchases from firm A by firm B

= 600 + (105-135)-180 **GVA of B = ₹390 lakhs**

(b) GDP_{fc} = GDP_{mp}-NIT = (165 + 390)-90 **GDPfc = ₹(555 -90) = ₹ 465lakhs**

5. Calculate: Net Value Added at factor cost

Items	₹ in lakhs
Purchase of machinery	100
Sales	200
Intermediate costs	90
Indirect taxes	12
Change in Stock	10
Excise Duty	6
Stock of raw material	5

Solution: 5 – NVAfc = Sales + Change in stock –IC –Dep –NIT

= 200 + 10 -90-(12-0)

NVAfc = 210-102 **NVAfc = ₹ 108 lakhs**

6. Calculate NVAfc

Items	₹. in lakhs
Net factor Income from Abroad	30
Sales	3500
Purchase of Intermediate goods	2000
Consumption of fixed Capital	500
Exports	400
Indirect taxes	350
Change in Stock	50

Solution: 6-- **NVAfc** = Sales + Change in Stock-IC-Dep-NIT

= 3500 + 50-2000-500-350 = **₹.700 lakhs**

7. Calculate GDPmp from the following data:

Items	₹ in Lakhs
Value of output in primary sector	2000
Intermediate Consumption by secondary sector	800
Intermediate Consumption by primary sector	1000

Net factor income from abroad	(-30)
Net indirect tax	300
Value of output in tertiary sector	1,400
Value of output in secondary sector	1,800
Intermediate Consumption by tertiary section	600

Solution: 7–GDPmp = V.A by primary sector + V.A by sec sector + V.A by Ter. Sec

= (2000-1000) + (1, 800 -800) + (1, 400 -600)

GDP_{mp} = ₹ 2800 lakhs

8. Calculate(a) Value of output, (b) Intermediate consumption and (c) Net value added at factor cost.

S.No	Particulars	₹ in Crores
1	Purchase of raw material from domestic market	500
2	Increase in unsold stock	50
3	Electricity Charge	20
4	Import of Machines	40
5	Value Added Tax(VAT)	20
6	Replacement of fixed capital	50
7	Subsidy	40
8	Exports	500
9	Import of raw material	100
10	Domestic Sales	1000
11	Goods used for self-Consumption	20

Answer: 8

a. Value of Output = Domestic Sales + Exports + Increase in unsold stock + Goods for self-consumption.

GVO = 1000 + 500 + 50 + 20 = ₹ 1570 crores

b. Intermediate Consumption = Purchase of raw material in the domestic market + Import of raw material + Electricity Charge

IC = 500 + 100 + 20 = ₹ 620 crores.

c. $NVA_{FC} = GVO_{MP}$-IC-Dep-NIT

NVA_{FC} = 1570-620- 50-(20-40) = 1570- 620-50 + 20 = 1590-670

NVA_{fc} = ₹ 920 crores

1.26 Income Method

The income method measures national income by adding all factor payments like, wages, rent, interest, profit etc. in an accounting year.

STEPS INVOLVED IN INCOME METHOD:

❖ Identify factors of production (land, labour, capital and enterprise).

❖ Classify factor payment received by them into **Compensation of employee, operating surplus and Mixed Income.**

❖ Sum up COE + OS + MISE to get Domestic Income (NDP_{fc} = COE + OS + MISE).

❖ Add NFIA to NDP_{fc} to get National Income (NNP_{fc} = NDP_{fc} + NFIA).

Precautions of Income Method

Items included:

> *Only factor income should be included.*

> *Direct Tax to be included like Income Tax, Corporate Tax should be included.*

> *Imputed rent and imputed production should be included.*

> *Commission or brokerage to the agent is included as he gets payment for his services.*

Items not included

> *Transfer income should not be included.*

> *Indirect Tax should not be included like excise duty, sales tax, custom duty etc.*

> *Imputed services should not be included like teacher teaching his own child, work done by housewife etc.*

> *Sale and purchase of second- hand goods should not be included because it is not current year production.*

> *Sale and purchase of shares and bonds should not be included as it is merely financial transaction.*

> *Wealth Tax and Gift tax should not be included as it is tax on past income.*

> *Income from illegal activities should not be included like smuggling, Black marketing, gambling etc.*

> *Income from windfall gain and lottery are not included because no new goods and services are produced.*

Formulas of Income Method

Domestic Income

NDPfc = COE + OS + MISE

NDPfc = Compensation of employees + Operating Surplus + Mixed Income

National income

NNPfc = COE + OS + MISE + NFIA

NDPfc = Private sector Income + Government sector income

NNPfc = Private sector Income + Government sector income + NFIA

NOTE:

Government Sector Income = *Income from property and entrepreneurship accruing to government administrative department + Savings of Non departmental Enterprise*

Net Factor Income from Abroad = Factor Income from Abroad –Factor income to Abroad

NFIA = (FIFA-FITA)

NOTE: Net Factor Income to Abroad [Use the value after changing the sign i.e, plus can be used as minus and vice versa].

Where, *Compensation of Employees* = **Salaries and wages in cash and kind + Bonus + Social Security Scheme by Employer.**

Note: Compensation of employee is the reward paid to employee for rendering their services .

Items includes in COE are- wages and salaries in cash and kind(rent free house, uniform,free meal,car or two wheeler for transport,bonus, dearness allowance,city compensatory allowance, leave travelling allowance, employers contribution to social security scheme etc.)

Items not included in COE are—{-Compensation to injured worker, Travel Allowance relating to business promotion, amount of loan, social security scheme by employee}

Social security scheme by employer includes-Contribution to life insurance,provident fund, pension scheme, welfare fund, casuality insurance etc.

NOTE:

Social Security by employees is not added separately in Compensation of employees as it is a part of the salary which is already included in compensation of employees[COE].

Operating Surplus = Rent + Interest + Profit + Royalty

Rent: Rent is that part of national income which arise out of ownership of land or building.Actual rent (rent on let out land) and imputed rent(rent of self-occupied properties).Imputed rent of owner occupied houses is calculated on the basis of market rental value of the house.

Royalty: It is income received for granting leasing rights of sub-soil assets. For example: Owners of coal mines, natural gas, iron mines etc.can earn income by giving rights of mining to the contractors.

Operating Surplus: **Operating Surplus = Income from property + Income from entrepreneurship**

Operating Surplus = Profit + Interest + Rent

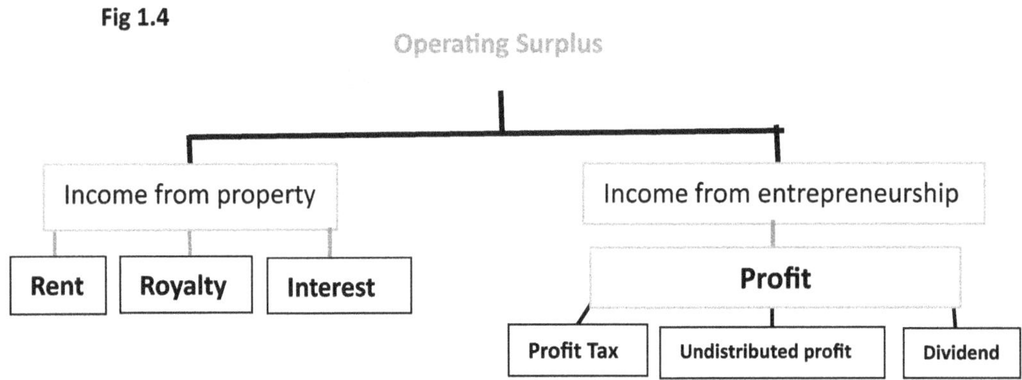

Profit = Corporate Tax + Undistributed Profit + Dividend

Profit (income accruing to corporation) : Profit is the reward to the entrepreneur for their contribution to the production of goods and services.It is the residual income which an entrepreneur gets after paying all the factors of production.

Profit is divided into three part:

a. **Profit tax:**It is that part of the profit which is paid to the government as direct tax.

   Corporate tax is also known as Profit Tax or Business tax.

b. **Undistributed profit**: It is that part of the profit which is kept as reserve to meet unexpected contingencies or for business expansion or diversification.

   Other names of undistributed profit are:

   ➢ Reserve Fund

   ➢ Net retained earnings of corporate sector

- ➢ Savings of Private corporate sector

- ➢ Surplus of private corporate sector

c. **Dividend**: It refers to that part of profit which is paid to the shareholders in proportion to their shareholdings. It is also called distributed profit.

Interest: Interest is the amount received for lending money for the production or business purpose.

Interest includes loan for productive purpose only.

*Interest income does not include:

i. Interest paid by government on public debt or interest paid consumers on the loan taken for consumption purpose.

ii. Interest paid by one firm to another firm

Mixed Income: Mixed Income is the income of Self Employed. It is the income generated by own- account workers (like farmers, barbers etc.) and unincorporated enterprises (like retail traders, small shopkeepers etc.) It is called mixed income because it is income of self -employed persons, whose income includes profits, rent, interest, wages etc. and these are not separated from each other.

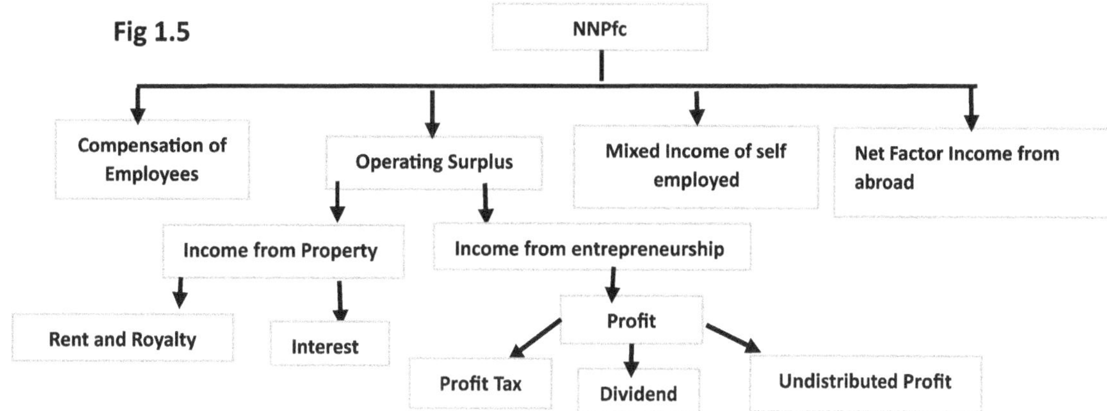

1.27 Numericals of Income Method

1. Calculate National Income and Domestic income:

Particulars	₹ in Crores
Compensation of employee	10000
Distributed profit	3000
Rent	2000
Interest	4000
Undistributed Profit	2000
Net Export	1000
Mixed Income	5000
Income paid to Abroad	-200

SOLUTION:1- NDPfc = COE + OS + MISE

NDPfc = 10000 + (3000 + 2000 + 4000 + 2000) + 5000

NDPfc = 26000 Crores

NNPfc = NDPfc + NFIA = 26000 + [0-(-200)] = 26000 + 200

NNPfc = ₹ 26,200 crores

2. Calculate GNP_{MP}:

Particulars	₹ in Crores
Mixed Income of self employed	400
Compensation of employees	500
Net factor Income from abroad	-20
Net indirect tax	100
Consumption of fixed capital	120
Profit	350
Rent	100
Interest	150

Solution:2- NNP_{fc} = COE + OS + MISE + NFIA

= 500 + (350 + 100 + 150) + 400 + (-) 20 NNP_{FC} = 1480

GNP_{MP} = NNP_{FC} + Dep + + NIT = 1480 + 120 + 100 = **₹1700 crores**

3. Calculate NNP_{fc} and GDP_{MP}

Particulars	₹ crores
Profit	700
Net Indirect Tax	110
Net Exports	-20
Compensation of Employees	1200
Rent	200
Interest	270
NFIA	30
Mixed income	600
Gross Domestic Capital Formation	700
Net Domestic Capital Formation	600

Solution: 3-NNP_{FC} = COE + OS + MISE + NFIA NNP_{FC} = 1200 + (700 + 200 + 270)600 + 30

NNP_{FC} = **₹3000 crores**

GDP_{MP} = NNPfc + Dep- NFIA + NIT = 3000 + (700-600) -30 + 110 = 3000 + 210-30 = ₹ 3180 crores

4. Calculate GNP_{MP}

Particulars	₹ crores
Mixed Income	200
Compensation of Employees	600
Net Factor Income From Abroad	-10
Net Indirect Tax	110
Depreciation	50
Rent	100
Interest	120
Profit	80

Solution: 4: GNPmp = COE + OS + MISE + Dep + NIT + NFIA

= 600 + (80 + 120 + 100) + 200 + 50 + 110 + (-10)

GNPmp = ₹ 1250 crores

5. Calculate GDP at MP and National Income

Particulars	₹ in Crores
Salaries and wages	1900
Rent	200
Interest	150
Operating Surplus	720
Net Indirect Taxes	400
Employees contribution of Social Security Scheme	100
Net Factor Income from Abroad	(-)20
Consumption of fixed Capital	100

Solution: 5-NNP_{FC} = COE + OS + MISE + NFIA

= 1, 900 + 720 + 0 + (-) 20

NNPfc = ₹ 2, 600 Crores

GDPmp = NNPfc + Dep + NIT-NFIA = 2, 600 + 100 + 400 − (-) 20

GDPmp = ₹ 3,120 Crores

6. Calculate Interest (2019-Foreign)

Particulars	Amount(₹ crores)
Indirect Tax	1, 500
Subsidies	700
Profits	1, 100
Consumption of fixed Capital	700
Gross domestic Product at market Price	17, 500
Compensation of Employees	9, 300
Interest	?
Mixed Income of self employed	3,500
Rent	800

Solution: 6

GDPmp = COE + (Rent + Interest + Profit) + MISE + Dep + NIT

17,500 = 9,300 + 800 + Interest + 1, 100 + 3,500 + (1500 -700) + 700

17, 500 = 16,200 + interest

Interest = ₹1,300 crores

7. Calculate Mixed Income of Self Employed: (2019- Foreign)

Particulars	Amount(₹ Crores)
Compensation of employees	17,300
Interest	1, 200
Consumption of fixed capital	1,100
Mixed Income	?
Subsidies	750
Gross Domestic Product at Market Price	27,500
Indirect Tax	2,100
Profits	1,800
Rents	2,000

Solution: 7

GDP mp = COE + (Interest + Profit + Rent) + MISE + Dep + NIT

27,500 = 17,300 + 1,200 + 1,800 + 2,000 + MISE + 1,100 + (2,100 -750)

27,500 = 24750 + MISE MISE = ₹ 2750 Crores

1.28 Expenditure Method

Expenditure method measures final expenditure on Gross Domestic Product at Market Price (GDP at MP) during a period of time.

By subtracting depreciation and Net Indirect Tax and adding NFIA to GDPmp we get National Income (NDPfc).

In this method final consumption expenditure and final investment expenditure are added to get GDPmp.

Steps of expenditure method:

❖ *Identification of final expenditure done by consuming sector, producing sector and government sector.*

❖ *Classify the final aggregate expenditure into-*

1. *Private final consumption expenditure*

2. *Government Final Consumption Expenditure*

3. *Gross fixed Capital formation*

4. *Change in stock*

5. *Net Exports(Exports-Imports)*

❖ *Sum up all the five components it will give GDPmp*

❖ *From GDPmp deduct Depreciation and NIT and add NFIA to estimate National Income (NNPfc).*

Precautions of Expenditure Method:

Items Included:

- Value of final expenditures done by household producers and government should be accounted.

- Imputed expenditure on own account (owner occupied house, production for self-consumption should be included.

Items Not Included:

- To avoid double counting, expenditure on intermediate goods and services should not be included. For Example, purchase of vegetables by a restaurant, expenses on electricity bill.

- Expenditure of government on transfer payments are not included. E.g. Old age pension, unemployment allowance because no productive services are rendered.

- Expenditure on second hand goods are not included as they are not currently produced goods.

- Expenditure on purchase of old and new shares are not included as they are merely financial transaction.

Components of GDP

1. Private Final Consumption expenditure(C): It is the money value of goods and services purchased by the households and non-profit institutions for current use during a given period of time. *It includes expenditure on all consumer goods and services. It includes good purchased from abroad by resident households. Purchase done in domestic market by the foreigners are deducted.*

2. Government Final Consumption Expenditure (G): Expenditure of Government on purchase of goods and services. Deduct sales done by the government. It includes salaries paid by the government, Expenses on administrative services, police, judiciary, defence, etc.

3. Gross fixed Capital Formation (GFCF): It includes increase in the stock fixed capital during a given year including depreciation. *It includes three items: -*

a) Business Fixed investment: Investment done by Businessman like purchase of machine, Buildings, Factories, equipment.

b) Residential Construction Investment: Expenditure on construction of residence.

c) Public Investment: Investment done by the Government like construction of roads, hospitals schools, dams etc.

Gross Domestic Capital formation is also known as Investment

Gross Domestic Capital Formation = Gross fixed Capital Formation + Change in stock

4. Change in stock: It is physical change in stocks of inventories like raw material, semi furnished goods and finished goods lying with the producers.

It is measured as Closing stock –Opening stock.

5. Net Exports (X-M): It is calculated as (**Value of Export – Value of Imports**).

When value of imports is more than value of exports, it is called Net imports

INVESTMENT HAS FOUR COMPONENTS

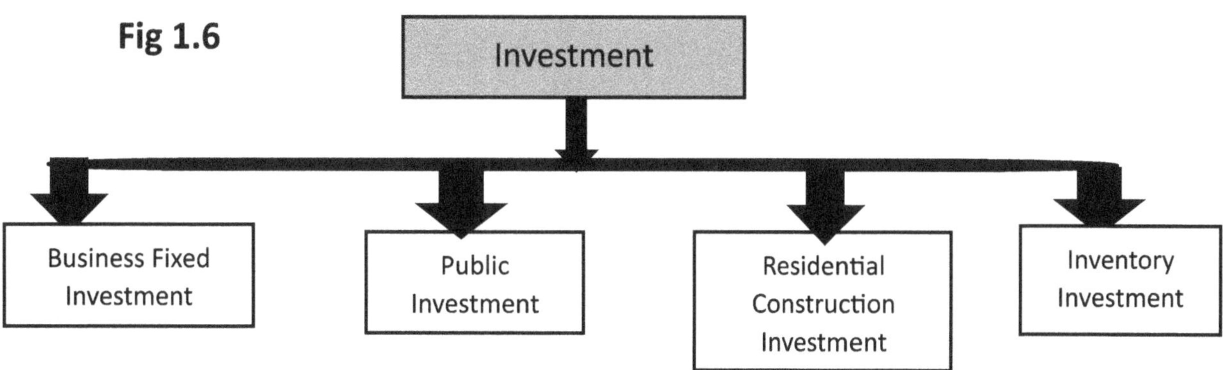

Note: In a question if Net import is given as -20 use it as + 20, or if Net Import is Given as + 80 use it as -80 in the formula GDPMP = C + G + GDCF + (X-M).

Exports are investment in foreign country and imports are disinvestment.

1.29 Formulas of Expenditure Method

Gross Domestic Capital Formation = Gross <u>Fixed</u> Capital Formation + <u>Change in Stock</u>

GDCF = GFCG + Change in Stock

<u>Gross</u> *Domestic Capital Formation = <u>Net</u> Domestic Capital Formation + <u>Depreciation</u>*

<u>Gross</u> *Domestic Capital Formation (GDCF) = Net Fixed Capital Formation (NDCF) + Depreciation + Change in Stock*

Gross Domestic Capital Formation is also known as Investment

1. GDPmp = C + G + (GFCF + Δ Stock) + (X-M)

2. GDPmp = C + G + GDCF + (X-M)

3. *GDPmp = C + G + (NDCF + Dep) + (X-M)*

4. *GDPmp = C + G + I + (X-M) where I is Investment*

5. *GDPmp = C + G + (Net Investment + Change in Stock) + (X-M)*

*The basic formula gives us **GDPmp** which can be converted into **NNPfc** (National Income)*

National Income (NNP$_{FC}$) *= GDPmp- Dep + NFIA-NIT*

Domestic Income (NDP$_{FC}$) = GDP$_{MP}$- Dep-NIT

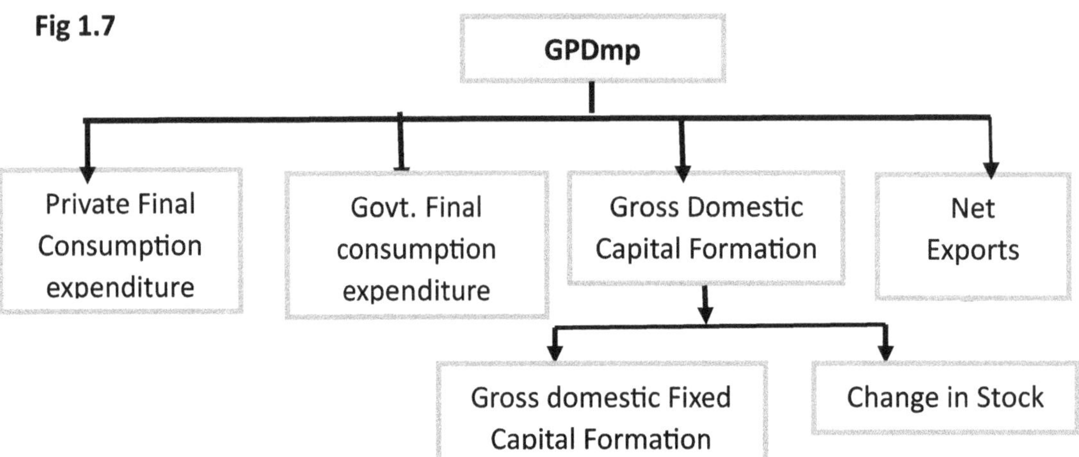

1.30 Numerical of Expenditure Method

1. Calculate GNP at FC by Income and Expenditure Method:

Components	₹ in Crores
Wages and Salaries	800
Mixed Income	160
Operating surplus	600
Undistributed profit	150
Gross Capital Formation	330

Change in Stock	25
Net Capital Formation	300
Employers contribution to Social Security Scheme	100
Net Factor Income From Abroad	-20
Exports	30
Imports	60
Private Final Consumption Expenditure	1000
Government Final Consumption Expenditure	450
Net Indirect Tax	60
Compensation of Employees paid by Government	75

Solution-1: *Income Method:* GNPfc = COE + OS + MISE + NFIA + Dep

= (800 + 100) + 600 + 160 + [-20] + (330-300) *(GCF-NCF = Dep) GNPfc = Rs. 1670 Crores*

Expenditure Method: GNPfc = C + G + GCF + (X-M) + NFIA –NIT

GNPfc = 1000 + 450 + 330 + (30-60) + (-20) -60

GNPfc = ₹1, 670 crores

2. Calculate National Income:

Component	₹ in Crores
Private Final Consumption Expenditure	400
Net current transfers from rest of the world	(-) 5
Indirect Taxes	65
Net Domestic Capital Formation	120
Government Final Consumption Expenditure	100
Consumption of fixed Capital	20
Subsidies	5
Exports	30
Net Factor Income From Abroad	(-)10
Imports	40

Solution: 2 *NDP fc = C + G + NDCF + (X-M) = 400 + 100 + 120 + (-)10*

NDPfc = Rs. 610 Crores

NNPfc = NDPfc + NFIA = 610 + (-) 10 **NNPfc** *= ₹600 Crores*

3. Calculate NNPfc with Income and Expenditure method:

Components	₹ in Crores
Interest	150
Rent	250
Government Final Consumption Expenditure	600
Private Final Consumption Expenditure	1200
Profits	640
Compensation of employees	1000

Net Factor Income to Abroad	30
Net Indirect Taxes	60
Net Exports	(-)40
Consumption of Fixed	50
Net Domestic Capital Formation	340

Solution:3 Income Method: NNPfc = COE + OS + MISE + NFIA

= 1000 + (150 + 250 + 640) + (-) 30

= ₹ 2010 Crores

Expenditure Method: NDPmp = C + G + NDCF + (X-M)

NDPmp = 1200 + 600 + 340 + (-) 40

$NDP_{mp} = 2100$

$NNP_{fc} = NDPmp + NFIA - NIT = 2100 - 30 - 60$

$NNP_{fc} = ₹ 2010$ **Crores**

4. Calculate GDPmp and GNPmp:

Components	₹ in Crores
Personal Consumption Expenditure	27,500
Government Consumption Expenditure	3,000
Gross Domestic Fixed Capital Formation	2,500
Imports of goods and services	500
Net factor income From Abroad	-250
Subsidy	250
Fall in Stock	300
Exports of goods and services	450
Depreciation	1,000
Net Indirect Tax	1, 000

Solution:4

GDPmp = C + G + GDFCF + Change in Stock + (X-M)

= 27,500 + 3,000 + 2,500 -300 + (450 – 500)

GDPmp = ₹ 32, 650 crores

GNPmp = GDPmp + NFIA = 32,650 + (-) 250 = ₹ 32,400 crores

5. Calculate GDP:

Components	₹ in Crores
Government Final Consumption Expenditure	43,201
Private Final Consumption Expenditure	52,302
Gross Fixed Capital Formation	5,109
Change in stock	2,055
Exports of goods and services	1,861
Import of goods and services	1,920

Solution:5

GDP = C + G + GFCF + Change in stock + (X-M)

GDP = 43, 201 + 52,302 + 5,109 + 2,055 + (1, 861- 1,920)

GDP = ₹1, 02, 608 crores

1.31 Net National Disposable income(NNDI) and Gross National Disposable Income(GNDI)

NNDI = National Income + Net Indirect Tax + Net current transfer from rest of the world.

NNDI = NNPmp + Net Current Transfer from ROW

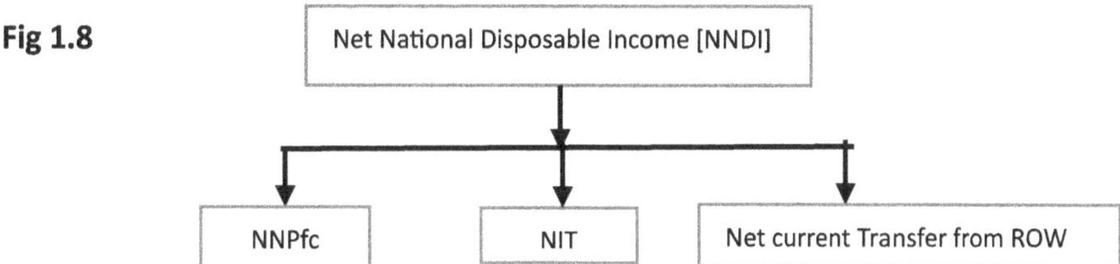

GNDI = National Income + Net Indirect Tax + Depreciation + Net current transfer from rest of the world.

GNDI = GNPmp + Net current transfer from Row

1.32 Domestic Income can be divided into two parts

Private sector Income and Government sector income. The income which is generated by private sector and the income which is generated by government sector. Income accruing to government sector is also called Income from domestic product accruing to government sector or surplus of government sector.

Government sector Income has two components:

 i. Income from property and entrepreneurship accruing to government administrative department and

 ii. Savings of non-departmental enterprises.

The income which is earned by private sector is called Income from property and entrepreneurship accruing to private sector.

1.31 Conversion of Nominal GNP into Real GNP

Nominal GNP can be converted into Real GNP with the help of GNP deflator.

GNP deflator = $\dfrac{Nominal\,GNP}{Real\,GNP}$ X100

Similarly

GDP deflator = $\dfrac{Nominal\,GDP}{Real\,GDP}$ X100

To neutralize the effect of rise in prices, we convert nominal GDP into Real GDP with the help of GDP deflator (current year Index Number).

Example: If Nominal GDP through expenditure approach is Rs.50, 000 crore and real GDP is Rs.40, 000 crores, then

$$\text{GDP deflator} = \frac{Nominal\ GDP}{Real\ GDP} \times 100 = \frac{50000}{40000} \times 100 = 125$$

Note: GDP deflator is Index Number of Current year

$$\textbf{Real GDP} = \frac{\textbf{Nominal GDP}}{\textbf{Index Number of current year}} \times \textbf{100}$$

$$\textbf{Real GNP} = \frac{\textbf{Nominal GNP}}{\textbf{Index Number of current year}} \times \textbf{100}$$

1. Can Real GDP be greater than Nominal GDP?

Ans. Yes, when base year price or output is more than current year.

1. When Current Year Price < Base Year Price

2. When Output of Current Year < Output of Base year

2. Can Real GDP be equal to Nominal GDP?

Ans. Yes, when base year and current year has equal price and output.

1. When Current Year Price = Base year Price

2. When Current Year Output = Base year output

3. Can Real GDP be smaller than nominal GDP?

Ans. Yes, when base year price or output is less than current year price or output.

1. When Current Year Price > Base Year Price

2. When Current Year Output > Base Year Price

1.32 Is GDP or GNP a correct Index of welfare?

Normally GDP or GNP is considered as an index of welfare of the people. Welfare means better living condition or improved standard of living. It depends on greater availability of goods and services. More production of goods and services means more consumption of these goods and services, thus increase in the standard of living. So it may be concluded that higher level of GDP is an index of well-being. But it has the following limitation:

i. **Unequal distribution of GDP**: An increase in the GDP or GNP may not increase economic welfare if distribution of income is unequal or wealth is concentrated in few hands or households. Unequal distribution will result in making rich richer and poor poorer.

ii. **Production of harmful material**: If GDP increases because of production of war material, liquor, weapons, cigarette, tobacco (pan masala and gutka), etc. It will not increase economic welfare.

iii. **Non-Monetary Work:** Many activities are not paid, it is done due to love and care which are not evaluated in terms of money. Services of housewife, Mother teaching her own children, barter exchange, social work etc. increases welfare (rejuvenate, energies and recreates, refresh, increase knowledge) but not included in measurement of GDP. Thus GDP under estimates welfare by not including non -monetary exchange.

i. **High Population Growth Rate:** If population growth rate is higher than growth of GDP or GNP than welfare will decrease.

ii.   **Externalities:** Any benefit or harm done by an individual or firm for which they are neither paid nor penalised is known as externalities. It can be of two types:

Positive Externalities: Work done by social workers or enjoying scenic beauty or relaxing in park increases welfare or rejuvenate people but they are neither paid nor included in GDP or GNP estimation.

Negative Externalities: Smoke of a factory pollutes the air and people may suffer from various diseases, noise pollution by factory results in health hazard and fall of social welfare but they are not penalised so it not accounted in GDP even though they create nuisance, health hazards, environment issues and loss of vegetation.

Conclusion: **Though GDP or GNP may not be correct index of welfare due to its limitations, yet it reflects some index of welfare. Increase GDP or GNP may increase standard of living of the people, reduces poverty or unemployment.**

GDP or GNP does not consider environment pollution or depletion of resources as a result of production which is considered in Green GDP or Green GNP. Only increase in GNP will not reflect improvement in quality of life

1.33 Green GNP

If GNP is an indicator of a sustainable use of natural resources and equitable distribution of benefits of development it is termed as Green GNP.

Three features of Green GNP:

i.   **Sustainable Economic Development:** Development should not deplete resources.

ii.   **Equitable distribution** of benefits of developments.

iii.   **Promote Economic welfare** for long time.

Green GNP = GNP-Net Fall in Stock of National Capital

1.34 *Items Include in Domestic Income and National Income*

1. Factor Income, Rent, wages, Interest, Profit

2. Imputed Production –production for self-consumption.

3. Imputed Rent or Services of owner-occupied house.

4. Commission or Brokerage to the agent as he is providing services.

5. Change in stock as it is a part of current production, included with value added and expenditure method.

6. Bonus as it is factor Payment.

7. Value of Final goods

8. Expenditure by Government on roads, railways etc.

9. Dividend is a part of profit, so it is included as factor Payment.

10. Salary in Kind like uniform, car etc.is a part of Compensation of employee.so it is factor payment.

11. Earnings from part time job is economic activity.

12. Expenditure on purchase of machine, Factories are included as it is investment. Included with expenditure method.

13. Interest on loan taken for **production purpose** is included.

14. Expenditure by household for consumption purpose is include as Private final consumption expenditure.

15. **Retirement pension** is included as it is Factor Payment.

16. Profit or income earned by foreign banks or company is a part of domestic income of the country where it is located but national income of the country of which the company or bank belongs to.

17. Income earned by the people (Indians) working in embassy of a particular country (United Kingdom) belongs to the Domestic income of United Kingdom but National Income of India.

18. Direct tax like income tax, corporate tax is included.

1.35 *Items which are not included in Calculation of Domestic Income and National Income*

1. Transfer income as it is unearned income like. Gifts, charity, scholarship, Subsidies.

2. Interest paid on loan taken **for consumption purpose like**, interest paid on loan taken for purchasing car.

3. Sale and purchase of shares and bonds either new or old are not included as it is merely financial transaction.

4. **Old age pension is** not included as it is transfer payment.

5. Imputed Services are not included as it not an economic activity.

6. Income from illegal activities are not included like smuggling, black marketing etc.

7. Lottery and windfall gain (gambling, horse race or lottery) are not included as no new goods or services are produced.

8. Social Security scheme by employees are separately not included as it is a part of salary again it should not be taken.

9. Indirect Tax are not included it tends to increases market price.

10. Direct tax like wealth tax and gift tax are excluded as they are paid from past savings.

11. Interest paid by the government of public debt or public borrowing. (it is taken for consumption purpose.)

12. Payment from past savings (gift tax, wealth tax, interest tax, death duty etc.) are not included as no new goods and services are produced.

13. Intermediate Cost or cost of inputs are not included separately as it value is already available in the final cost of the product. If value of intermediate cost is included it will lead to double counting.

14. Value of second hand goods/sale and purchase of second hand good is not included in calculation of domestic income and national income because its value was included in first time it was produced.

15. Goods which are purchased for resale or future sale are considered as intermediate goods so its value is not included in calculation of Domestic income or National Income.

16. Capital gains like profit due to increase in the value of land, flats, buildings, shares etc. are not included as no new goods and services are produced.

17. Capital Loss like destruction in building, damage due to flood or earthquake is not included in the calculation of Domestic or National Income.

1.36 Main Uses of National Income Accounting

1. It reflects performance of the economy and shows strength and failures.

2. Helps to find out structural changes in the economy.

3. It helps to make nation wise comparison.

4. Helps to formulate economic policy and welfare programs.

5. It helps to know contribution of different sector in the economy.

6. It helps in research and strategy making.

1.37 Important Formulae

VALUE-ADDED

Gross Value Added at MP = Value of output(GVO)-Value of Inputs(IC) [GVA_{MP} = GVO-IC]

Value of Output (GVO) = Sales + Change in Stock
Sales = Price X Quantity
GVA_{MP} = Sales + Change in Stock-IC

Change in Stock = {Closing stock –Opening stock}
NVAmp = GVAmp-Depreciation
NVAFc = GVAmp-Depreciation-Net indirect tax
NVA_{fc} = Sales + change in stock –IC-Dep-NIT
NNP_{fc} = Sales + Change in Stock-IC-Dep-NIT + NFIA

INCOME METHOD

Domestic Income

NDPfc = Compensation of employees + Operating Surplus + Mixed Income(NDPfc = COE + OS + MISE)

National income

NNPfc = COE + OS + MISE + NFIA

NDPfc = Private sector Income + Government sector income

NNPfc = Private sector Income + Government sector income + NFIA

NOTE:

Government Sector Income = *Income from property and entrepreneurship accruing to government administrative department + Savings of Non departmental Enterprise*

Net Factor Income from Abroad = Factor Income from Abroad –Factor income to Abroad

NFIA = (FIFA-FITA)

EXPENDITURE METHOD

Gross Domestic Capital Formation = Gross <u>Fixed</u> Capital Formation + <u>Change in Stock</u>

GDCF = GFCG + Change in Stock

Gross Domestic Capital Formation = <u>Net</u> Domestic Capital Formation + <u>Depreciation</u>

Gross_Domestic Capital Formation (GDCF) = Net Fixed Capital Formation (NDCF) + Depreciation + Change in Stock

Gross Domestic Capital Formation is also known as Investment

1. GDPmp = C + G + (GFCF + Δ Stock) + (X-M)

2. GDPmp = C + G + GDCF + (X-M)

3. GDPmp = C + G + (NDCF + Dep) + (X-M)

4. GDPmp = C + G + I + (X-M) where I is Investment

5. GDPmp = C + G + (Net Investment + Change in Stock) + (X-M)

The basic formula gives us **GDPmp** which can be converted into **NNPfc** (National Income)

National Income (NNP$_{FC}$) = GDPmp- Dep + NFIA-NIT

Domestic Income (NDP$_{FC)}$ = GDP$_{MP}$- Dep-NIT

1.38 Terms to Remember: [Understanding terms having same meaning]

1	Depreciation	• Consumption of fixed capital • Current replacement cost • Capital consumption allowance • Replacement cost of fixed capital
2	Undistributed Profit	• Saving of private corporate sector • Net retained earning • Reserve fund
3.	Dividend	• Distributed Profit
4.	Profit	• Income accruing to corporation • Surplus of corporate sector
5	Profit Tax	• Corporate Tax • Business Tax
6	Factor income	• Earned Income • Factor Payment
7	Transfer Income	• Unearned Income • Transfer Payment
8	NDPfc	• Domestic Income • Net value added at factor cost • Sum of factor income
9	NNPfc	• National Income • National Product
10	Capital formation	• Investment • Addition in capital stock
11	Income Method	• Distributive Share Method • Factor Payment Method
12	Intermediate Consumption	• Intermediate goods • Intermediate Purchases • Value of inputs

13	Imputed rent	• Services of owner occupied house • Self -owned and occupied house
14	Imputed Production	• Subsistence production • Production for self- consumption
15	GDP deflator	• Price Index • Index number
16	Nominal National income	• National income at current Price
17.	Real National Income	• National income at constant Price
18	Inventory Investment	• Change in stock
19.	Expenditure Method	• Income Disposal Method
20	Value Added Method	• Product method • Output Method
21	Compensation of employees	• Emolument of employees
22.	Operating surplus	• Income from property and entrepreneurship
23	Gross domestic capital formation	• Gross Investment • Gross capital formation
24.	Net factor Income From abroad	• Net earned income from abroad • Net earned income from foreign
25.	Private final consumption expenditure	• Household final consumption expenditure • Personal consumption expenditure.
26	Domestic territory	• Economic territory
27	Real Flow	• Physical Flow
28.	Money Flow	• Nominal Flow

1.39 Revision of Key Points

1. Domestic Territory refers to the geographical territory administered by a government within which persons, goods and capital circulate freely.

2. Normal resident refers to an individual or an institution who ordinarily resides in the country for a period more than one year and whose centre of interest also lies in that country. Factor Income is the income received by the factors of production for rendering factor services in the process of production

3. Transfer Income refers to the income received without rendering any productive service in return.

4. Final Goods refer to those goods which are used either for consumption or for investment.

5. Intermediate Goods refer to those goods which are used either for resale or for further production in the same year.

6. Owner occupied house is called imputed rent and it is included in the calculation Domestic Income and National Income.

7. Tax is a transfer income so it is not included in calculation of Domestic Income and National Income even though tax is paid from income or profit of the corporate sector. Income and profit will be included while calculating national income and domestic income.

8. Production for self-consumption or subsistence farming is included while calculating Domestic income and National Income as per its market value of the produce.

9. Imputed services like work done by housewives, teacher teaching her own child, doctor treating his children, gardening or repairing electrical fault etc. are not included in the calculation of national income and domestic income

1.40 Practice Question-Answers

Multiple Choice Questions:

1. Identify stock variable:

a. Wealth

b. Savings

c. Income

d. Change in stock.

   Answer. (a) Wealth

2. Domestic income is more than national income:

a. NFIA is Zero

b. NFIA is Negative

c. NFIA is Positive

d. None of the above.

   Answer. (b) NFIA is negative

3. Which of the following is not included in the calculation of national income?

a. Services of owner occupied house

b. Imputed production

c. Services of housewives

d. Investment.

   Answer. (C) Services of housewives

4. Transformation of Physical good into other good takes place in:

a. Joint sector

b. Primary sector

c. Tertiary sector

d. Secondary sector.

   Answer. (d) Secondary sector

5. Change in stock:

a. Opening stock + closing Stock

b. Opening- Closing stock

c. Closing stock- Opening stock

d. None of these

Answer. (C) Closing stock- Opening stock

6. Value of output:

a. Sales + Change in stock

b. Sales + closing stock

c. Sales + opening stock

d. Sales- opening stock

Answer. (a) Sales + Change in stock

7. Which of the following is not a part of compensation of employees?

a. Social security scheme by employers.

b. Social security scheme by employees.

c. Bonus

d. Salary in kind

Answer. (b) Social security scheme by employees.

8. **Which of the following is not included in calculation of national income?**

a. Gift

b. Free medical facilities to the employee

c. Subsidised lunch

d. Retirement Pension

Answer. (a) Gift

9. NVAfc =

a. Σ Factor payment

b. Σ Current Transfer Payment

c. Σ Net current transfer from ROW

d. Σ Transfer Payment

Answer. (a) Σ Factor payment

10. NDP_{mp} will be equal to:

a. NNP_{fc} + NIT

b. NNP_{fc} + Depreciation -NIT

c. NDP_{fc} + Depreciation -NIT

d. NNP_{fc} –NFIA + NIT

Answer. (d) NNP_{fc} –NFIA + NIT

11. Income is an example of

a. Stock

b. Flow

c. Inventory

d. None.

Answer. (b) Flow

12. Which of the following is a not factor payment? [CBSE 2020]

a. Free uniform to defense personal.

b. Salaries to the members of Parliament.

c. Rent paid to the owner of a building.

d. Scholarship given to the students.

Answer. (d)Scholarship given to the students

13. With a rise in real national income, welfare of the people. [All India 2018]

a. Rises

b. Falls

c. Remains unchanged.

d. None of the above

Answer. (a) Rises

14. Foreign embassies in India are a part of India's: [Delhi 2017 C]

a. Economic territory

b. Geographical territory

c. Both (a) and (b)

d. None of the above

Answer. (b)Geographical territory

15. Real GDP is considered as an index of:

a. Price level in the economy

b. Welfare of the people

c. Profit maximisation

d. None

Answer. (b)Welfare of the people

16. Which of the following is not included in calculation of the national income:

a. Bonus paid by company

b. Old age pension

c. Construction of factory

d. Subsidies food

Answer. (b) Old age pension

17. Which among the following is not Undistributed Profit:

a. Dividend

b. Net retained earning

c. Saving of corporate sector

d. Reserve Fund

Ans. (a) Dividend

18. Nominal GDP is calculated by:

a. Current Price X Current Output

b. Base year Price X Current Output

c. Base year Price X Base Year Output

d. None of these.

Answer. (a) Current Price X Current Output

19. Which of the following is included in calculation of Domestic Income?

a. Investment

b. Intermediate purchase

c. Cost of raw material

d. Transport Cost

Answer. (a) Investment

20. Which is not included in Operating Surplus includes:

a. Rent

b. Salary

c. Interest

d. Profit

Answer. (b) Salary

21. Which among the following is not a part of profit:

a. Reserve Fund

b. Dividend

c. Corporate tax

d. Bonus

Answer. (d) Bonus

22. If GDP deflator is 125, nominal GDP is ₹15,000 crores, then real GDP will be:

a. ₹10,000

b. ₹12,000

c. ₹ 15,000

d. ₹14000

   Answer. (b) ₹12000

23. Which of the following is included in the calculation of domestic income of India:

a. Profit earned by State bank of India in Japan.

b. Salary of the employees working in Indian embassy in Russia.

c. Remittance from abroad send to the parents.

d. Sale of shares.

   Answer. (b) Salary of the employees working in Indian embassy in Russia.

24. Which among the following is indirect tax?

a. Forfeiture

b. Escheat

c. Octroi

d. None

   Answer. (c) Octroi

25. 'Income from property and entrepreneurship accruing to Government administrative department' is a part of:

a. Private sector income

b. Government sector income

c. Entrepreneurs' income

d. Mixed Income

   Answer. (b) Government sector income

26. Net factor income will be negative when:

a. Exports are more than imports

b. Imports are more than exports

c. Factor income from abroad is less than factor income to abroad

d. Factor income to abroad is less than factor income from abroad.

   Answer. (c) Factor income from abroad is less than factor income to abroad

27. Compensation of employee does not include:

a. Loan given to the employee

b. Uniform from the company

c. Bonus

d. Social security scheme by employer

   Answer. (a) Loan given to the employee

28. Which one of the following is not indirect tax?

a. Value Added Tax

b. Estate duty

c. Excise Duty

d. Custom duty

Answer. (b) Estate Duty

29. Expenditure method focuses on measurement of national income at:

a. Phase of production of goods and services.

b. Phase of income disposition

c. Phase of income distribution

d. All the above

Answer. (b) Phase of income disposition

30. Gross domestic capital formation is equal to:

a. Gross fixed capital formation + Change in stock

b. Net fixed Capital formation + depreciation

c. Net Domestic capital formation + Change in stock

d. None of the above

Answer. (a) Gross fixed capital formation + Change in stock

31. Brokers commission on sale and purchase of second hand goods is included in national income because:

a. It is a part of operating surplus

b. It is factor income paid for rendering services.

c. It is a part of sale

d. None of the above

Answer. (b) It is factor income paid for rendering services.

32. National Income is sum of factor income accruing to:

a. Nationals

b. Economic territory

c. Residents

d. Both residents and Non-residents.

Answer: (c) Residents

33. Factor income paid to non- residents within the domestic territory of a country leads to:

a. Increase in domestic income

b. Decrease in national income

c. Both(a) and (b)

d. None of these

Answer. (c) Both (a) and (b)

34. "Operating surplus" refers to:

a. Income from property.

b. Income from entrepreneurship

c. Income from property and entrepreneurship.

d. None of these

Answer. (c) Income from property and entrepreneurship

35. A closed economy does not include:

a. Households

b. Firms

c. Government

d. Foreign Exchange

Answer. (d) Foreign Exchange

36. Real Flow refers to:

a. Consumption expenditure

b. Factor Payments

c. Exchange of goods and services

d. Both (a) and (b)

Answer. (c) Exchange of goods and services

37. Which of the following is the characteristic of a good?

a. Intangible

b. Cannot be transferred

c. Can be stored

d. Production and consumption happens simultaneously.

Answer: c) Can be stored.

TRUE / FALSE Questions:

1. Nominal national income provides reliable data for comparison. (True/False)

   Ans.: False.

2. National income is affected by both transfer income and factor income. (True/False).

   Ans.: False

3. Nominal GDP can never be less than real GDP. (True/False)

   Ans.: False

4. Increase in stock of goods held by consumer will be a part of capital formation. (True /False)

   Ans.: False, It is considered as final goods as it is purchased by consumer.

5. Imputed rent is a part of National Income. (True/False)

Ans.: True

6. NDP at factor cost is equal to NDP at market price in two sector economy. (True/False). Give reason.

Answer: True, Because the concept of Indirect tax and subsidy is absent in two sector economy as there is no government.

7. Gross domestic capital formation is always greater than gross fixed capital formation.

Answer: False, Gross domestic capital formation can be less than gross fixed capital formation if change in stock is negative.

8. When intermediate consumption is zero, Value added is equal to value of output. (True/False)

Answer: True, GVA = GVO-IC, GVA = GVO-0.

9. Emoluments of employees are also called compensation of employees. (True/False)

Answer: True

10. Interest received on loans taken by the government is included in national income. (True/False)

Answer: False, because it is taken for consumption purpose.

11. In a closed economy GDP is always equal to GNP. (True/False)

Answer: True, as NFIA is zero.

12. Gross investment can be equal to net investment. (True/False)

Answer: True, when depreciation is zero.

13. Market price is always more than factor cost. (True/False)

Answer: False, Market price can be less than factor cost when subsidies are more than indirect tax. MP = FC when NIT is zero.

14. Capital gain from sale of property is a part of domestic factor income. (True/False)

Answer: False, Sale of property does not create new goods.

15. Income tax is not a part of domestic income. (True/False)

Answer: False, Income tax is a part domestic income as it is paid from the salary which is a part of compensation of employee.

16. Goods produced for self -consumption is not a part of national income.

Answer.: False, it is a part of national income as goods are produced.

Identify Correct Match:

1. **Identify the correctly matched items in the Column 1 to that of Column II:**

Column I	Column II
(A) Compensation of employees	(i) Social security scheme by employees
(B) Mother cooking food	(ii) Economic Welfare
(C) Smoke from a factory	(iii)Externalities
(D)NDP fc	(iv)Real GDP

Alternatives: (a) A-(i) (b) B-(ii) (c) C-(iii) (d) D-(iv)

Answer. (c) C-(iii)

2. **Identify the correctly matched items in the Column 1 to that of Column II:**

Column I	Column II
(A) Indian embassy in Turkey	(i) Domestic territory of India
(B) Nominal GDP	(ii) Base year price to measure GDP
(C) Production of War material	(iii) Welfare of the people
(D) Wealth	(iv) Flow Variable

Alternatives: (a) A-(i) (b) B-(ii) (c) C-(iii) (d) D-(iv)

Answer. (a) A- (i)

3. **Identify the correct pair from the following Column I and Column II:**

Column I	Column II
(A) Income method	(i) Distributive share method
(B) GDP deflator	(ii) Distributed property
(C) Inventory investment	(iii) Gross investment
(D) Dividend	(iv) Price Index

Alternatives: (a) A-(i) (b) B-(ii) (c) C-(iii) (d) D-(iv)

Answer: (a) A-(i)

4. **Identify the correctly matched items in the Column 1 to that of Column II:**

Column I	Column II
(A) Real Flow	(i) Market Price
(B) Money Flow	(ii) Expenditure on goods
(C) Trade flow	(iii) Factor services
(D) Wealth	(iv) Inventory

Alternatives: (a) A-(i) (b) B-(ii) (c) C-(iii) (d) D-(iv)

Answer. (b) B -(ii)

5. **Identify the correctly matched items in the Column 1 to that of Column II:**

Column I	Column II
(A) Compensation of employees	(i) Rent
(B) Profit	(ii) Social security scheme by employees
(C) Mixed Income	(iii) Dividend
(D) GDP deflator	(iv) Price Index

Alternatives: (a) A-(i) (b) B-(ii) (c) C-(iii) (d) D-(iv)

Answer. (d) D-(iv)

Assertion - Reason and statement questions and answers:

1. Read the following statement -Assertion (A) and Reason (R). Choose one of the correct alternatives given below:

Assertion (A): Public goods are non-excludable and non-rivalries in nature.

Reason (R): Public goods cannot be provided by market mechanism.

Alternatives:

(a) Both Assertion (A) and Reason (R) are true and Reason (R) is the correct explanation of Assertion (A).

(b) Both Assertion (A) and Reason (R) are true and Reason (R) is not the correct explanation of Assertion (A).

(c) Assertion (A) is true but Reason (R) is false.

(d) Assertion (A) is false but Reason (R) is true.

Answer:(a) Both Assertion (A) and Reason (R) are true and Reason (R) is the correct explanation of Assertion (A).

2. **Assertion (A):** Stationary purchased by an office is intermediate good so it is not a part up domestic income.

Reason (R): Intermediate goods are consumed up during the production process.

Answer: a) Both Assertion (A) and Reason (R) are true and Reason (R) is the correct explanation of Assertion (A).

3. **Assertion (A):** Refrigerator purchased by a restaurant is intermediate good.

Reason (R): Intermediate goods get consumed during the process of production.

Answer:(d) Assertion (A) is false but Reason (R) is true.

4. **Assertion (A):** Nominal national income can inflate due to price.

Reason (R): Nominal national income is used for year wise comparison.

Answer. (c) Assertion (A) is true but Reason (R) is false.

5. **Assertion (A):** Stock variables are not having time dimension.

Reason (R): Stock variable are measured over a period of time.

Answer:(c) Assertion (A) is true but Reason (R) is false.

6. **Assertion (A):** Indian Embassy in Riyadh is not a part of domestic territory of India.

Reason (R): Income generated in Indian embassy will be included in domestic income of India.

Answer. (d) Assertion (A) is false but Reason (R) is true.

7. **Assertion (A):** Capital loss is depreciation.

Reason (R): Depreciation is fall in the value of fixed assets due to normal wear and tear or expected obsolesces.

Answer:(d) Assertion (A) is false but Reason (R) is true.

Read the following statements carefully and identify the correct statement.

1. **Statement 1**: A normal resident must live in a country for more than a year and his Centre of economic interest should lie in that country.

Statement 2: Crew members of aircraft are normal resident of their own country.

In the light of the given statements, choose the correct alternative from the following:

(a) Statement 1 is true and statement 2 is false

(b) Statement 1 is false and statement 2 is true

(c) Both statements 1 and 2 are true.

(d) Both statements 1 and 2 are false

Answer. (c) Both statement 1 and 2 are true.

2. Statement 1: Chalk and duster purchased by a school is a final good.

Statement 2: Final goods are used to satisfy human wants.

Answer: (b) Statement 1 is false and statement 2 is true.

3. Statement 1: Retirement pension is a part of compensation of employees.

Statement 2: Retirement pension is unearned income.

Answer: (a) Statement 1 is true and statement 2 is false.

4. Statement 1: GDP does not include externalities.

Statement 2: Externalities are non-monetary work or services.

Answer. (c) Both statements 1 and 2 are true.

5. Statement 1: Durable goods get transformed during the production process.

Statement 2: Capital goods raise the production capacity of the labour.

Answer. (b) Statement 1 is false and statement 2 is true.

Numerical Questions:

1. **Calculate Gross Value Added at Market Price from the following:**

   [AI 2004 C]

	Particulars	₹ in lakhs
i.	Intermediate cost	8
ii.	Closing stock	5
iii.	Sales	30
iv.	Net Indirect Tax	6
v.	Subsidy	1
vi.	Depreciation	3
vii.	Opening stock	4

2. **Calculate Gross Value Added at Market Price from the following:**

   [AI 2004 C]

	Particulars	₹ in lakhs
i.	Purchase of materials	30
ii.	Depreciation	12
iii.	Sales	200

	Particulars		₹ in lakhs
iv.	Excise Tax		20
v.	Opening Stock		15
vi.	Intermediate consumption		48
vii.	Closing Stock		10

3. **Calculate Net Value Added at Market Price from the following:**

[AI 2004 C]

	Particulars	₹ in lakhs
i.	Opening stock	10
ii.	Net Indirect Tax	7
iii.	Subsidy	2
iv.	Intermediate cost	12
v.	Closing stock	8
vi.	Sales	40
vii.	Depreciation	5

4. **From the following data of firm X. Calculate Gross Value Added at Factor Cost by it: [Delhi 2005]**

	Particulars	₹ in lakhs
i.	Sales	500
ii.	Opening stock	30
iii.	Closing Stock	20
iv.	Purchase of intermediate Product	300
v.	Purchase of machinery	150
vi.	Subsidy	40

5. **From the following data of firm 'A'. Calculate Gross Value Added at Market Price by it: [AI 2005]**

	Particulars	₹ in lakhs
i.	Sales	700
ii.	Change in stock	40
iii.	Depreciation	80
iv.	Net Indirect Tax	100
v.	Purchase of machinery	250
vi.	Purchase of intermediate Product	400

6. From the following data, calculate 'gross value added at factor cost'.

[**Foreign 2006**]

Particulars	₹ in Lakhs
Sales	500
Change in stock	30
Subsidies	40
Consumption of fixed capital	60
Purchase of intermediate product	350
Profits	70

7. From the following data, calculate 'gross value added at factor cost.

[**Delhi 2006**]

Particulars	₹ in Lakhs
Sales	180
Rent	5
Subsidies	10
Change in stock	15
Purchase of raw material	100
Profits	25

8. From the following data, calculate 'Gross Value Added at factor cost': [A I 2006]

Particulars	₹ in Lakhs
Net Indirect Tax	20
Purchase of intermediate Cost	120
Purchase of machine	300
Sales	250
Consumption of Fixed Capital	20
Change in Stock	30

9. Calculate Value added by firm X and firm Y from the following data:

Particulars	₹ in Lakhs
Closing stock of firm X	20
Closing stock of firm Y	15
Opening stock of firm Y	10
Opening stock of firm X	5
Sales by firm X	300
Purchase by firm X from firm Y	100

Purchase by firm Y from firm X	80
Sales by firm Y	250
Import of raw material by firm X	50
Exports by firm Y	30

10. **Calculate 'Intermediate Consumption' from the following data:**

[**Delhi 2008**]

ParticularsC	₹ in Lakhs
Value of output	200
Net Value added at factor cost	80
Sales Tax	15
Subsidy	5
Depreciation	20

11. **Calculate 'Sales' from the following data; [Delhi 2008].**

Particulars	₹ in Lakhs
Net Value added at factor Cost	300
Intermediate Consumption	200
Indirect Tax	20
Change in stock	(-)50
Depreciation	30

12. **Calculate 'Value of Output' from the following data: [Foreign2008]**

Particulars	₹ in Lakhs
Subsidy	10
Intermediate Consumption	150
Net addition to stocks	(-)13
Depreciation	30
Excise Duty	20
Net Value Added at Factor Cost	250

13. **Calculate 'Gross Value Added at Factor Cost' from the following data: [A I 2008]**

Particulars	₹ in Lakhs
Sales Tax	20
Sales	400
Purchase of raw material	250
Excise Duty	30

Change in Stock	(-)40
Import of raw material	12
Depreciation	9

14. **Calculate 'Net Value Added at Factor Cost' from the following data. [Foreign 2008]**

Particulars	₹ in Lakhs
Purchase of raw material	300
Import Duty	20
Excise Duty	30
Net addition to stocks	50
Value of output	500
Depreciation	10

15. **Calculate 'Net Value Added at Factor Cost' from the following data. [Foreign 2009]**

Particulars	₹ in Lakhs
Purchase of raw material to be used in the production unit	
Sales	400
Intermediate Cost	200
Indirect taxes	90
Change in Stock	12
Excise duty	10
Stock of raw material	6
	5

16. **Calculate Gross Domestic Product at market Price:**

Particulars	₹ in crores
Value of output of primary sector	3000
Intermediate cost of secondary sector.	900
Intermediate Cost of primary sector	1000
Net factor Income from abroad	(-20)
Net Indirect Tax	400
Value of output of secondary sector.	1,500
Value of output of tertiary sector.	1,700
Intermediate consumption of tertiary sector	500

17. **Given the following data, find the missing value of 'Private Final Consumption Expenditure' and 'Operating Surplus'**

S. No	Particulars	Amount (in ₹ cores)
1	National Income	50,000
2	Gross Domestic Capital Formation	18,000
3	Government Final Consumption Expenditure	12,000
4	Mixed Income of self-employed	13,000
5	Net factor Income from Abroad	600
6	Net Indirect Tax	1,000
7	Profits	2,000
8	Wages and Salaries	10,000
9	Net exports	2,000
10	Private Final Consumption Expenditure	?
11	Consumption of Fixed Capital	500
12	Operating Surplus	?

18. **Given the following data, find the missing value of 'Government Final Consumption Expenditure' and 'Mixed Income of self-employed'.**

S. No	Particulars	Amount (₹ cores)
1	National Income	70,000
2	Gross Domestic Capital Formation	10,000
3	Government Final Consumption Expenditure	?
4	Mixed Income of self-employed	?
5	Net factor Income from Abroad	5,000
6	Net Indirect Tax	1,000
7	Profits	1,200
8	Wages and Salaries	10,000
9	Net exports	5,000
10	Private Final Consumption Expenditure	30,000
11	Consumption of Fixed Capital	4,000
12	Operating Surplus	30,000

19. **Calculate (a) National Income and (b) Depreciation from the following data**

S. No	Particulars	Amount (₹ cores)
1	Employer's Contribution to the Provident Fund	1000
2	Gross Domestic Product	8,000
3	Interest	200
4	Rent	100
5	Net factor Income from Abroad	200
6	Indirect Tax	300
7	Profits	400
8	Wages and Salaries	5000

9	Subsidies	100
10	Private Final Consumption Expenditure	300
11	Royalty	100

20. **Calculate (a)GDP $_{MP}$ and (b) Closing stock**

S. No	Particulars	Amount (₹ in cores)
1	Private final consumption expenditure	500
2	Rent	100
3	Government final consumption expenditure	100
4	Indirect taxes	50
5	Profit	300
6	Interest	150
7	Subsidies	20
8	Mixed Income of Self employed	50
9	Opening stock	10
10	Consumption of Fixed Capital	20
11	Gross Fixed Capital Formation	300
12	Compensation of employees	300
13	Net Factor Income from abroad	(-)10
14	Net Exports	(-)20

21. **Calculate National Income by (a) GDP at FC (b)Factor Income to Abroad. [CBSE 2010]**

S. No	Particulars	Amount (₹ cores)
1	Compensation of employees	800
2	Profits	200
3	Dividends	50
4	GNP at MP	1400
5	Rent	150
6	Interest	100
7	Gross Domestic Capital formation	300
8	Net Fixed Capital formation	200
9	Change in Stock	50
10	Factor income from abroad	60
11	Net Indirect Tax	120

22. **Calculate value of 'Rent' from the following data:**

S. No	Particulars	Amount (₹ cores)
1	Gross Domestic Product at market price	18,000
2	Mixed income of self employed	7,000
3	Subsidies	250
4	Interest	800
5	Rent	?

6	Profits	975
7	Compensation of Employees	6,000
8	Consumption of Fixed Capital	1,000
9	Indirect Tax	2000

23. **Calculate National income with income method and expenditure method. [CBSE 2009]**

S. No	Particulars	₹ in Crores
1	Interest	150
2	Rent	250
3	Government Final Consumption Expenditure	600
4	Private Final Consumption Expenditure	1200
5	Profits	640
6	Compensation of employees	1000
7	Net Factor income from abroad	30
8	Net Indirect Tax	60
9	Net Exports	(-) 40
10	Consumption of fixed Capital	50
11	Net Domestic Capital Formation	340

24. **Find out (i) Gross National Product at Market Price and (ii) Net Current Transfer to Abroad. [All India 2012]**

S.No	Particulars	₹ in Crores
1	Private Final consumption Expenditure	1000
2	Depreciation	100
3	Net National disposable income	1500
4	Closing stock	20
5	Government Final consumption Expenditure	300
6	Net Indirect Tax	50
7	Opening Stock	20
8	Net Domestic Fixed Capital Formation	110
9	Net Exports	15
10	Net factor income from abroad	(-) 10

25. **Calculate (i) GDPmp and (ii) Factor Income from abroad from the following data: [All India 2010]**

S.No	Particulars	₹ in crores
1	Profit	500
2	Exports	40
3	Compensation of employees	1500
4	GNP_{fc}	2800
5	Net Current Transfer From rest of the world	90
6	Rent	300
7	Interest	400
8	Factor Income to Abroad	120

9	Net Indirect Taxes	250
10	Net Domestic Capital Formation	650
11	Gross fixed Capital formation	700
12	Change in stock	50

26. Calculate National Income by output method and Income Method:

S.No	Particulars	₹ in crores
1	Value of output	800
2	Value of intermediate consumption	400
3	Subsidies	10
4	Indirect Tax	60
5	Factor income received from abroad	10
6	Factor income paid abroad	10
7	Mixed income of self employed	20
8	Rent and royalty	120
9	Interest and profit	40
10	Wages and salaries	20
11	Consumption of fixed capital	50
12	Employer's contribution to social security scheme	10

27. Calculate National Income from the following. [CBSE 2013]

S.No	Particulars	₹ in crores
1	Govt .Final consumption Expenditure	100
2	Subsidies	10
3	Rent	200
4	Wages and Salaries	600
5	Indirect Taxes	60
6	Private final consumption Expenditure	800
7	Gross Domestic capital Formation	120
8	Social security contribution by employers	55
9	Royalty	25
10	Net factor income to abroad	30
11	Interest	20
12	Consumption of fixed capital	10
13	Profit	130
14	Net Exports	70
15	Change in stock	50

28. From the following data, calculate NNP at by (a) Expenditure method (b) income method. [NCERT]

S.No	Particular	₹ in crores
1	Personal Consumption Expenditure	700
2	Wages and salaries	700

3	Employer's contribution to Social Security Scheme	100
4	Gross business fixed investment	60
5	Gross residential construction Investment	60
6	Gross Public Investment	40
7	Inventory Investment	20
8	Profits	100
9	Govt. Purchase of goods and services	200
10	Rent	50
11	Exports	40
12	Imports	20
13	Interest	40
14	Mixed Income	100
15	Net Factor Income From Abroad	(-) 10
16	Depreciation	20
17	Subsidies	10
18	Indirect Taxes	20

29. **Calculate compensation of employee from the following data: [CBSE SQP-2020].**

S.No	Particulars	₹ in crores
1	Profit after Tax	20
2	Interest	45
3	Gross Domestic Product at Market Price	200
4	Goods and Service Tax	10
5	Consumption of fixed capital	50
6	Rent	25
7	Corporate tax	5

30. **Given the following data, find the missing value of 'Wages and salary 'and 'Gross Domestic Capital Formation'. [CBSE, DELHI 2019]**

S.No	Particulars	₹ in crores
1	Mixed Income of self employed	3500
2	Net Indirect Tax	300
3	Wages and Salaries	?
4	Government Final Consumption Expenditure	14000
5	Net Exports	3000
6	Consumption of fixed capital	300
7	Net factor Income from Abroad	700
8	Operating Surplus	12000
9	National Income	30000
10	Profit	500
11	Gross Domestic Capital Formation	?
12	Private Final Consumption Expenditure	11,000

31. **Calculate National Income:**

S. No	Particulars	Amount (₹ cores)
1	Compensation of employees	2000
2	Profits	800
3	Consumption of fixed capital	120
4	Rent	300
5	Interest	250
6	Mixed Income of self-employed	7000
7	Net current transfer to abroad	200
8	Net exports	-(100)
9	Net Factor income to abroad	60
10	Net Indirect Tax	1500

Answers of Numerical Questions

1. GVA_{MP} = Sales + Change in stock-IC

   = 30 + (5-4)-8 GVA_{MP} = ₹23 lakhs

2. GVA_{MP} = Sales + Change in stock-IC

   = 200 + (10-15)-48 GVA_{MP} = ₹ 147 Lakhs.

3. NVA_{MP} = Sales + Change in stock –IC-Depreciation

   NVA_{MP} = 40 + (8-10)-12-5 NVA_{MP} = ₹21 lakhs

4. GVA_{fc} = Sales + Change in stock-IC-NIT

   = 500 + (20-30) -300- (0-40) GVA_{fc} = ₹ 230 lakhs

5. GVA_{MP} = Sales + Change in Stock-IC

   = 700 + 40-400 GVA_{MP} = ₹340 lakhs

6. GVA_{fc} = Sales + Change in stock-IC-NIT

   = 500 + 30-350-(0-40)

   = 570-350 GVA_{fc} = ₹220 lakhs

7. GVA_{fc} = Sales + Change in stock-IC-NIT

   = 180 + 15-100-(0-10)

   GVA_{fc} = ₹105 lakhs

8. GVA_{fc} = Sales + Change in stock-IC-NIT

   = 250 + 30-120-20

   = 280-100 GVA_{fc} = ₹140 lakhs

9. Value added by firm X = Sales of X + Change in stock of firm X- Purchase by firm X from firm Y- Import of raw material by firm X.

   = 300 + (20-5)-100-5- = ₹165 lakhs

Value added by firm Y = Sales by firm Y + Change in stock by firm Y- Purchase by firm Y from firm X

= 250 + (15-10)-80 = ₹175 Lakhs

10. NVA fc = GVO- IC-NIT-Depreciation

80 = 200-IC-(15-5) -20

80 = 170-IC

IC = ₹90 lakhs

11. NVAfc = Sales + Change in Stock-IC-Depreciation-NIT

300 = Sales + (-50)-200-30-20

Sales = 300 + 300 = ₹600

12. NVAfc = GVO-IC-Dep-NIT

250 = GVO-150-30-(20-10)

250 = GVO-190

GVO = ₹440 Lakhs

13. GVA_{fc} = Sales + Change in stock-IC-NIT

= 400 + (-40)-250-(20 + 30)

= 400-340 GVAfc = ₹60 lakhs

14. NVAfc = GVO-IC-Dep-NIT

= 500-300-50-10

= 500-360 NVAfc = ₹140

15. NVAfc = Sales + Change in stock-Ic-Dep-NIT

= 200 + 10-90-12-5

NVAfc = ₹103 lakhs

16. GDPmp = Value of Output-Value of Inputs

GDPmp = (3000 + 1500 + 1700)-(1000 + 900 + 500)

GDPmp = 6200-2400 GDPmp = ₹3800 crores

17. **Operating Surplus** = NI- (COE + MISE + NFIA) = 50,000-(10,000 + 13,000 + 600)

O S = ₹ 26,400 crores

NNPfc = GDPmp –DEP- NIT + NFIA

Private Final Consumption Expenditure (C) = NI-(G + GDCF + (X-M) + NIT + Dep-NFIA

C = 50,000-(12,000 + 18,000 + 2000) + 500 + 1,000-600 PFCE = ₹ 18900 Crores

18. Mixed Income = National Income-(COE + OS + NFIA) = 70,000-(30,000 + 10,000 + 5000)

Mixed Income of Self Employed = ₹25,000 crores.

Government Final Consumption Expenditure (G) = NI-(C + GDCF + (X-M) + NIT + Dep-NFIA

G = 70,000-(30,000 + 10,000 + 5000) + 4000 + 1000-5000

Government Final Consumption Expenditure (G) = ₹ 25,000 crores.

19. NNPfc = COE + OS + MISE + NFIA

    = (5000 + 1000) + (200 + 100 + 400 + 100) + 200

    NNPfc (National Income) = ₹7000 crores

    NNPfc = GDPmp-Dep + NFIA –NIT

    7000 = 8000-Dep + 200-(300-100)

    7000 = 8000-Dep + 200-200

    Dep = 8000-7000 **Depreciation = ₹1000**

20. **NDPfc = COE + OS + MISE = 300 + (300 + 150 + 100) + 50 = ₹ 90 crores**

    GDPmp = COE + OS + MISE + Dep + NIT

    = 300 + (300 + 150 + 100) + 50 + 20 + (50 -20) **GDPmp = ₹ 950 crores**

    (b)Closing Stock

    GDPmp = C + G + (GFCF + Change in Stock) + (X-M)

    950 = 500 + 100 + 300 + Closing Stock-10 + (-)20

    950 = 870 + Closing Stock

    Closing Stock = 950-870 = 80

    Closing Stock = ₹ 80 Crores.

21. (a) GDP at FC = NDP at FC + Depreciation [Dep = GDCF-(NFCF + Δ Stock) = 300-250] [Dep = 50]

    GDP at FC = (800 + 200 + 150 + 100) + 50 = ₹1300 crores

    NFIA = GNPmp-GDPmp = 1400- (1300 + 120) NFIA = -20

    NFIA = FIFA-FITA

    -20 = 60- FITA

    FITA = ₹80 crores

22. GDPmp = NDPfc + Depreciation + Net Indirect Tax

    18,000 = 6000 + 7,000 + {800 + 975 + Rent} + 1000 + {2,000-250}

    18,000 = 17,525 + Rent

    Rent = ₹ 475 Crores

23. **Income Method:** NNP_{fc} = COE + OS + MISE + NFIA = 1000 + (150 + 250 + 640) + 30 NNP_{fc} = ₹ 2070 crores.

    Expenditure method: NNPfc = C + G + NDCF + (X-M) –Dep + NFIA = 1200 + 600 + 340 -40-60 + 30 NNP_{fc} = ₹ 2070 crores

24. **(i) Expenditure Method:**

    GDP_{mp} = C + G + [NDFCF + (CS-OS) + CFC] + Net Exports-Net Factor Income to Abroad

    = 1000 + 300 + [110 + (20-20) + 100] + 15 –(-10) GDP_{mp} = ₹1535 Crores

    (ii)NNDI = NNP_{mp} + NIT + NCTFA

1500 = (1535-100)-Net current from abroad

1500-1435 = Net current from abroad

Net current from abroad = ₹65 Crores

25. NDP_{fc} = COE + OS + MISE = 500 + 1500 + 300 + 400 = 2700

Depreciation = [GFCF + change in Stock] –NDCF

Dep = 700 + 50-650 = 100

(i)GDPmp = NDP_{fc} + Dep + NIT

= 2700 + 100 + 250 = **₹3050 crores**

(ii)NFIA = NNPfc-NDPfc = [2800-100]-2700

NFIA = 0

NFIA = FIFA-FITA

0 = FIFA-120

Factor Income from abroad = 120

26. National Income by Output Method:

NNP_{fc} = GVO-IC-Depreciation- NIT + NFIA

= 800-400-50- [60-10] + [10-20] NNP_{fc} = ₹290 crores.

National Income by income method:

NNPfc = COE + OS + MISE + NFIA

= [110 + 10] + [40 + 20] + 120 + [10-20]

NNPfc = ₹290 crores

27. (a) NNP_{fc} (By income Method) = Coe + OS + MISE + NFIA

= 200 + 600 + 55 + 25 + (-30) + 20 + 130 = ₹1000Crores.

NNP_{fc}(By Expenditure Method) = C + G + GDCF + (X-M) + NFIA –DEP-NIT

= 800 + 100 + 120 + 70-30 -10-[60-10] NNP_{fc} = ₹1000 Crores

28. Expenditure Method:

GDP_{fc} = C + G + I + (X-M)- NIT

= 700 + [60 + 60 + 40 + 20] + 200 + (40-20) + [10-20]

GDP_{fc} = **₹1,090 Crores**

(b)Income Method:

GDP_{fc} = COE + OS + MISE + DEP = 700 + 100 + 100 + 50 + 40 + 100-10-10 + 20

GDP_{fc} = 1,090Crores

29. COE = GDPmp- Depreciation-Rent- Interest –Profit- NIT

COE = 200-50-25-45-20-5-10 COE = ₹ 45 crores

30. NNP_{fc} = COE + OS + MISE + NFIA

30000 = Wages and Salaries + 12000 + 3500 + 700

Wages and Salaries = 30000- (12000 + 3500 + 700) = ₹13,800 crores

31. National Income = COE + OS + MISE + NFIA

= 2000 + {800 + 300 + 250} + 7000-60 = 2000 + 1350 + 7000-60

National Income = ₹10,290 crores

Question-Answer on Real and Nominal GDP

31. If the Real GDP is ₹ 400 and Nominal GDP is ₹450, Calculate the Price Index. (Base = 100) [A I2015 Set-1]

32. If the Real GDP is ₹ 500 and Price Index (Base = 100) is 125, Calculate the Nominal GDP. [AI 2015 Set 2]

33. If the Nominal GDP is ₹600 and Price Index is 120, Calculate the Real GDP. (Base = 100) [AI 2015 Set-3]

34. If the Real GDP is ₹ 200 and Price Index is 110, Calculate the Nominal GDP. (Base = 100) [Delhi,2015 Set-1]

35. If the Nominal GDP is ₹1200 and Price Index is 120, Calculate the Real GDP. (Base = 100). [Delhi, Set-2].

36. If the Real GDP is₹ 300 and Nominal GDP is₹ 330, calculate Price Index. (Base = 100) [Delhi, 2015 Set-3]

Answers of questions on Real and Nominal GDP:

31. **Real GDP** = Base Year Price X Current Year Production

400 = 100 X Current Year Production

Current Year Production = $\dfrac{400}{100}$ = 4

Nominal GDP = Current Year Price X Current Year Production

450 = Current Year Price X 4

Current Year Price = $\dfrac{450}{4}$ = 112.5

Price Index = $\dfrac{Current\ Year\ Price}{Base\ Year\ Price}$ = $\dfrac{112.5}{100}$

Price Index = 1.125

32. **Step-1: Real GDP** = Base Year Price X Current Year Production

500 = 100 X Current Year Production

Current Year Production = $\dfrac{500}{100}$ = 5

Step-2: Nominal GDP = Current Year Price X Current Year Production = 125 X 5 = 625 **Nominal GDP = 625**.

33. **Nominal GDP** = Current Year Price X Current Year Production(Quantity)

600 = 120 X Current Year Quantity

Current Year Quantity = $\dfrac{600}{120}$ = 5

Real GDP = Base Year Price X Current Year Production

Real GDP = 100 X 5 **Real GDP = 500**

34. **Step-1: Real GDP** = Base Year Price X Current Year Production

200 = 100 X Current Year Quantity

Current Year Quantity $= \dfrac{200}{100} = 2$

Real GDP = 500

Step-2: **Nominal GDP** = Current Year Price X Current Year Production(Quantity)

Nominal GDP = 110 X 2 = **220**

35. Step-1: **Nominal GDP** = Current Year Price X Current Year Production

1200 = 120 X Current Year Quantity

Current Year Quantity $= \dfrac{1200}{120} = \mathbf{10}$

Step-2: **Real GDP** = Base Year Price X Current Year Production

Real GDP = 100 X10 **Real GDP = 1000**

36. Step-1: **Real GDP** = Base Year Price X Current Year Production

300 = 100 X Current Year Production

Current Year Production $= \dfrac{300}{100} = 3$

Step-2: **Nominal GDP** = Current Year Price X Current Year Production

330 = Current Year Price X 3

Current Year Price $= \dfrac{330}{3} = 110$

Step-3: Price Index $= \dfrac{Current\,Year\,Price}{Base\,Year\,Price} = \dfrac{110}{100}$ **Price Index = 1.1**

Question and Answers (3marks, 4 marks,6marks)

1. **Do you agree that an increase in real GDP always leads to an increase in the welfare of the people? Explain.**

   Answer: Normally it is considered that higher level of GDP is higher index of well-being. But this is not correct due to following limitation:

   i. **Unequal distribution of GDP**: An increase in the GDP or GNP may not increase economic welfare if distribution of income is unequal or wealth is concentrated in few hands or households. Unequal distribution will result in making rich richer and poor poorer.

   ii. **Production of harmful material**: If GDP increases because of production of war material, liquor, weapons, cigarette, tobacco (pan masala and gutka), etc. It will not increase economic welfare.

   iii. **Non**-Monetary Work: Many activities are not paid, it is done due to love and care which are not evaluated in terms of money. Services of housewife, Mother teaching her own children, barter exchange, social work etc. increases welfare (rejuvenate, energies and recreates, refresh, increase Knowledge) but not included in measurement of GDP. Thus GDP under estimates welfare by not including non -monetary exchange.

   iv. **High Population Growth Rate:** If population growth rate is higher than growth of GDP or GNP than welfare will decrease.

   v. **Externalities:** Any benefit or harm done by an individual or firm for which they are neither paid nor penalised is known as externalities. It can be of two types:

vi. ***Positive Externalities***: Work done by social workers, park increases welfare but they are neither paid nor included in GDP or GNP estimation.

Negative Externalities: Smoke of a factory pollutes the air, noise pollution by factory results in fall of social welfare but they are not penalised so it not accounted in GDP even they though they create nuisance, health hazards, environment issues and loss of vegetation.

Conclusion: Though GDP or GNP may not be correct index of welfare due to its limitations, yet it reflects some index of welfare. Increase GDP or GNP may increase standard of living of the people, reduces poverty or unemployment.

2. **Cash transfer of subsidy on LPG raises annual income of the households. Does it increase domestic? Give reason for your answer.**

Answer: No, cash transfer of subsidy will be treated as transfer income so domestic income will not increase as transfer income cannot be added in calculation of domestic income.

Annual income of the households will increase but it will be treated as transfer income not factor income.

3. **Yusi purchased a car of worth 7 lakhs Indian rupees to go to her office. Should it be treated as an intermediate consumption or final consumption? How will you treat it in the calculation of national Income**

Answer: Car purchased by Yusi will not be treated as intermediate good but a final good. Car purchased by her is not used for adding value or for resale so it is not intermediate good. It will be included with expenditure method as private final consumption expenditure in the calculation of National Income.

4. **How will the following affect Net domestic product at factor?**

    i.   Consumption of fixed capital

    ii. Net indirect tax

    iii. Net factor income from abroad

    iv. Net exports of goods and services.

    Answer:

    i.   Consumption of fixed capital: It is deducted from GDP to arrive NDP. So consumption of fixed capital reduces NDP.

    ii. It is deducted from NDP_{MP} to get NDP_{FC}.

    iii. Net factor income from abroad: It is not included in domestic income.

    iv. Net exports of goods and services. It is included in domestic income. Increases NDP.

5. **Sate whether the following statements are true or false. Give reason for your answers.**

    i.   Capital formation is a flow.

    ii. Bread is always a consumer good.

    iii. Nominal GDP is never less than Real GDP.

    iv. Gross domestic capital formation is always greater than gross fixed capital formation.

    Answer:

    i.   True, Capital formation is flow as it is measured over a period of time.

ii.   False, Bread is not always a consumer good. It depends on the end use of bread whether it is a consumption good or production good (intermediate good). If bread is used by the households, it is consumer good but if it is used by a restaurant for making sandwiches or sweets then it is producer good (intermediate good).

iii. False, Nominal GDP can be less than real GDP when price of goods and services produced in the base year is more than price of goods and services in the current year.

iv.   False, it is not always true. Gross domestic capital formation = Gross fixed Capital Formation + Change in stock.

v.   GDCF can be less or more than GFCF.

Case-Study based Question:

1. Read the following news report and answer the questions on the basis of the same.

There are three main justifications for imposing a tax on a specific good. Firstly, it raises money for the government.

Secondly, its use inflicts costs on third parties that are not factored into its price. The third rationale for imposing sin taxes is to discourage the use of undesirable goods. Critics of such taxes have argued that they are ineffective because the goods they target tend to be addictive, making consumers relatively unresponsive to changes in price. In fact, study after study has shown that sin taxes do tend to reduce consumption.

Without intervention from the government, the economy will produce too many goods that foul up the atmosphere and that benefits both manufacturers and consumers, but harms everyone who breathes in the by-products. Proponents of so- called "sin taxes" apply this logic to goods deemed to be socially undesirable. Many studies have a tendency to overstate the magnitude of such externalities, since they present gross costs instead of net ones. **The Economist; July 31st,2018**

a.   Goods purchased to satisfy human wants are:

   i.   Capital goods

   ii. Intermediate goods

   iii. Consumption goods

   iv. None of these

b.   Pollution created by factories is an example_____________ externality. (Positive/Negative)

c.   Total addition of capital goods to the existing stock of capital during the given year is known as:

   i.   Depreciation

   ii. Gross Costs

   iii. Gross Investment

   iv. Net investment

Answers:

a.   **(iii) Consumption good**

b.   **Negative Externality**

c.   **(iii) Gross Investment**

2. Read the following and answer the questions on the basis of the same.

The reserve bank of India in its latest bulletin has dedicated a chapter on the state of economy to highlight the key indicators of India's economic health. The RBI has now started 'now casting' or in simpler term 'the prediction of present or very near future of the state of economy'. The first 'now cast' has predicted the country's economy will shirk by 8.6% in the second quarter (July, August, September) of the current fiscal year. This means that India has entered in technical recession in the first half of current fiscal year for the first time in history. It is important to note that the GDP has shrunk by 23.9% in the first quarter (April, May, June). India's GDP growth contracts by 23.9%.

The RBI Bulletin, March 27th,2020

1. The continuous fall in the GDP leads to ____________(choose the correct alternatives)

    a.   Rise in national income

    b.   Fall in national income

    c.   No change in national income

    d.   Fall in general price level

2. What is term used for the prediction of present or very near future of the state of economy?

3. Second quarter of the fiscal year includes:

    a.   January, February, March

    b.   April, May, June

    c.   June, July, August

    d.   September, October, November

Answers:

1. **(b) fall in national Income**

2. **Now cast**

3. **(c) June, July, August**

3. Read the following and answer the questions on the basis of the same.

Capital goods are used make consumer goods. It is used again and again during the production process. Capital goods are investment or fixed assets. They undergo wear and tear during the process of production. Machine tool used for production in a factory. A grinder juicer machine in a juice shop or a sewing machine in a tailoring shop is example of capital good. There are intermediate goods which are used in the production. Intermediate goods get transformed during the production process. There are certain goods which are used as intermediate goods by some producers and final goods by some consumers. It is end used which helps to differentiate between final and intermediate goods. Milk used by the household is a consumer good. Milk used by a restaurant to make sweet is an intermediate good. While calculating GDP or GNP of a country value of intermediate good is not included only value of final goods are included. GDP is the measurement of the market value of all final goods and services. To avoid double counting, market value of intermediate good is not included in the calculation of GDP.

a.   Purchase of biscuits by the household for consumption will be considered as:

    i.   Intermediate good

    ii.   Consumer good

    iii.   Capital good

    iv.   None

b. A mixer juicer purchased by a household is a _______________ good, when it is purchased by a restaurant, it is _______________good.

   i.   Capital good/ consumer good

   ii. Consumer good/Capital good

   iii. Intermediate good/capital good

   iv. Consumer good/Intermediate good

c. The inclusion of market value of bread purchased by a restaurant while calculating the GDP will lead to____________(single counting/double counting).

d. Which kind of goods are known as final goods?

   i.   First use of product

   ii. End-use of product

   iii. No use of product

   iv. Full use of product

Answers:

a. **ii. Consumer good**

b. **ii. Consumer good/Capital good**

c. **Double counting**

d. **ii. End-use of product**

Case study:

4. Read the following and answer the questions on the basis of the same:

Gift, grants, pocket money are merely transfer income from one person to another. No new goods are produced or income is generated. Hence, it is not included in calculation of GDP or GNP. Income earned through illegal activities like black marketing, gambling, pick-pocketing, smuggling is not included while calculating GDP or GNP because they are unlawful activities and there is problem of estimation. Services of housewives, gardening done as a hobby, repair of some electrical fault at home or a teacher teaching her own child at home are not included in domestic income or national income as estimation of these work is difficult. If a teacher teaches other children and she is paid or a maid comes and cleans house or a house help cooks food, their work will be included in calculation of GDP or GNP as their income is factor income. Imputed rent of owner occupied house and production for self-consumption are include in the calculation of GDP or GNP as per market value of it. Value of second hand good is not included while value of goods produced in the current year is included in estimation of domestic income and national income. Inclusion of value of second hand good will lead to double counting as it was included in the year it was produced. Brokerage for sale and purchase of second hand good is included as the broker renders services and he is paid for it. Income from lottery or windfall gain should not be included in estimation of national income as no new goods are produced.

a. Money earned from gambling is _______________in the calculation of national income. (included/ not included).

b. Value of vegetables produced in the kitchen garden is considered as:

   i.   Marketable good

   ii. Non-marketable good

iii.   Capital good

iv.   Both (i) and (ii)

c.   Pension paid by a company to its retired employee is:

i.   Factor payment

ii.   Transfer payment

iii.   Unearned income

iv.   Private Income

d.   Value of following activity is not included in GNP:

i.   Economic activities

ii.   Non-economic activities

iii.   Leisure time activities

iv.   Both ii. and iii

Answers:

a.   **Not included**

b.   **ii. Non-marketable good**

c.   **i. Factor Income**

d.   **iv. Both ii. and iii**

Practice Test Paper

GENERAL INSTRUCTIONS:

Read the following instructions very carefully and strictly follow them:

All questions are compulsory

i.   *Question No. 1-20 are 1- mark questions and are to be answered in one word/sentence.*

ii.   *Question No. 21 is a 3- mark question.*

iii.   *Question No. 22 is 3- marks question. Numerical*

iv.   *Question No. 23 is 4 marks question. Numerical Explanation.*

Q.-1:Why are the intermediate goods not included in the National Income while measuring National Income?

(A) To avoid double counting
(B) It decreases income
(C) Intermediate goods are not good
(D) All of these

Q-2: Calculation of National Income at Market Prices is known as:

(A) Money income
(B) Real income
(C) Non-monetary income
(D) None of these

Q-3: Accounting of National Income at constant prices is known as:

(A) Money income
(B) Real income
(C) Current income
(D) Domestic income

Q-4: Which of the following items are excluded from GNP measurement?

(A) Purely financial transactions
(B) Transfer of used goods and non-market goods and services
(C) Illegal activities and the value of leisure
(D) All of these

Q-5: Increase in Stock of Capital is known as:

(a) Capital Loss
(b) Capital Profit
(c) Capital Formation
(d) None of these

Q-6: Which of the following is included in real flow?

(a) Flow of Goods
(b) Flow of Services
(c) Both (a) and (b)
(d) None of these

Q-7: Give reason and categories the following into stock and flow.

(a) Balance of payment account
(b) Capital Formation
(c) GDP
(d) Profits
(e) Capital
(f) Income
(g) Inventory.

Q-8: Read the following statements carefully:

Statement 1 - Net investment is a stock concept.

Statement 2 - Capital is a flow concept.

In the light of the given statements,

Choose the correct alternative from the following:

(a) Statement 1 is true and statement 2 is false
(b) Statement 1 is false and statement 2 is true
(c) Both statements 1 and 2 are true
(d) Both statements 1 and 2 are false

Q-9: Product method of calculating national income is also known as:

a) Income Method
b) Expenditure Method
c) Value Added Method
d) Distribution Method

Q-10: Identify the correctly matched pair of the items in Column A to those in Column B:

Column 1	Column 2
1.Money Flow	(a) Depreciation
2.Real Flow	(b) Factor Service
3.Trade	(c)House Work by Housewife
4.CapitalFlow	(d) Inventory

(A) 1 – (a)
(B) 2 – (b)
(C) 3 – (c)
(D) 4 – (d)

Q-11: Unforeseen obsolescence of fixed capital assets during production is:

(A) Consumption of fixed capital
(B) Capital loss
(C) Income loss
(D) None of the above

Q-12: Identify which of the following statements is true:

(A) Durable goods get transformed in the production and consumption process.
(B) More sophisticated and heavy capital goods raise the ability of a labour to produce goods.
(C) Intermediate goods do not pass through any more stages of production.
(D) Final goods refers to that good which is purchased for the purpose of further production/resale.

Q-13: Which of the following statements is incorrect?

(A) Gross Domestic Product (GDP) at Market Price = GDP at Factor Cost + Net Indirect Taxes
(B) Net National Product (NNP) at Market Price = NNP at Factor Cost.
(C) Gross National Product (GNP) at Market Price = GDP at Market Price + Net Factor Income from Abroad
(D) Net National Product (NNP) at Factor cost = National Income

Q-14: National Income is the sum of factor incomes accruing to:

(A) Nationals
(B) Economic territory
(C) Residents
(D) Both residents and non-residents

Q-15: Read the following statements: Assertion (A) and Reason (R). Choose one of the correct alternatives given below:

Assertion (A): Money received from the sale of second-hand cars will be considered while estimating national income.

Reason (R): Their value is already included and it does not contribute to the current flow of goods and services.

Alternatives:

(a) Both Assertion (A) and Reason (R) are true and Reason (R) is the correct explanation of Assertion (A).
(b) Both Assertion (A) and Reason (R) are true and Reason (R) is not the correct explanation of Assertion (A).
(c) Assertion (A) is true but Reason (R) is False.
(d) Assertion (A) is False but Reason (R) is true.

Q-16: Read the following statements: Assertion (A) and Reason (R). Choose one of the correct alternatives given below:

Assertion (A): Real GDP shows the change in the level of economic activity and facilitates inter-regional and international comparison.

Reason (R): It is an inflation-adjusted index and accounts for an increase in the level of production in response to the price changes.

Alternatives:

(a) Both Assertion (A) and Reason (R) are true and Reason (R) is the correct explanation of Assertion (A).
(b) Both Assertion (A) and Reason (R) are true and Reason (R) is not the correct explanation of Assertion (A).
(c) Assertion (A) is true but Reason (R) is False.
(d) Assertion (A) is False but Reason (R) is true.

17. Read the following statements: Assertion (A) and Reason (R). Choose one of the correct alternatives given below:

Assertion (A): Production of services for self-consumption is not included in national income.

Reason (R): Domestic Services are already included in the value of final goods. If they are included again, it will lead to double counting.

Alternatives:

(a) Both Assertion (A) and Reason (R) are true and Reason (R) is the correct explanation of Assertion (A).
(b) Both Assertion (A) and Reason (R) are true and Reason (R) is not the correct explanation of Assertion (A).
(c) Assertion (A) is true but Reason (R) is False
(d) Assertion (A) is False but Reason (R) is true.

18. Read the following statements: Assertion (A) and Reason (R). Choose one of the correct alternatives given below:

Assertion (A): Imputed value of owner-occupied lands are a part of both domestic income and national income.

Reason (R): Factors of production are bound to give their services regardless of the fact that it is giving its services to the owner or an outsider.

Alternatives:

(a) Both Assertion (A) and Reason (R) are true and Reason (R) is the correct explanation of Assertion (A).
(b) Both Assertion (A) and Reason (R) are true and Reason (R) is not the correct explanation of Assertion (A).
(c) Assertion (A) is true but Reason (R) is False
(d) Assertion (A) is False but Reason (R) is true.

19. Can domestic income be more than national income? Give reason.

20. Is bread a final good? Give reason for your answer.

21. How will you treat the following while estimating domestic factor income of India?

(i) Remittances from non-resident Indians to their family in India.

(ii) Rent paid by the embassy of England in India to a resident Indian.

(iii)Profit earned by branches of foreign bank in India.

Q-22: Calculate Value of output from the following data:

Items	₹ in (Lakhs)
Subsidy	10
Intermediate consumption	150
Net addition to stock	(-)13
Consumption of fixed capital	30
Excise Duty	20
Net value added at factor cost	250

Q-23: Calculate Net Value Added at market price.

Items	(₹ in lakh)
i) Fixed capital good with a life span of 5 years	15
ii) Raw Materials	6
iii) Sales	25
iv) Net Change in Stock	(-) 2
v) Taxes on production	1

Answers of Test Paper:

1. **(A) To avoid double counting.**
2. **(A) Money Income.**
3. **(B) Real Income.**
4. **(D)-All of these.**
5. **(C) Capital Formation.**
6. **(C) Both (a) and (b)**
7. (b), (c), (d), (f) are flow as they are measured over a period of time.

    (a), (e) and (g) are stock variable as they are measured at a point of time
8. **(d) Both 1 and 2 are false.**
9. (c) Value Added Method
10. **2-(B)**
11. **(B) Capital Loss**
12. (B) More sophisticated and heavy capital goods raise the ability of a labourer to produce goods.
13. (B) Net National Product (NNP) at Market Price = NNP at Factor Cost.
14. (C) Residents
15. (d) Assertion (A) is False but Reason (R) is true
16. (a) Both Assertion (A) and Reason (R) are true and Reason (R) is the correct explanation of Assertion (A).
17. (C) Assertion (A) is true but Reason (R) is False .

18. (a) Both Assertion (A) and Reason (R) are true and Reason (R) is the correct explanation of Assertion (A)

19. Yes, Domestic Income can be more than National Income when NFIA(Net Factor Income From Abroad) is negative.

20. Bread is final good if it is purchased by the household for final consumption.

Bread is intermediate good if it is purchased for resale or by a restaurant for making dishes to sell.

21. **(i) Remittances from non-resident Indians to their family in India—It is not included in calculating Domestic Income and National Income as remittance from abroad is a Transfer Income.**

(ii) Rent paid by the embassy of England in India to a resident Indian-----It is included in calculation of Domestic Income as rent is factor Income.

(iii)Profit earned by branches of foreign bank in India-------- It is included in calculation of Domestic Income as Bank is located in India.

22. $\textbf{NVA}_{\textbf{fc}}$ **= (Sales + Change in stock) –IC-Dep-NIT**

250 = GVO-150-30-(20-10)

250 = GVO- 190 GVO = 250 + 190 GVO = ₹ 440 lakhs

23. Value of Output = Sales + Change in Stock

Value of Output = iii) + iv) = 25 + (– 2) = 23

Gross Value Added at MP = Value of Output – Intermediate Consumption

GVA at MP = ₹ 23 – ₹ 6 = ₹ 17

Net Value Added at MP = GVA at MP – Consumption of fixed Capital

Consumption of Fixed Capital = Total value of fixed Capital/life span = 15/5 = ₹ 3 lakh

NVA at MP = ₹17 – ₹ 3 = **₹ 14**

X---X

(Note: Private Income, Personal Income, Personal Disposable Income are not in the present syllabus of CBSE)

NDPfc	COE	Rent	Interest	UDP	Profit Tax	Dividend	Mixed Income	Govt. Sector Income		
NNPfc	COE	Rent	Interest	UDP	Profit Tax	Dividend	Mixed Income	Govt. Sector Income	NFIA	
Private Income	COE	Rent	Interest	UDP	Profit Tax	Dividend	Mixed Income		NFIA	Transfer Income
Personal Income	COE	Rent	Interest			Dividend	Mixed Income		NFIA	Transfer Income

Domestic Income = Private sector Income + Government sector income

National Income = Private sector Income + Government sector income + NFIA

National Income = Domestic Income + NFIA

Private Income: Private income is sum total of all types of income received by the private households and enterprise. It includes both factor income and transfer income from the country as well as from abroad

Private Income = Private Sector Income + NFIA + Transfer Incomes

Pvt. Income = NDPfc – Govt. Sector Income + NFIA + Transfer Income

Pvt. Income = NNPfc- Govt. Sector income + Transfer Income

Pvt. Income = Personal Income + Corporate Tax + Undistributed Profit.

Note: Private sector Income and Private Income are different. Private sector Income includes only factor income earned by private sector within the domestic territory.

Private Income is a wider concept as it includes Private sector income , NFIA and all types of transfer Income within and outside the country.

Transfer Income = National debt Interest + Current transfer from the Government + Net current Transfer From rest of the world.

Personal Income: It is the sum of all income earned by the households with in the domestic territory and from abroad both factor and transfer income. It means income of an individual both earned and unearned income.

Personal income = Private income- Profit tax – Undistributed profit.

Personal Income = National Income – Govt. Sector Income- UDP-Profit Tax + Transfer Income.

Personal Income = Domestic Income- Govt. Sector Income-UDP-Profit Tax + NFIA + Transfer Income.

Personal Income = Private sector income-UDP-Profit Tax + NFIA + Transfer Income

Personal Disposable Income: That part of an individual's income which is available with him at his disposal, which he/she can spent on consumption or save. An individual has to pay tax and fees and fines to the government from his income. The amount left after paying tax and other charges to the government is called Personal Disposable Income(PDI).

Personal Disposable Income = Personal Income –Personal Tax- Misc. Receipt of the Government.

Personal Disposable Income = Personal Consumption Expenditure + Personal Savings.

UNIT: 2
MONEY AND BANKING

2.1 Evolution of Money

Money is a matter which facilitates exchange of goods.

Evolution of money was mainly through commodity money, metallic money, paper money, plastic money and e-money.

Money is the most important invention of modern time. It has undergone a long process of historical evolution.

- **Barter System:** Direct exchange of goods against goods is known as barter system. The inconvenience and drawbacks of barter system led to the gradual use of common medium of exchange.

- **Commodity Money:** Commodities like seashells, pearls, precious stones, tea, tobacco, leather, clothes, salt, wine etc. have been used as a medium of exchange. These were called commodity money. But commodity money lack uniformity and storing for long time was not possible.

- **Metallic Money:** Inconvenience of commodity money and barter system lead to evolution of metallic money. In the beginning it was gold and silver coins but purity and uniformity of weight of precious metal lead to private and public coinage and later government took the charge of minting money.

- **Paper Money:** Lack of uniformity of weight and purity of precious metals and difficulty in carrying gave way to paper money and cheap metal currency which is in use even today.

- **Bank money:** When volume of transaction increased, paper money and coin became inconvenient to use for large transaction. Bank money in the form of cheques, drafts, bill of exchange came into use.

- **Plastic Money:** Plastic money in the form of credit card and debit card is most convenient and safe money. It is most popular mode of payment without carrying cash and eliminates many types of risk.

- **E-Money:** The most modern mode of payment and transaction is done through electronic transfer which is done from one bank to another without actual use of money in cash, so it eliminates many risks.

In the contemporary era paper money, cheap metallic coins, bank money and plastic money all are simultaneously in use.

2.2 Important Concept

1. **Barter system**: A system in which goods are exchanged for goods.

2. **Double coincidence of wants**: It means that goods in possession of two different persons must be useful and needed by each other.

3. **Legal definition of money**: Legally, money is anything which is used as a medium of exchange on the instruction of government or as per law of the land. Paper notes and coins (together called currency) is money in present time.

4. **C-C Economy**- Exchange of commodity for commodity is called barter system or C-C Economy.

5. **Money**: Anything which has general acceptability as a medium of exchange and can be converted into any assets without losing its time and value.

6. **Legal Definition of Money**: Anything which has legal sanction by the government behind it is legal tender money.

7. **Fiat Money**: Any money which is backed by the order of the government to act as money. Fiat money is generally created and circulated at the time of crisis like war or emergency. It is issued without any backing of gold, silver or other reserves, it is not convertible into anything.

8. **Fiduciary Money**: The money which is accepted as money on the basis of trust that the issuer commands. Example: Cheque, Draft, bill of exchange.

9. **Standard and Token money**: Standard coins are those coins whose face value (printed) is equal to its intrinsic value. It is also called full bodied money.It means value printed on the coin is equal to metal value.

10. **Token Coins**: It refers to those coins whose face value is much greater than its intrinsic value. All the Indian coins like Rs.5, Rs.2, and Rs.1 these coins are made of cheap metals like nickel copper aluminum.

11. **Credit Money**: Credit money refers to the money whose intrinsic value is less than face value. All currency notes and token coins are credit money.

    In day to day language bank money is called credit money which refers to the bank deposits of the people, which can be withdrawn by cheque.

12. **Near money:** It is close substitute of money rather than cash and currency. It is not real money because it has no legal sanction. Assets which are close substitute of money are near money. Example Bonds, equity shares, National Saving Certificates, Commercial Bills etc.

13. **Narrow definition of money (M = C + DD)** = It is based on medium of payment function only. (M is money, C is Currency and DD is demand deposits).

14. **Broad definition of money (M = C + DD + TD + SD):** Broad definition of money includes all function of money. Medium of exchange & store of value. It has high degree of liquidity.

    Where, M is money, C is Currency and DD is demand deposits,

    TD is Time Deposit SD is saving deposits.

15. **Legal Tender Money**: Money which has legal sanction by the government behind it, is called legal tender money. It is money under the law of land which cannot be refused by any person in payment. No one can refuse to accept it, non-acceptance is an offence.

    In India currency notes and coins are legal tender money but Demand deposits is not legal tender money because a person can legally refuse to accept it.

Legal tender money is of two types:

a) Limited legal tender money: It is money which is accepted to a certain maximum limit fixed by law. In India, all coins of ₹5, ₹10, ₹25, ₹50 paisa etc. are accepted up to maximum sum ₹1000. One can refuse payment in small coins beyond a sum of ₹1000.

b) Unlimited legal tender money: It is the money for which there is no limit to settle the payments of unlimited value. All currency notes in India.

16. **High Powered Money**: It refers to the money produced by RBI and government of India. H = C + R + OD

    Where, C = Currency held by Public (notes and coins)

    R = Cash Reserve of Commercial Bank

    OD = Other deposit of RBI

17. **Money Supply**: It is the stock of money held by the public at a point of time in the economy. It includes currency held by public and net demand deposits in the banks.

18. **Sources of Money Supply**: (1) Government which issues one rupees and all other coins.

    (2) RBI or central bank which issues paper currency of 2 rupee and above.

    (3) Commercial Banks which creates credit on the basis of demand deposits.

19. **Alternative measures of money supply**: Reserve Bank of India uses four alternative measures of money supply called M_1, M_2, M_3, M_4. M1 is the most commonly used measure of money supply as it is highly liquidity.

    (1) M1 = C + DD + OD where C is currency notes, DD is demand deposits and OD is other deposits.

    (2) M2 = C + DD + OD + SD, where SD is saving deposits with post office.

    (3) M3 = C + DD + OD + TD, where TD is time deposits of banks.

    (4) M4 = C + DD + OD + TD + SD, (excluding NSC)

    Note: Post office savings and fixed deposits of commercial bank

    lacks the function of medium of exchange due to lack of cheque facility so it is not counted as money. M4 is least liquid.

20. **Liquidity** of money: Money is perfectly liquid as it can be converted into any asset without loss of value.

21. **Money Multiplier**: Money multiplier (m) is the ratio of total money supply (M) to the stock of High-Powered Money (H) in the economy. $m = \dfrac{M}{H}$ Money supply in the economy depends on money multiplier and amount of high-powered money.

    Example: m is 2 and H is 1000 then

    M (money Supply) = 2 x 1000 = 2000

    $\text{Money Multiplier} = \dfrac{1}{LRR} \text{ x Initial Deposit}$

22. **Demand Deposits**: These are the deposits which can be withdrawn from the bank anytime by the depositor. No interest is paid on it.

23. **Cheque**: It is bank paper that instructs the bank to transfer funds from cheque issuer's account to receiver account.

24. **Time Deposits:** These are the deposits which can be withdrawn after a specified period of time. It is also known as fixed deposit.

25. **Liquidity trap**: It is a situation of very low rate of interest rate where people expect the interest rate to rise in future and consequently bond prices to fall. So, it becomes totally unattractive to invest money in bonds causing capital loss.

    People hold their money and no investment is done, speculative demand for money is infinite. This situation is called liquidity trap because money supply gets trapped.

26. In India, monetary system is 'Paper Currency Standard'. It is also known as Managed Currency Standard' because any amount of notes can be issued with minimum back up of gold. RBI maintains a minimum reserve of ₹ 200 crore of which ₹ 115 crore is in gold and remaining ₹ 85 crore in the form of foreign securities.

2.3 Drawbacks of Barter System

Barter system of exchange has the following difficulties:

1. **Lack of double coincidence of want:** Barter system is possible if goods produced by two people are needed by each other. It is called double coincidence of want.

   It is difficult to find such person every time. Money which is a common medium of exchange removes this problem.

2. **Lack of divisibility**: In barter system difficulty of divisibility of commodity arises. It is difficult to exchange goods of unequal value. A goat and bread are not of equal value, neither goat can be divided into pieces to exchange with bread. It makes exchange impossible or difficult.

3. **Difficulty in storing wealth**: It is difficult to store goods like wheat, rice, vegetables, cattle etc. as wealth for future use. As it decays with time or needs proper and costly storage system.

4. **Lack of common measure of unit:** In barter system there is no common measure of value. Different commodities are of different value so exchange becomes difficult. Even if buyers and sellers of each other commodity meet, the problem in what proportion the two goods to be exchanged. When thousands of goods are produced and exchanged, there will be unlimited number of exchange ratio, absence of common denominator makes exchange difficult. Money removes these problem as it has a common unit of value.

5. **Lack of standard of deferred payment**: In barter system future payments are stated in goods and services. There could be disagreement regarding the quality of the goods or services to be repaid and there could be change in the value of goods.

Fig 2.4

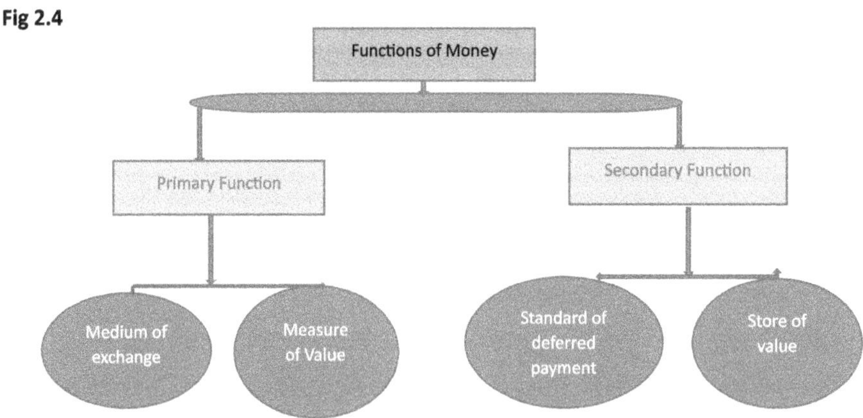

2.4 Functions of Money: "Money is a Matter of Function Four, A Medium, A Measure, A Standard, A Store"

(1) Medium of Exchange:

i. As a medium of exchange money helps to overcome the problem of barter system like lack of double coincidence of wants.

ii. People can use money to buy anything they want as it has general acceptability and liquidity.

iii. Money facilitates exchange and promotes trade.

iv. It facilitates business activity and productivity. It plays effective role in specialisation.

v. The use of money allows sale and purchase of goods and services independently without connecting with any other commodity.

(2) Measure of Value /Unit of account:

i. Money is a common unit of account. It is a common denominator to measure value of all the goods and services.

ii. Money value of goods can be expressed in terms of price. Pricing makes exchange easy to calculate and understand.

iii. Value of goods and services can be compared with help of price which in expressed in terms of money.

iv. It has helped in organized marketing and production.

(3) Standard of deferred payment:

i. Payment which are made in future are called deferred payment or delayed payment.

ii. Loans are taken and paid in terms of money because money has general acceptability, durability and identity.

iii. Debts are expressed in terms of money. Debtors can make promise to the creditor that loan will be returned on some future date.

iv. Money has simplified lending and borrowing operation.

v. It facilitates capital market, investment and stock exchange as it has general acceptability, durability and stability.

(4) Money as a store of Value:

i. Store of wealth was difficult in barter system as goods can decay and spoil after sometime.

ii. Money can be stored without loss of its value. Wealth can be stored in terms of money for future without losing its value.

iii. Holding money is holding liquid assets because it can be easily converted into any other things. This is known as liquidity preference.

iv. People normally keep a part of their wealth in the form of money because saving in terms of good is difficult. Money is the best form of store of value.

2.5 Qualities of Good Money

1. **General acceptability**: It should have general acceptability. No one should refuse to accept money as a medium of exchange.

2. **Portability:** Money should possess high value in small bulk. Currency notes are light weighted and easily to carry.

3. **Homogeneity**: Uniformity in quality, weight and value makes the money a common medium of exchange without fear or distrust in its value.

4. **Durability**: It must not easily deteriorate, spoil, decay or evaporate. It should not easily destroy due to wear and tear. It should not rust. It should have long lasting quality.

5. **Divisibility**: It should be capable of division. The bigger denomination should be easily divided into small denominations.

6. **Cognizability**: Capacity to recognize and distinguish from other substances. It should have some distinct mark and authenticity of government. It should have impression or legal sanction.

7. **Stability in value**: Its value should remain stable in its value. Fluctuating standard of value may lead to distrust in money.

2.6 Classification of Money

Money can be classified on the basis of value of money as a commodity; there are broadly three categories:

1. **Full Bodied money**: The money whose face value is equal to its commodity value (intrinsic value). Example when coins were made of gold and silver the value inscribed on coin was equal to the metal value of that coin.

2. **Representative Full-bodied Money**: When the value of money is much higher than the commodity value (paper or metal) of which it is made. It is accepted as money as it can be easily used for all types of transaction. Example paper money which is 100% backed by reserve of gold or silver and it can be redeemed on the demand of the holder.

There are two types of representative money:

    a. **Convertible Paper Money**: Currency notes which can be freely convertible into gold or silver on the demand of the holder (full bodied). It is to be noted that 100% backing of gold and silver is not required as all the notes in circulation are not demanded for conversion at a time.

    b. **Inconvertible Paper Money**: Currency notes which cannot be convertible into gold or silver on the demand of the holder (full bodied). This money is in circulation as per the command of government. This money does not have any backing of bullion or standard coins. Indian rupee note is an example of inconvertible paper money.

3. **Credit Money**: The money whose intrinsic value is much lower than its face value. Which means money value is more than the commodity Value. For example: A note of ₹ 50 has much less commodity value then its face value. Credit cards, Demand draft etc. are also credit money. There is various form of credit money:

    i. **Token Coins: All coins of various denominations like** ₹5, ₹10,₹ 2 are token coins since the face value of these coins are much more than the value of metals it is made.

    ii. **Representative Token Money**: It is 100% backed and fully redeemable in commodities like gold or silver. Its face value is higher than the paper of which it is made.

    iii. **Promissory notes**: The currency notes which are issued by the Reserve Bank of India with the statement, 'I promise to pay the bearer the sum of ₹ 10 or ₹ 50 ……. Signed by the governor of Reserve Bank of India. The intrinsic value of promissory notes is much less than face value.

iv. **Demand Deposits**: Deposits are claimed by the depositors (creditors) when they need it. These deposits can be withdrawn from the bank or transferred to others through cheques, drafts or e- transfer. Such deposits do not have any backing in terms of bullion (gold or silver). The commodity value of drafts and cheques are much less than amount written on it.

Demand deposits has made easy and convenient transactions of huge amount as it has removed the risk of carrying large amounts of cash.

2.7 Definition of Money

Increase in the volume of economic activity, large scale transactions, domestic and international business and industrial development has become possible due to use of money as a common medium of exchange as it has general acceptability, uniformity, durability, portability and government authenticity.

Money can be defined in different ways on basis of different criteria:

1. **Legal definition of money**:

   Legal tender money: Money that has legal sanction behind it is called legal tender money. Anything which is used as money as per order of the government or law of the land is called legal tender money. It is issued by the government or the monetary authority of the country which no one can refuse in payment for any kind of transaction. Everyone has to accept it in exchange of goods and services and for payment of debts. No one can refuse to accept it. Non-acceptance will be considered as non- abiding by the law of land so it will be offence. In India, currency notes and coins are legal tender money which cannot be refused in payment of transactions.

   Whereas cheques and drafts are non- legal tender money, so anyone can refuse to accept the payments through cheques.

   Legal tender money is of two types:

   a. **Limited legal tender Money**: It is the money which can be accepted as payment of transaction only up to limit fixed by the government. Example: In India coins are limited legal tender because coin of 5,10, 25 paisa are accepted up to maximum limit of Rs1000. Anyone can refuse to accept payments in small coins beyond the sum of 1000.

   b. **Unlimited Legal Tender Money**: Money which is accepted for payment to any amount at a time. No one refuse to accept it for the settlement of any amount of payment. In India all paper notes are unlimited legal tender money.

2. **Functional Definition of money**:

   Money is anything which can be accepted as medium of exchange and for the payment of debt. Anything which is accepted by the people as medium of payment and settling the debt is treated as money even if legal sanction is not there.

   In India, money supply includes currency held by public and demand deposits in the banks.

3. **On the basis of components of money: Narrow and Broad Money**:

   a. **Narrow definition of money ($M = C + DD$)**: This is based on medium of payment function only. Other functions of money like store of value and deferred payment is not included here. Only currency(C) and demand deposits (DD) of banks are included here. Narrow definition includes only what is included in money supply (C + DD).

   b. **Broad definition of money ($M = C + DD + TD + SD$)**: According to broad definition of money all the functions of money is included. Money is that commodity which functions as a medium of exchange, measure of value, store of value and means of deferred payment. Time deposits(TD), Saving deposits (SD) is included in broad money because it is financial assets which has liquidity too. Saving Deposits and Time deposits can be converted into demand deposits or cheques or drafts on demand in short notice.

4. **On the basis of liquidity - Money and near Money:**

   a. Money is anything which has general acceptability as a medium of exchange with legal sanction of the government. It is highly liquidity as it can be converted into anything anytime without losing its value. In India all currency notes and coins are considered as money.

   b. Near Money are actually not legal money but close substitute of it. It includes financial assets, commercial bill of exchange, national saving certificate, equity, bonds etc. Near money cannot be used to purchase goods and services directly as it can be done with cash and bank money. Near money can be converted into money easily within short period of time.

2.8 Money Supply and its Components

Money supply can be defined as the total volume of money held by the public at a point of time in an economy. [Money Supply = Currency + Demand deposits]

Currency and coins with Public: It consists of currency notes and coins held by public. All denomination of notes and coins. It is called legal tender money or fiat or order from the government to act as money.

Demand Deposits of commercial Banks: It refers to the deposits of the people which they can withdraw any time by issuing cheques. It does not need any prior notice. It is easily accepted as a means of payment.

Features of money supply:

1. It is stock concept as it is measured at a point of time.

2. It includes money held by the public (households and business entity).

3. It does not include money held by the government and banks as they are creator of money. The money held by them is not put into circulation.

Alternative measures of money supply:

Reserve Bank of India uses four alternative measures of money supply called M_1, M_2, M_3, M_4

M1 is the most commonly used measure of money supply as it is highly liquidity.

(1) M1 = C + DD + OD where C is currency notes, DD is demand deposits and OD is other deposits.

(2) M2 = C + DD + OD + SD, where SD is saving deposits with post office.

(3) M3 = C + DD + OD + TD, where TD is time deposits of banks.

(4) M4 = C + DD + OD + TD + SD, (excluding NSC)

Note: Post office savings and fixed deposits of commercial banks does not perform the function of medium of exchange due to lack of cheque facility, so it is not counted as money. M4 has least liquidity.

2.9 Demand for Money

People demand goods and services to satisfy their wants. Money does not have any utility in itself but it is a means to satisfy human wants. All the goods and services can be purchased by money.

There are three main motives for which people demand for money:

(a)Transaction Motive (b)Precautionary Motive (c)Speculative Motive

1. **Transaction Demand for money:** It refers to the demand of money for fulfilling household needs of the people, like food, clothes, educational expenses, transport expense and so on. Even businessman and entrepreneurs need money for purchasing raw materials and other expenses. Normally salary is earned monthly but expenses are there throughout the month, so amount of money people hold as cash. The transaction demand for money is done to meet current transaction requirement of the households and business entity.

   Note: According to Keynes, transaction demand for money is positively associated with the level of income i.e. higher the income more amount of money people will keep as cash for transaction.

2. **Precautionary Demand for money**: People keep some amount of money in cash form for unforeseen contingencies or uncertainty like sickness, accident etc. The amount of money kept as precaution depends on the nature of the individual, his lifestyle and his income. Higher the income, more cash money will be kept for emergency.

3. **Speculative Demand for money**: It refers to the demand to keep cash balance as some alternative assets like shares, bonds etc.

2.10 Banking

Bank: It is an institution which borrows and lends money.

Banking: Banking is a system of accepting for the purpose of lending or investment of money from the public.

Central Bank: It is the apex institution of monetary and banking system of the country.

Commercial Bank: It is a financial institution which accepts deposits from public and advance loans to public with the motive to earn profit.

Money Multiplier or Credit Multiplier: When the primary cash deposit in the banking system leads to multiple expansion in the total deposits, it is known as money multiplier.

Bank Rate: It is the rate of interest at which central bank lends (long term) to commercial banks without any collateral.

Repo rate: It is the rate of interest at which commercial bank borrows from the central banks for short term by selling their financial securities.

Reverse Repo Rate: It is the rate at which central bank borrows money from commercial banks.

Cash Reserve Ratio: It refers to the minimum percentage of the bank's total deposits, which the bank is required to keep with central bank.

Statutory liquidity Ratio: It refers to minimum percentage of deposits that a commercial banks has to maintain in the form of liquid cash, gold or other securities with themselves.

Open Market Operation: Buying and selling of government securities and bonds in open market by central bank.

Margin Requirement: Commercial bank gives credit against security. The amount of loan given by the bank is always less than the value of collateral. The difference between value of collateral and loan amount is called marginal requirement.

Moral Suasion: Persuasion, request, informal suggestion, advice and appeal by the central bank to the commercial bank to cooperate with general monetary policy is called moral suasion.

Quantitative measures of Monetary Policy (general tools): These are the measures of monetary policy that affect overall supply of money/credit economy.

Qualitative measures of Monetary Policy (Selective Tools): The measures which are used to regulate the direction of credit is known as Qualitative measure.

Selective Credit Controls (SCCs): When central bank gives direction to the commercial banks not to give credit for certain purposes or give more credit for particular purposes or preferences to some sectors.

Reserve Deposit Ratio (RDR): It is ratio of total deposits which commercial banks keep as reserve.

Liquidity Trap: A situation of very low interest rate where people are ready to hold money in bank with the expectation that rate of interest will rise in future and bond price will fall.

Spread: The difference between borrowing rate of interest and lending rate of interest of commercial bank is called spread.

Post office are not banks because they accept deposits but do not give loan.

Lending Rate of Interest: The rate of interest at which commercial bank lends loan to the public or investors is called lending rate of interest.

Borrowing Rate of Interest: The rate of interest offered to the depositors by the commercial bank is called borrowing rate of interest.

2.11 Functions of Commercial Bank

PRIMARY FUNCTIONS:

1. It accepts deposits: A commercial bank accepts deposits in the form of current, saving and fixed deposits. It collects the surplus balances of the individuals, firms and finances the temporary needs of commercial transaction.

(1) Current Account:

- Deposits are payable on demand so they are called demand deposits.
- No interest is paid on the deposited amount.
- Maintained by Businessman and Industrialists.
- Overdraft facility is given.

(2) Fixed deposits or time Deposits:

- Deposits are fixed for a specified period of time can be withdrawn after maturity. No cheque facility.
- High interest rate is given on fixed deposit.
- It is not a part of money supply.

(3) Saving account Deposits:

- Deposits are done by individual households.
- Payable on demand so cheque facility is given but with restriction.
- Rate of interest is low.

2. It gives loan and advances: Banks give loan and advances to businessman and industrialists and earn interest. A part is kept by bank and rest of the deposits are given as loan in the form of cash credit, demand loans and short term loans overdrafts etc.

a. **Cash credits**: Loans are sanctioned with some security and allowed to withdraw a certain amount. Interest is charged on withdrawn amount.

b. **Demand loans**: Loan that can be recalled on demand. Entire loan is paid in lump sum to the borrower. Security brokers whose credit needs fluctuate, they take loan on personal security and financial assets.

c. **Short term loan**: Loans given on security for short period. The entire amount is repaid in one instalment or in a number of instalments.

SECONDARY FUNCTIONS

3. **Overdraft facility**: Advance given to the current account holder without security. Interest is charged only on withdrawn amount and on daily basis.

4. **Agency Functions:** Bank acts as agent of its customers.

It transfers funds like telegraphic transfer, e- transfer.

Collect the funds on behalf of its customers through cheques, drafts ,bill and hundies.

It makes payment on behalf of the customers like tax payment, insurance bills and other payments.

Collection of dividend and interest on shares and debentures.

Purchase and sale of shares and security.

Acts as a trustee and executor of property of its customers.

Letter of references are given to its customers.

6. **General Utility Function**: Travelers cheque, locker facility, Purchase and sale of foreign exchange.

7. **Credit Creation by Commercial Banks or Money creation by commercial bank:**

Commercial banks increase the supply of money by creating credit which is known as money creation. Total deposits of a bank are of two types

i. Primary deposits is the initial deposits by the public.

ii. Secondary deposits are the deposits created due to loans given by the banks which are assumed to the redeposited in the bank.

Money creation by commercial banks is depends on two factors:

i. Primary deposits i.e., initial cash deposit.

ii. Legal Reserve Ratio (LRR) i.e., minimum ratio of deposits which is legally compulsory for the commercial banks to keep as cash in liquid   form(LRR = CRR + SLR).

When a bank receives cash deposits from the public, it keeps a fraction of deposits as cash reserve (LRR) and uses the remaining amount for giving loans. In the process of lending money, banks are able to create credit through secondary deposits many times more than the initial deposits.

Process of Credit Creation or Money Creation by Commercial Banks

Commercial banks are the factory of credit creation. They create credit multiple time of the initial deposits in the bank.

It can be explained with the help of following example; Let us assume

1. Entire commercial banking system is one -unit call banks.

2. All the transactions are routed through banks. Payments are given and received in the form of cheque and drafts.

Suppose initial deposit in the bank is ₹1000 by the people.

Banks cannot use the entire amount to give loan. It keeps a certain percentage of its deposit as cash called Legal Reserve Ratio (LRR). LRR is fixed by central Bank. Suppose LRR is 10%.

The bank will give loan of ₹ 900 in the first round to a person A and ₹100 will kept as LRR. The bank opens an account of the borrower and credits money in that account. The borrower withdraws the whole amount and spends it, the receiver of the amount will deposit the money in the bank as all transactions are routed to the bank.

Thus ₹ 900 comes back to bank as secondary deposits. Again bank keeps 10% of it as LRR i.e.

₹ 90 and ₹ 810 is given as loan to a person B in the second round. He spends ₹ 810 and receiver of that amount deposit it in the bank. ₹ 810 come to the bank and 10% of it that is ₹81 is kept as LRR and ₹729 is given as loan to person C. This process continues round after round until derivative deposits become zero.

Stage	Deposits (₹)	Loans (₹).	LRR (10%) ₹
Initial	1000	900	100
Round 1	900	810	90
Round 2	810	729	81
------	------	-----	-----
-------	------	-----	-------
Total	10,000	9,000	1,000

Loan is given 10 times more than initial deposits.

Money multiplier $\dfrac{1}{LRR} = \dfrac{1}{10\%} = \dfrac{100}{10} = 10$

Thus, credit creation will be 10 times more than the initial deposits.

Credit Creation = Initial deposits x $\dfrac{1}{LRR}$ = 1000 x $\dfrac{1}{10\%}$ = 1000 x $\dfrac{100}{10}$

= ₹10, 000

2.12 Central Bank

FUNCTIONS OF CENTRAL BANK

1. ***Issue of Currency:*** *The central bank has the sole monopoly to issue currency in order to control over the volume of currency and credit.*

   - *These notes circulate throughout the country as legal tender money. It has to keep a reserve of gold and foreign securities as per statutory rules against notes issued by it.*

   - *RBI issues all currency notes of 2 rupees and above.*

   - *Under the instruction of RBI **one rupees notes and coins** are issued by the government mints.*

   When government expenditure is more than its revenue, then government sells it security bills to RBI, and issues one rupee note. This is called monetisation of budget deficit **or deficit financing**.

2. **Banker to the Government**: Central bank functions as the banker to the government both Central and State Government.

   - It carries all banking business of the government.

   - Government keeps cash in the current account of central Bank.

   - It accepts receipts and make payments on behalf of the government.

- It carries out exchange, remittance and other banking operations on behalf of the government.
- Central gives loans to the governments for temporary periods.
- It manages Public debt.

3. **Bankers bank and supervisor:** Central bank regulates and supervise all the banks for their proper functioning.

Central bank act as banker's bank in three capacities-

a. It is the custodian of cash reserve of all the commercial banks in the form of Cash Reserve Ratio(CRR). All the commercial banks are required to keep a certain percentage of deposits with the Central Bank.

b. Central bank is the lender of last resort for all the commercial banks.When commercial banks are in liquidity crisis and they are not able to meet the obligation of it depositors, Central Bank gives loan and advance to safeguard them from financial crisis.

c. It acts as bank of central clearance and settlements house, provides remittance and transfers facility.

It supervises, regulates and controls the activities of commercial banks.

Its moral persuasion is very effective for commercial banks.

4. **Controller of Credit and money supply:**

Quantitative Measures:

i. **Bank rate and repo rate:** The rate at which central bank lends to commercial bank for short period is called repo rate and long period loan is called bank rate.

   When bank rate or repo rate increases, commercial bank increases its rate of interest, loan becomes costlier. People take less loan and thus credit and supply of money is curtailed. Decrease in repo rate will in turn decrease rate of interest and thus credit and money supply increases as loan become cheaper for people.

ii. **Cash Reserve Ratio (CRR):** Commercial banks are required to keep certain percentage of their cash deposits with the central bank called Cash Reserve Ratio. When central bank wants to control credit and money supply, it increases CRR, which means more money is to be kept with central bank and less will be left with commercial bank to give loan. Decrease in CRR, increases money supply and credit.

iii. **Statutory Liquidity Ratio (SLR):** All the banks are required to keeps fixed percentage of its assets as cash called liquidity ratio. When central bank increases SLR, credit creation capacity of commercial bank decreases and vice versa.

iv. **Open Market operation:** Buying and selling government securities by central bank to public and banks to influence money supply. Sale of government securities to commercial banks means flow of money into central bank which reduces cash of commercial bank and thus less loan can be given to the people. When central bank wants to increase credit and money supply it buys government securities thus money flow to the banks.

Qualitative Measures

These are the qualitative measures to regulate and channelize credit for specific purpose.

5. **Margin requirement:** Margin requirement refers to difference between security deposit(collateral) amount and loan amount. Security amount is always excess of loan amount and excess amount is called margin requirement. To check depression, Central bank reduces margin requirement (Security) of loan which increases borrowing capacity of the people and vice versa.

6. **Moral Suasion:** The Central bank request, advises, appeals, admonish and persuades commercial banks to be liberal in lending and giving credit during recession and be strict during inflation.

7. **Direct Action:** The Central Bank may take direct action against those banks which do not comply with its direction.

8. **Rationing of credit:** This means fixation of quotas for loan to be given for different business activities.

9. *Custodian of foreign exchange its Control:* Central bank is the custodian of foreign exchange and nation's gold. It keeps a close watch on external value of its currency. Central Bank controls exchange value of the money. Every citizen of India should deposit all foreign currency to Central Bank if they have, whenever foreign exchange is needed by any citizen, they can get from Central bank.

10. **Lender of last Resort:** Central bank functions as the lender of last resort for the commercial banks. When commercial banks fail to meet the obligation of its creditors. The commercial banks are in liquidity crisis; they can approach central bank as a last resort. Central bank gives financial support by

    i. Rediscounting their securities and bills of exchange.

    ii. By granting loan against their securities.

    Central bank saves banking system by providing temporary financial assistance and saves financial structure of the country from collapse.

11. *Clearing house function:* Banks receive cheques drawn on the other banks from their customers which they have to realize from drawee banks. Cheques on a particular bank are drawn and passed into the hands of other banks which have to realize them from drawee banks. Independent realisation of each cheque would take a lots of time. Central bank provides clearing facilities. All the banks come together every day and set off their chequing claims.

12. **Collection and Publication of Data:** Central bank collects and compiles statistical information related to banking and financial sector of the economy.

2.13 Distinguish between Commercial Bank and Central Bank

Commercial Bank	Central Bank
It is a unit of banking structure.	It is Apex bank of the country.
Aim is to earn profit.	Aim is Public Welfare
It cannot issue currency but creates credits.	It has sole monopoly to issue currency.
It deals with the public.	It does not deal with public.
It is not custodian of gold and foreign reserve.	It is custodian of gold and foreign reserve.
It follows the monetary policy decided by the central bank.	It decides the monetary policy of the country.
It is the bank for the public and not for government.	It is the banker to the government.

2.14 Some Schemes of Government

1. **Pradhan Mantri Jan Dhan Yojana(PMJDY):** This scheme was launched in August 2014 as a national mission of financial inclusion at an affordable cost to low income segments. It aimed to promote banking activity among the financially excluded people and reduce poverty.

   Any individual can open an account under this scheme, who has no bank account in his/her name previously.

No minimum balance is required. It covers life and accident insurance. Account opened before 28th August 2018- ₹ 1 lakh and account opened after that ₹2 lakhs.

An overdraft facility up to ₹10 lakhs is available for such account.

2. **Pradhan Mantri Mudra Yojana**: Under this scheme, small borrowers can borrow from banks, MFIs, NBFCs for loan up to ₹10 lakhs for non- farm activities. It is given to Micro Small Enterprises without collaterals.

Practice Question-Answer

Multiple Choice Question-Answers:

1. Quantitative instrument of RBI can be:

   a. Cash reserve ratio

   b. Bank rate

   c. Open market operation

   d. All of them

   Answer:(d) All of them.

2. In order to control credit:

   a. Increase in CRR and Decrease in Bank Rate

   b. Decrease in CRR and Increase in Bank Rate

   c. Increase in CRR and Bank rate

   d. Decrease in CRR and Bank Rate

   Answer: (c) Increase in CRR and Bank rate.

3. The effect of increase in CRR will be reduced or nullified when:

   a. Bank rate is reduced

   b. Security is sold in open market.

   c. SLR is increased

   d. None

   Answer: (a) Bank rate is reduced

4. Money supply is

   a. Demand Deposits

   b. Currency held by public

   c. Currency held by public + Demand deposits

   d. None of these

   Answer:(c) Currency held by public + Demand deposits

5. The value of money multiplier is:

    a. Inverse of legal reserve ratio

    b. Proportionate of legal reserve ratio

    c. Both (a) and (b)

    d. None of these

    Answer. (a) Inverse of legal reserve ratio

6. Which of the following bank creates credit?

    a. (a) Commercial Bank

    b. (b) Central Bank

    c. (c) Both (a) and (b)

    d. (d)None of these

    Answer: (a) Commercial Bank

7. Banks use the major portion of the deposits to:

    a. To meet their daily needs

    b. Extend Loan

    c. To invest in business

    d. Keep in reserve for the depositors to withdraw.

    Answer: (b) To extend Loan.

8. In India supplier of money is

    a. Government of India

    b. Banking System

    c. Both (a) and (b)

    d. None of these.

    Answer:(c) Both (a) and (b)

9. The primary function of money is:

    a. Transfer of value

    b. Store of value

    c. Medium of exchange

    d. Standard of deferred payment

    Answer. (c) Medium of exchange

10. The ratio of total deposits that a commercial bank has to keep with reserve bank of India is called: [Delhi 2017]

    a. Statutory liquidity Ratio

    b. Deposit Ratio

c. Cash Reserve Ratio

d. Legal reserve Ratio

Answer. (c) Cash Reserve Ratio.

11. The value of Money Multiplier is:

a. $\dfrac{1}{CRR}$

b. $\dfrac{1}{SLR}$

c. $\dfrac{1}{LRR}$

d. $\dfrac{1}{MPS}$

Answer. (c) $\dfrac{1}{LRR}$

12. Which of the following is not a function of Central Bank [All India 2018]?

a. Banking facilities to government.

b. Banking Facilities to public.

c. Lending to the government

d. Lending to the commercial banks.

Answer:(b) Banking facilities to public

13. Printing of one-rupee note is done by:

a. Reserve Bank of India.

b. Commercial Bank

c. Central Bank

d. Ministry of finance.

Answer: (d) Ministry of finance

14. In a situation of deficient demand, Bank rate should be:

a. Increase

b. Decrease

c. Constant

d. None

Answer: (b) Decrease

15. The Central Bank appeals to the commercial Bank through:

a. Open market operation

b. Bank Rate

c. Moral Suasion

d. Reserve Ratio

Answer: (c)Moral Suasion

16. Which monetary measure is the affective method to control excess demand:

    a. Increase in Public expenditure.

    b. Decrease in public Expenditure.

    c. Increase in deficit financing

    d. Increase in Margin Requirement.

    Answer: (d) Increase in Margin Requirement.

17. Printing of one- rupee note is known as:

    a. Deficit Financing

    b. Fiscal deficit

    c. Primary Deficit

    d. None

    Answer. (a) Deficit financing

18. No interest is paid on:

    a. Saving account deposit

    b. Term deposit

    c. Fixed Deposit

    d. Current account Deposit

    Answer. (d) Current account deposit

19. The essential condition to become a bank:

    a. Accept deposits

    b. Advance Loan

    c. Create credit

    d. Both (a) and (b)

    Answer:(b) Both (a) and (b)

20. Calculate initial deposit when value of LRR is 25%, whereas total deposit created is ₹ 12,000 crores.

    a. ₹ 4000

    b. ₹ 5000

    c. ₹ 3000

    d. 2000

    Answer. (C) ₹3000

21. What will be the value of legal reserve ratio, when initial deposit is ₹ 500 and total deposit is ₹2000.

    a. 25%

    b. 20%

c. 5 %

d. 4%

Answer: (a) 25%

22. The rate at which Central bank takes loan from commercial bank:

    a. Bank Rate

    b. Repo rate

    c. Reverse repo rate

    d. Interest rate

    Answer: (c) Reverse repo rate

23. Which of the following is not included in the money supply of the country?

    (Fill up the blank with correct alternative)

    a. Time deposits

    b. Coin and currency

    c. Demand deposits

    d. None of the above

    Answer. (a) Time deposit.

24. Paper currency is the example of which type of money?

    a. Commodity money

    b. Fiat money

    c. Fiduciary money

    d. None of the above

    Answer: (b) Fiat money

25. What step Central Bank should take to encourage greater investment in the economy?

    a. Increase in Cash Reserve Ratio

    b. Reduce Cash Reserve Ratio

    c. Increase Bank Rate

    d. Sell government security in the open market.

    Answer: (b) Reduce Cash Reserve Ratio.

26. Money has separated the act of __________ and ___________.

    a. sale, purchase

    b. Goods, services

    c. Bank and credit

    d. None

    Answer: a) sale, purchase

True/False- Questions

1. Credit created by commercial bank is always equal to the deposits they have in the bank. (True/False)

   Answer: False.

2. Financial institutions are called banks. (True/False).

   Answer: False

3. There is inverse relation between reserve ratio and money multiplier (True/False)

   Answer: True.

4. RBI acts as a banker to the government and commercial bank is the banker to the people government.

   Answer: True

5. Commercial bank does not contribute to the money supply as they are not producer of money.

   Answer: False, Commercial bank contribute to money supply by creating credit.

6. Increase in cash reserve ratio adversely affects credit creation capacity of commercial banks.

   Answer: True

7. LIC is not termed as bank. (True/False).

   Answer: True.

   Identify the correct Match.

8. Identify the correct pair from the following Column I and Column II:

Column I	Column II
A. Money Multiplier	(i) $Initial\ Deposit \times \frac{1}{LRR}$
B. Bank Rate	(ii) Primary function
C. Deficit Financing	(iii) Interest Rate
D. Medium of exchange	(iv) One-rupee note

   Alternatives: (a) A-(i) (b) B-(ii) (c) C-(iii) (d) D-(iv)

   Answer. a) A-(i)

10. Identify the correct pair from the following Column I and Column II:

Column I	Column II
i. RBI	(i) Accepts deposits from the public
ii. Money Supply	(ii) Quantitative measure to control credit.
iii. CRR	(iii) Currency held by public and demand deposits.
iv. High powered money	(iv) Monetary authority of the country.

   Alternatives: (a) A-(i) (b) B-(ii) (c) C-(iii) (d) D-(iv)

   Answer. d) D-(iv)

12. Choose the correct alternative:

Column I	Column II
A. Bill of exchange	v. Broad Money
B. SLR	vi. Kept a fixed proportion with RBI.
C. CRR	vii. Maintaining a fixed percentage of assets in cash or liquid form in the Commercial bank.
D. M3	viii. Near Money

Alternatives:

a. (a) A-(iv) (b) B-(iii) (c) C-(ii) (d) D-(i)

b. (a) A-(ii) (b) B-(i) (c) C-(iii) (d) D-(iv)

c. (a) A-(i) (b) B-(iii) (c) C-(iv) (d) D-(ii)

d. (a) A-(i) (b) B-(iii) (c) C-(ii) (d) D-(iv)

Answer: (a) A-(iv) (b) B-(iii) (c) C-(ii) (d) D-(i)

Assertion-Reason Question.

Read the following statement -Assertion (A) and Reason (R). Choose one of the correct alternatives given below:

1. **Assertion (A):** Reserve Bank of India is solely responsible for supply of money and credit.

   Reason (R): Currency notes are issued by RBI to have control over volume of currency and credit.

   Alternatives:

   a. Both Assertion (A) and Reason (R) are true and Reason (R) is the correct explanation of Assertion (A).

   b. Both Assertion (A) and Reason (R) are true and Reason (R) is not the correct explanation of Assertion (A).

   c. Assertion (A) is true but Reason (R) is false.

   d. Assertion (A) is false but Reason (R) is true.

   Answer: (d) Assertion (A) is false but Reason (R) is true.

2. **Assertion (A):** Printing of one-rupee note is called monetization of budget deficit.

   Reason (R): One -rupee note is printed to overcome financial deficit

   Answer: a) Both Assertion (A) and Reason (R) are true and Reason (R) is the correct explanation of Assertion (A)

3. **Assertion (A):** Credit creation capacity increases when the value of legal reserve ratio increases.

   Reason (R): There is inverse relation between money multiplier and legal reserve ratio.

   Answer: (d) Assertion (A) is false but Reason (R) is true.

4. **Assertion (A):** Credit creation capacity depends on reserve ratio.

   Reason (R): Reserve Bank of India issues credit to public.

   Answer: (c) Assertion (A) is true but Reason (R) is false.

5. **Assertion (A):** Demand deposits are a part of money supply.

   Reason (R): Money supply includes all the money which is held by public at a point of time.

   Answer: a) Both Assertion (A) and Reason (R) are true and Reason (R) is the correct explanation of Assertion (A).

6. **Assertion (A):** Store of value is the primary function of money.

   Reason (R): Money is the common medium of exchange.

   Answer: (d) Assertion (A) is false but Reason (R) is true

7. **Assertion (A):** One- rupee note is a promissory note.

   Reason (R): One- rupee note is printed by finance ministry under instruction of the government.

   Answer: (d) Assertion (A) is false but Reason (R) is true.

8. **Assertion (A):** Cheques are fiduciary money.

   Reason (R): Cheques are accepted on the basis of trust.

   Answer: a) Both Assertion (A) and Reason (R) are true and Reason (R) is the correct explanation of Assertion (A).

9. **Assertion (A):** High LRR results into high credit creation.

   Reason (R): Money multiplier is inversely related to LRR.

   Answer: (d) Assertion (A) is false but Reason (R) is true.

Statement Questions:

1. Read the following statements carefully:

   Statement 1: Credit creation capacity of commercial bank is checked and monitored by reserve bank of the country.

   Statement 2: All paper currency is promissory notes.

   In the light of the given statements, choose the correct alternative from the following:

   a. Statement 1 is true and statement 2 is false

   b. Statement 1 is false and statement 2 is true

   c. Both statements 1 and 2 are true.

   d. Both statements 1 and 2 are false.

   Answer: a) Statement 1 is true and statement 2 is false.

2. **Statement 1:** Money multiplier is inversely related to the legal reserve ratio.

   Statement 2: Google pay is an example of e-money.

   Answer: c) Both statements 1 and 2 are true.

3. **Statement 1:** A bank is a financial institution whose demand deposits are accepted as money.

   Statement 2: Central bank is a financial institution which accept deposits and advances loan to the public.

   Answer: (a) Statement 1 is true and statement 2 is false.

4. **Statement I:** Money is a commodity which is generally accepted as a medium of exchange.

   Statement 2: Money does not solve the problem of double coincidence of wants.

   Answer: (a) Statement 1 is true and statement 2 is false.

5. **Statement1:** No interest is paid to current account holders.

   Statement 2: M4 measure of money has maximum liquidity.

   Answer: (a) Statement 1 is true and statement 2 is false.

6. **Statement1:** Credit creation is one of the important function of Central Bank.

   Statement 2: Money multiplier is directly related to legal reserve ratio.

   Answer: (d) Both statements 1 and 2 are false.

7. **Statement 1:** Fiscal policy is decided by Reserve bank of India.

   Statement 2: Central Bank has the sole monopoly to issue currency notes.

   Answer: (b) Statement 1 is false and statement 2 is true.

8. **Statement 1:** Commercial bank affect money supply by creating credit.

   Statement 2: Selling of government security increases money supply.

   Answer: (a) Statement 1 is true and statement 2 is false.

9. **Statement 1:** Post Office is a bank as it accepts deposits.

   Statement 2: Commercial bank is the custodian of foreign exchange.

   Answer: (d) Both statements 1 and 2 are false.

Question- Answers (3 marks, 4 marks, 6marks)

1. What is monetary policy? State any three instruments of monetary policy.

Answer: It is the policy of central bank to regulate and control credit and money supply.

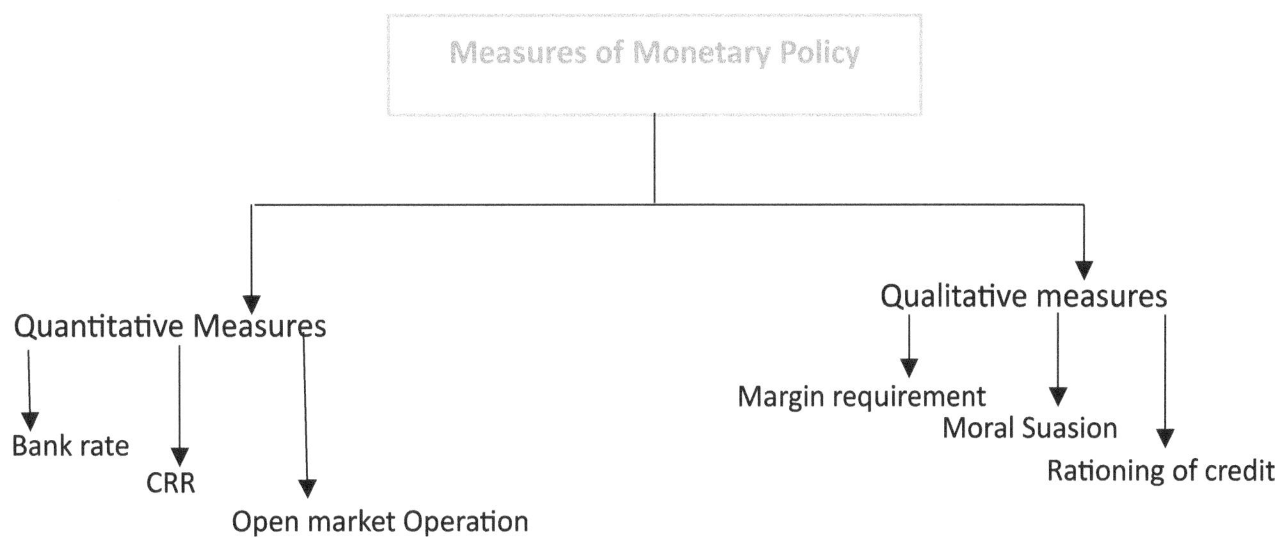

i. **Bank rate and repo rate**: The rate at which central bank lends to commercial bank for short period is called repo rate and long period loan is called bank rate.

When bank rate or repo rate increases, commercial bank increases its rate of interest, loan becomes costlier, people take less loan and thus credit and supply of money is curtailed. Decrease in repo rate will in turn decrease rate of interest and thus credit and money supply increases.

ii. **Cash Reserve Ratio (CRR)**: Commercial banks are required to keep certain percentage of their cash deposits with the central bank called Cash Reserve Ratio. When central bank wants to control credit and money supply, it increases CRR, which means more money is to be kept with central bank and less will be left with commercial bank to give loan.

iii. **Statutory Liquidity Ratio (SLR)**: All the banks are required to keeps fixed percentage of its asset as cash called liquidity ratio. When central bank increases SLR, credit creation capacity of commercial bank decreases and vice versa.

iv. **Open Market operation**: Buying and selling government securities by central bank to public and banks to influence money supply. Sale of government securities to commercial banks means flow of money into central bank which reduces cash of commercial bank and thus less loan can be given to the people.

When central bank wants to increase credit and money supply it buys government securities thus money flow to the banks.

Qualitative Measures

These are the qualitative measures to regulate and channelize credit for specific purpose.

Margin requirement: Margin requirement refers to difference between security deposit(collateral) amount and loan amount. Security amount is always excess of loan amount and excess amount is called margin requirement. To check depression, Central bank reduces margin requirement (Security) of loan which increases borrowing capacity of the people and vice versa.

Moral Suasion: The Central bank request, advises, appeals, admonish and persuades commercial banks to be liberal in lending and giving credit during recession and be strict during inflation.

Direct Action: The Central Bank may take direct action against those banks which do not comply with its direction.

Rationing of credit: This means fixation of quotas for loan to be given for different business activities.

2. Differentiate between demand deposit and Time deposit.

Answer:

Demand Deposit	Time Deposit
1.Money can be withdrawn on demand.	1. Money cannot be withdrawn on demand.
2.Low interest is given to the depositor.	2. High interest rate is paid to the depositor.
3. Overdraft facility is provided.	3. No overdraft facility is given.

3. Define Credit Multiplier. What role it plays in credit creation power of the banking system? Use numerical example to explain.

Answer:

The amount of credit a commercial bank in generating from the initial deposits is known as credit multiplier.

Credit creation by commercial bank is inversely related to Legal Reserve Ratio(LRR).

Higher the LRR, less credit will be generated and vice versa.

Numerical Example: Suppose the initial deposit in a bank is ₹1000 and LRR is 10%. ₹100 rupees will be kept with the bank and₹ 900 will be given loan to borrowers. The borrowers will spend money on goods and services and the money is assumed to come back to the banks as all transactions are rooted through banks.

In the second round out of ₹900 (derivative deposit) 10% i.e., ₹90 will kept as LRR and ₹810 will be given as loan to the borrowers. They will again spend this money which will come back to the bank again. Out of this ₹810, 10% i. e.,₹ 81 will be kept as LRR and ₹729 will be given as loan to the borrowers. This process will continue round after round till derivative deposit becomes zero.

$$\text{Money Multiplier} = \frac{1}{LRR} = \frac{1}{10\%} = \frac{1}{0.10} = 10$$

Credit creation = Initial deposit x Money Multiplier = 1000 x 10 = ₹10,000

4. How 'Jan–Dhan Yojana' be used as an instrument to increase money supply by commercial bank?

Answer: As we know that opening a bank account needs some document and processing. A large section of people in India do not keep their money in the bank specially the people with low income. 'Jan–Dhan Yojana' helped the people to open account without balance and hassle-free. When more account is opened some cash balance will surely be deposited in the bank which was earlier lying idle at home. Once deposit increases in bank, credit creation capacity of bank will also increase and thus money supply will increase.

5. Explain the following:

   a.   Fiat Money

   b.   High powered Money

   c.   Clearing House Function of RBI.

   d.   Fiat Money: Any money which is backed by the order of the government to act as money. Fiat money is generally created and circulated at the time of crisis like war or emergency. It is issued without any backing of gold, silver or other reserves, it is not convertible into anything

   e.   High Powered Money: It refers to the money produced by RBI and government of India. H = C + R + OD

   Where, C = Currency held by Public (notes and coins)

   R = Cash Reserve of Commercial Bank

   OD = Other deposit of RBI

   f.   **Clearing house function of RBI**: Banks receive cheques drawn on the other banks from their customers which they have to realize from drawee banks. Cheques on a particular bank are drawn and passed into the hands of other banks which have to realize them from drawee banks. Independent realisation of each cheque would take a lots of time. Central bank provides clearing facilities. All the banks come together every day and set off their chequing claims.

Case Study Questions:

1. Read the following news report and answer the following questions on the basis of the same.

Keeping in the view the continuing hardship faced by the banks in terms of social distancing of staff and consequent strain on reporting requirements, the reserve bank of India has extended relaxation of the minimum daily maintenance of the CRR of 80% for up to 25th September 2020. Currently CRR is 3% and SLR is 18.5%.

An announcement in the statement of development and regulatory policies of 27th March 2020 the minimum daily maintenance of CRR was reduced from 90% to the prescribed CRR of 80% effective from the fortnight beginning from 28th March 2020 till 26th June 2020, that was now extended up to 25th September 2020, said RBI.

a. What will be the value of money multiplier?

   i. 3.33

   ii. 5.4

   iii. 4.65

   iv. None of these.

b. Decrease in CRR will lead to:

   i. A fall in aggregate demand

   ii. A rise in aggregate demand

   iii. No change in aggregate demand

   iv. A fall in general price level

c. SLR implies:

   i. Certain percentage of total bank deposit to be kept with current account of RBI.

   ii. The minimum percentage of deposits that a commercial bank has to maintain in the form of liquid cash, gold or other securities.

   iii. Certain percentage of net demand deposit to be kept with the RBI.

   iv. None of the above

Solution:

a. (iii) 4.65

b. (ii) A rise in aggregate demand

c. (ii) The minimum percentage of deposits that a commercial bank has to maintain in the form of liquid cash, gold or other securities.

2. Read the following and answer the questions on the basis of the same.

The RBI announced a host of measures today aimed at increasing liquidity in the liquidity in the economy. As a consequence, individuals may see bank reducing their margins on interest rates charged on loans. However, fixed income earner should be aware of these steps might exert downward pressure on interest rate offered to the fixed deposits by banks, as per some experts. However, the impact of these announcements will not be immediate and may be marginal.

a. Reduction in the interest rates charged on loans will lead to ____________(decrease/increase/no change) in the overall demand in the economy.

b. Deceasing interest rate on fixed deposits by banks will(increase/decrease) the purchasing power of the people in general.

c. Increasing liquidity in the economy is generally done when there is:

i) Excess aggregate demand ii) Deficient aggregate demand

iii) Excess aggregate supply iv) neither(i) nor (ii)

d.   Which of the qualitative measures taken by the Central Banks to ease liquidity in the market?

   i.   Increase Margin Requirement

   ii.   Decrease Margin Requirement

   iii.   Increase in Repo Rate

   iv.   Decrease in Repo Rate

Answer-2:

   a.   **i) increase**

   b.   **ii) increase**

   c.   **iii)Deficient aggregate demand**

   d.   **iv) Decrease in Margin Requirement**

3. Read the following and answer the questions on the basis of the same.

The monetary policy is the policy formulated by Reserve bank of India for controlling credit and money supply. This includes measures like repo-rate, reserve repo-rate, bank rate, cash reserve ratio, open market operation and statutory liquidity ratio. The central bank of the country decides about distribution of credit, rationing of credit, availability and cost of credit in the economy. How much credit is distributed among various users, what should be the lending rate and borrowing rate etc. also a part of monetary policy of RBI. Instruments like direct action, moral suasion and margin requirements are the tools of selective credit control. The bank rate, repo-rate, reverse repo rate, CRR etc. remained unchanged as an after effect of pandemic.

   A.   Who plays important role in controlling credit and money supply of the country?

   i.   Fiscal Policy

   ii.   Selective Credit Policy

   iii.   Monetary policy

   iv.   None

   B.   Identify the incorrect sentence.

   i.   RBI did not change any policy due to pandemic.

   ii.   Repo-rate, Bank rate and open market operation are tools of monetary policy.

   iii.   Monetary policy is regulated by central Bank.

   iv.   Borrowing and lending rate is not decided by Central Bank.

   C.   Which of the following is not a part of selective credit control by RBI?

   i.   Direct Action

   ii.   Moral suasion

   iii.   Margin requirement

   iv.   Open market operation

   D.   Bank rate, repo-rate, reverse repo rate was changed as an after effect of pandemic. (True/False)

   Answers: A. iii. Monetary Policy

   B. iv. Borrowing and lending rate is not decided by Central Bank.

C. iv. Open market operation

D. False

4. Read the following and answer the questions on the basis of the same:

A new form of banking has emerged in India which is called e-banking or on- line banking. Banking system is no more confined to the branches where the physical presence of customer is needed for depositing or withdrawing cash. Passbook is no more an important document to know the account balance or statement of account. Now customers can withdraw money from ATM. People can also deposit money through ATM. The customer can transfer fund, pay electric bills, Tax, rent, etc. E- banking offers facilities like bank statement, loan application etc. e- banking has made life easier and banking faster for both customers and banks.

Unified Payments Interface (UPI) is an Indian instant payment system that powers multiple bank accounts into a single mobile application developed by the National Payment corporation of India. UPI was introduced on 11th April 2016. The mobile number of the device is required to be registered with bank. The UPI ID of the recipient can be used to transfer money. Indian banks started making their UPI enabled apps available on Google Play Store on 25 August 2016.

UPI has emerged as a game-changer in India's digital future. UPI has revolutionised India's payment sector and helped in transformation into cashless economy. By eliminating the need to disclose sensitive account information, it provides an impregnable fortress against vulnerabilities and cyber-attack.

It is one of the most widely used payment systems in the world, in terms of number of users and transactions. India has shared its UPI technology with many countries including France, Australia, Singapore, UAE, Saudi Arabia, Oman, Nepal, Bhutan, Sri Lanka etc.

a. **E- Banking offers many features except:**

   i.   Cash withdrawal

   ii. Bank statement

   iii. Fund transfer

   iv. E-Bill payment

b. **Statement 1**: E-Banking allows customers to monitor all their accounts in one place.

   Statement 2: Customer can avail all banking services from any computer with electric connection.

   In the light of the given statements, choose the correct alternative from the following:

   i.   Statement 1 is true and statement 2 is false.

   ii. Statement 1 is false and statement 2 is true.

   iii. Both statements 1 and 2 are true.

   iv. Both statements 1 and 2 are false.

c. **When was UPI introduced in India?**

   i.   25 August 2016

   ii. 16 April 2016

   iii. 11 April 2016

   iv. 11 August 2016

d. **In which method is sensitive account information is not required and it also safe from cyber-attack:**

   i.   E-Banking

   ii.   UPI

   iii.   Net Banking

   iv.   On-Line banking

Answers:

a. (i) Cash- transfer

b. (i) Statement 1 is true and statement 2 is false.

c. (iii)11 April 2016

d. (ii)UPI

X--X

UNIT: 3

DETERMINATION OF INCOME AND EMPLOYMENT

3.1 Approaches of Macro Economics

There are two theories of macroeconomics- the first one is classical theory which was given by the classical economists like Adam Smith, Ricardo, Malthus, they believed that in a capitalist economy, there is *full employment* and never over production is found in the economy. Which means whatever is produced in an economy is sold. But the great depression of 1929-1933 fully shattered the classical myth. The western countries were highly industrialised, they had well developed transport and communication system and all other basic requirement for production like power, fuel, capital and financial institutions etc. but still there was continues fall in the income, employment and output. At this time an English economist J.M. Keynes wrote his famous book *"General Theory of Employment, Interest and Money" in 1936* which brought a revolution in economic thoughts called Keynesian revolution. He discarded the assumption of full employment of an economy given by the classical economists.

CLASSICAL THEORY OF INCOME AND EMPLOYMENT

Classical economist like Adam Smith, Ricardo and Malthus and Neo classical like Marshall, Pigou, Robbins believed that

1. An economy as a whole always functions at full employment, means all the people are employed and resources are fully utilized. There could be temporary unemployment which can be cured by free play of economic forces.

2. **Supply creates its own demand**: It is called **Say's law of market** which states that supply creates its own demand. It means the whole output is sold and there is never deficiency in aggregate demand and no possibility of overproduction or unemployment.

3. Flexible system of price, wages and interest rate:

    i. Price brings equilibrium between demand and supply.

ii.   Flexibility in interest rate brings equilibrium between savings and investment.

iii.   Flexibility in wage rate brings full employment equilibrium.

3.2 Keynesian Theory of Income and Employment

Keynes criticized the classical theory which was based on assumption of full employment of the economy. The great depression of 1929-33 proved it wrong.

Keynesian Theory states that:

1. **An economy can be in equilibrium even at less than full employment**: In real world an economy never works at full employment. An economy can be at equilibrium even at less than full employment.

2. **Demand creates its own supply**: It is not supply which creates its own demand rather it is demand which creates its own supply. Aggregate demand which determines the level of output, income and employment.

3. **Equilibrium level of income and employment is determined by aggregate demand and aggregate supply**: Equilibrium in an economy is determined by aggregate demand and aggregate supply but not necessary at full employment. There can be equilibrium at less than full employment known as underemployment equilibrium.

In short run, aggregate supply does not change because technology does not change in short period, so it is aggregate demand which brings change in income and employment.

3.3 Components of Aggregate Demand

Aggregate demand refers to total demand for final goods and services in an economy.

Components of Aggregate Demand:

1. **Household (Private) consumption demand [C]**

2. **Private Investment Demand[I]**

3. **Government demand for goods and services [G]**

4. **Net Export Demand [X-M]**

1. Household or Private Consumption Demand (C): Value of goods and services that households are able and willing to buy. Household demand includes consumption demand for goods like demand on purchase of foods, cloths, furniture, books, television etc.

2. Private Investment Demand (I): It is the demand for creation of new capital assets like machines, buildings and raw materials by the entrepreneurs. It includes Investment demand to maintain present level of production as well as demand for increase in production capacity in future.

3. Government demands for goods and services (G) : If includes government demand to purchase goods and services. It includes demand to purchase consumer and capital goods to fulfil common needs of the society.It is expenditure on hospitals, roads, railways ,dams water supply etc.

4. Net Exports (X-M) : It is the difference between export demand and import demand for goods and services. The difference between demands for domestic goods in foreign countries over demand for foreign goods in domestic market.

$$AD = C + I + G + (X\text{-}M)$$

Since determination of income and employment is studied in the context of two sector economy (Households and Firms). Aggregate demand includes household demand and investment demand only.

$$AD = C + I$$

1. Aggregate demand Curve is positively sloped which means when income increases aggregate demand also increases.

2. AD does not originate from point O which shows consumption is never zero, minimum consumption is required at zero level of income.

3. Investment is constant in short period, so

   The investment curve is parallel to X axis.

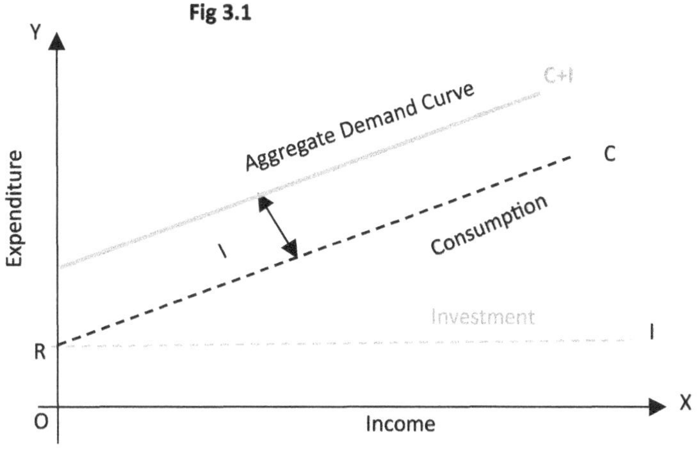

3.4 Aggregate Supply (AS)

Aggregate supply refers to total output of goods and services produced for sale in an economy. **Aggregate supply means national income of the country. Aggregate supply = Total Output = National Income**

$$AS = C + S \quad Y = C + S$$

C is consumption demand for goods and services.

S is saving, Y is national Income

Aggregate supply or national income is represented by 45^0 line.

45^0 line is equidistance from X-Axis and Y- Axis. Each point on this line indicates Expenditure (AD) = Income (AS).

45^0 line is also called Guide line or line of reference or income line.

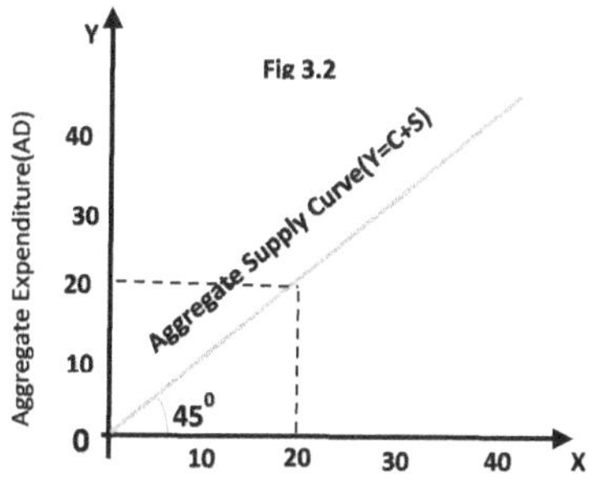

Aggregate Supply/National Income(AS)

It is assumed that in short period technology remains constant, so output (AS) increases only by employing more resources, mainly labour. Thus AS increases only when employment increases.

3.5 Consumption Function

The functional relationship between consumption and income is called consumption function or marginal propensity to consume.

$$C = f(Y)$$

$$C = \bar{c} + b\,Y \text{ (Consumption function equation)}$$

C = consumption function f = function b = MPC Y = Income

$\bar{c}$ = autonomous consumption

$\bar{c}$ = autonomous consumption is consumption at zero level of income or very low level of income which is needed for survival.

$b\,Y$ = Induced consumption, which means as income increases, consumption also increases.

Consumption function with schedule and diagram

Consumption function shows functional relationship between income and consumption.

1. Consumption is never zero, even at zero level of income there is some minimum amount of consumption is needed for survival. This is called **autonomous consumption.** Income can be zero but consumption is never zero. In the figure 3.3 OR shows autonomous consumption.

2. As income increases consumption also increase. This is called **induced consumption.** So consumption curve is positively sloped towards right. Income and consumption are directly related.

National Income(Y) ₹	Consumption(C) ₹
100	140
200	220
300	300
400	380

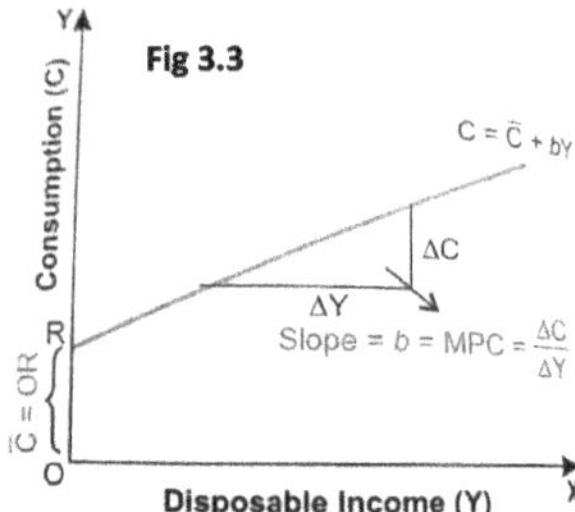

Consumption function Equation: C = $\bar{c}$ + b Y

3. Slope of consumption curve is MPC. MPC = b = $\dfrac{\Delta C}{\Delta Y}$

4. Slope of consumption curve (MPC) is constant so we get a linear straight line consumption curve.

3.5 Keynesian Psychological Law of Consumption

1. Consumption is never zero. Some amount of consumption is needed for survival.

   Consumption at zero level of income which is needed for survival is called autonomous consumption.

2. As income increases consumption also increases but consumption expenditure does not increase at the same rate as that of income. A lesser portion of increased income is used for consumption. This is known as induced consumption.

3.6 Propensity to consume are of two types: APC & MPC

Average Propensity to Consume and Marginal Propensity to Consume

(APC & MPC)

Average Propensity to Consume {APC}: It is the ratio of total consumption to total income. **APC = $\dfrac{C}{Y}$**

Example: National Income in an economy is ₹50000 and total consumption expenditure is ₹40000.

APC = $\dfrac{40000}{50000}$ = 0.8

Which means 80%of the income is spent on consumption.

3.7 Features of Average Propensity to Consume

1. **APC can be greater than 1(APC > 1):** When consumption expenditure is more than income. Example, Income is ₹ 500 and consumption expenditure is ₹1000. APC = $\dfrac{1000}{500}$ = 2

2. **APC is can be less than 1 (APC< 1):** When consumption expenditure is less than income. Example, Income is ₹ 2000 and consumption expenditure is ₹1000. Then APC = $\dfrac{1000}{2000}$ = 0.5

3. **APC is never zero** because consumption is never zero, even when income is zero some amount of consumption is needed for survival. Income can be zero but consumption cannot be zero.

4. **APC = 1, when consumption expenditure is equal to income (C = Y). It is known as break-even point.**

5. **APC falls when income increases** because the whole increased income is not consumed. When income increases consumption also increases but less than increase in income (Lesser portion of increased income is consumed).

    This can be explained with the following example:

    Let us assume that consumption function, **C = 50 + 0.50Y**

    a. **When income is 100, C = 20 + 0.50 X100 = 70 APC =** $\dfrac{70}{100}$ **= 0.7**

    b. **When income is 300, C = 20 + 0.50 X 300 = 170 APC =** $\dfrac{170}{300}$ **= 0.56**

Here we can notice that when income was ₹100 APC was 0.7 and when income has increased to ₹300 APC has decreased to 0.56.

3.8 Marginal Propensity to Consume (MPC)

The ratio of change in consumption (ΔC) due to change in income (ΔY)

i.e., MPC = $\dfrac{\Delta C}{\Delta Y}$

Marginal means additional. Propensity to consume means tendency to consume. Delta (Δ) means change.

Marginal Propensity to Consume means that amount of additional consumption which is spent from increased income.

3.9 Features of MPC

1. The value of MPC is always more than 0 but less than1 (0<MPC<1). When income increases, consumption also increase but the entire increase in income is not consumed.

    a. If the entire increased income is spent on consumption then ΔC = ΔY, so MPC = 1. When MPC is 1, it is called Break Even Point.

    b. If entire increased income is saved, ΔC = 0, so MPC = 0.

2. MPC falls with the increase in income. As the income increases, people consume smaller portion of their increased income in general.

3. MPC is assumed to be constant for a straight-line consumption curve.

4. The slope of consumption curve is MPC.

Increase in MPC reflects increase in consumption due to increase in income. Thus when consumption demand increases, production will increase and it will further increase income and employment.

3.10 Distinguish Between APC and MPC

APC	MPC
It is ratio of total consumption to total income. APC $= \dfrac{C}{Y}$	It is ratio of change in consumption to change in income. MPC $= \dfrac{\Delta C}{\Delta Y}$

• APC can be greater than 1, when consumption expenditure is more than income. • APC can be less than 1 when consumption expenditure is less than income. • APC is 1 when consumption is equal to Income. • APC is never 0 as consumption is never 0.	• MPC is greater than 0 and less than 1. $$0 < MPC < 1$$ • MPC falls with increase in income because as people become richer, they tend to spend less amount of their increased income. • When income increases both APC and MPC falls but fall in MPC is faster. • MPC is the slope of consumption curve.

3.11 Saving Function (Propensity to Save)

The relationship between saving and income is called saving function.

S = f (Y) S = saving, Y = income

Saving depends upon income. Saving directly depends on income.

Y = C + S so, S = Y-C

Saving Function Equation: S = - $\overline{c}$ + (1-b) Y

- $\overline{c}$ = dissaving (1-b) = MPS

$$MPS = \frac{\Delta S}{\Delta Y}$$

3.12 Break-Even Point

The point at which consumption expenditure is equal to income is known as Break-Even Point. At Break–Even Point, **savings are 0** because Income is equal to Consumption.

Income ₹	Consumption ₹	Savings ₹
1000	900	100
1500	1350	150
2000	2000	0
2500	2300	200

When income and consumption is equal to 2000 and saving is 0, it is called break-even point.

3.13 Relation between Income and saving

There is direct relationship between income and saving. When income increases saving also increases. At zero level of income or very low income saving is negative which means there is some amount of dissaving because consumption expenditure is more than income.

S = f(Y) saving depends upon income.

Income(Y) ₹	Consumption(C) ₹	Saving(S) ₹
0	60	-60
100	100	0
200	150	50

| 300 | 230 | 70 |
| 400 | 310 | 90 |

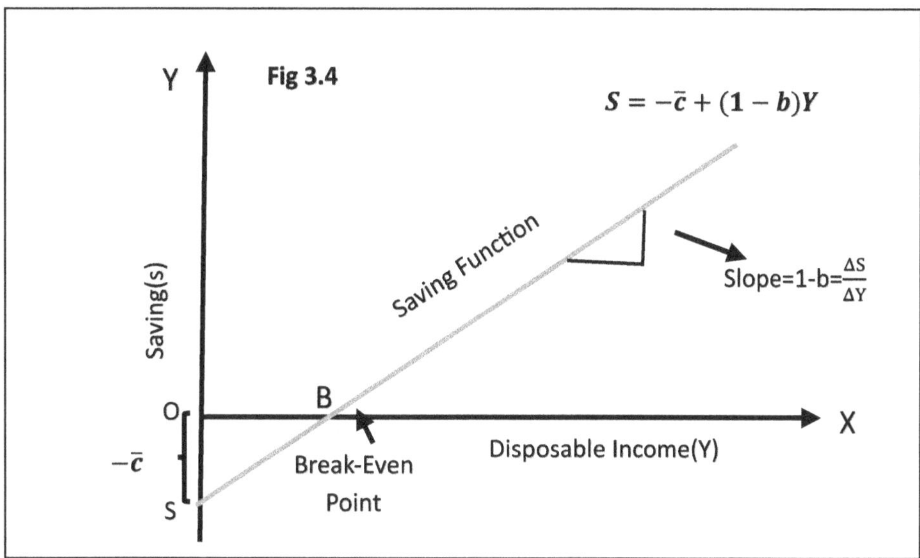

3.14 Average Propensity to Save and Marginal Propensity to Save (APS & MPS)

Average Propensity to Save (APS): The ratio of total saving to total income is known as average Propensity to Save. APS = $\dfrac{S}{Y}$

Features of APS:

1. Value of APS can be negative when consumption expenditure is more than income.

   Example: Y = 1000   C = 1200   S = Y-C

   S = 1000-1200   S = -200

   APS = $\dfrac{S}{Y}$ = $\dfrac{-200}{1000}$ = -0.2

2. Value of APS can be 0 when saving is 0, i.e., income is equal to consumption. When APS is 0 it is called Break–Even Point.

   Y = 1000   C = 1000   S = 0

   APS = $\dfrac{S}{Y}$ = $\dfrac{0}{1000}$ = 0

3. APS can never be 1 or more than 1 because saving can never be equal to income or more than income.

4. APS increases with increase in income.

3.15 Marginal Propensity to Save (MPS)

MPS is the ratio of change in saving to change in income.

MPS = $\dfrac{\Delta S}{\Delta Y}$

(Additional saving as proportion to additional income.)

Value of MPS lies between 0 to1.

0<MPS<1

MPS = 0, when increased income is entirely consumed and change in saving is 0.

MPS = 1, when increased income is fully saved.

Example: $\Delta S = 100 \qquad \Delta Y = 100$

$$MPS = \frac{\Delta S}{\Delta Y} = \frac{100}{100} \qquad MPS = 1$$

3.16 Features of MPS

1. Value of MPS lies between 0 to1. If entire increased income is consumed, then there is no saving making MPS = 0.

   If entire increased income is saved, then MPS = 1. ($\Delta S = \Delta Y$).

2. MPS can never be negative.

3.17 Difference Between APS and MPS

APS	MPS
$APS = \dfrac{S}{Y}$ It is ratio of total saving to total income.	$MPS = \dfrac{\Delta S}{\Delta Y}$ It is ratio of change in saving to change in income.
The value of APS can be negative if consumption expenditure is more than income.	The value of MPS cannot be negative.
The value of APS cannot be 1 as income cannot be fully saved.	The value of MPS can be 1 when increased income is fully saved.

3.18 Relationship Between APC and APS, MPC and MPS

APC + APS = 1, because income is either consumed or saved.

Y = C + S

APC = 1-APS

APS = 1-APC

MPC + MPS = 1, because when income increases either consumption expenditure will increase or savings will increase.

$\Delta Y = \Delta C + \Delta S$

$$\frac{\Delta Y}{\Delta Y} = \frac{\Delta C}{\Delta Y} + \frac{\Delta S}{\Delta Y} \quad \text{It means } 1 = MPC + MPS$$

MPC = 1-MPS

MPS = 1-MPC

1. If APS is 0.6, find APC?

   Ans. APC = 1- APS = 1-0.6 = 0.4

2. If MPS = 1, find MPC?

   Ans. MPC = 1-MPS

   = 1-1 = 0

3. MPC is 0.70, find MPS.

   Ans. MPS = 1-MPC

   = 1-0.7 = 0.3

4. APC = 0.9, find APS

   Ans. APS = 1-APC

   = 1-0.9 = 0.1

5. Complete the following: [Delhi 2005]

Income	Consumption	MPC	MPS
400	240		
500	320		
600	395		
700	460		

Answer: 5

Income Y	Consumption C	Saving S = Y-C	ΔY	ΔC	ΔS	MPC = $\Delta C / \Delta Y$	MPS
400	240	160	-	-	-	-	-
500	320	180	100	80	20	0.8	0.2
600	395	205	100	75	25	0.75	0.25
700	460	240	100	65	35	0.65	0.35

6. Complete the following. [All India 2005]

Income	Consumption	MPC	MPS
1000	900		
1,200	1,060		
1,400	1,210		
1,600	1,350		

Answer:6

Income	Consumption	ΔY	ΔC	MPC	MPS
1000	900	-	-	-	-
1200	1060	200	160	0.8	0.2
1400	1210	200	150	0.75	0.25
1600	1350	200	140	0.70	0.30

7. **Complete the following:** [Delhi 2007]

Income	Consumption	MPS	APS
2000	1900		
3000	2700		
4000	3400		
5000	4000		

Answer:7

Income	Consumption	Saving	ΔY	ΔS	MPS	APS
2000	1900	100	-	-	-	0.05
3000	2700	300	1000	200	0.2	0.10
4000	3400	600	1000	300	0.3	0.15
5000	4000	1000	1000	400	0.4	0.20

8. **Complete the following:** [All India 2009]

Income	MPC	Saving	APS
0	-	-90	
100	0.6		
200	0.6		
300	0.6		

Answer:

Income	MPC	MPS = 1-MPC	ΔS = MPS X ΔY	MPS	APS
0	-	-	-	-90	-
100	0.6	0.4	40	-50	-0.50
200	0.6	0.4	40	-10	-0.05
300	0.6	0.4	40	30	0.10

9. **Complete the following:** [Delhi 2009]

Income	Consumption	MPS	APS
0	40		
50	70		
100	100		
150	120		

Answer:

Income	Consumption	Saving	MPS	APS
0	40	-40	-	-
50	70	-20	0.4	-0.40
100	100	0	0.4	0
150	120	30	0.4	0.2

10. **Complete the following:** [Delhi 2009]

Income	Saving	MPC	APS
0	-12		
20	-6		
40	0		
60	6		

Answer:

Income	Saving	Consumption	$MPC = \dfrac{\Delta C}{\Delta Y}$	$APS = \dfrac{S}{Y}$
0	-12	12	-	-
20	-6	26	0.7	-0.30
40	0	40	0.7	0
60	6	54	0.7	0.10

11. **Complete the following:** [CBSE 2013]

Income	Saving	APC	MPC
0	-40		
50	-20		
100	0		
150	30		
200	50		

Answer:

Income	Saving	Consumption	APC	ΔC	MPC
0	-40	40	-	-	-
50	-20	70	1.4	30	0.6
100	0	100	1	30	0.6
150	30	120	0.8	20	0.4
200	50	150	0.75	30	0.6

12. **Complete the following table:** [CBSE 2013]

Income	Consumption	MPS	APS
0	80	-	-
100	140	0.4	-
200	-	-	0
-	240	-	0.2
-	260	0.8	0.35

Answer:

Income	ΔY	Consumption	Saving(APS x Y)	ΔS	MPS	APS
0	-	80	-80	-	-	-
100	100	140	-40	40	0.4	-0.4
200	100	200(Y-S)	0	40	0.4	0
$\dfrac{C}{APC} = 300$	100	240	60	60	0.6	0.2
$\dfrac{C}{APC} = 400$	100	260	40	80	0.8	0.35

3.20 Derivation of Saving Function from Consumption Function with the help Diagram

Income = Consumption + Savings because income is either consumed or saved.

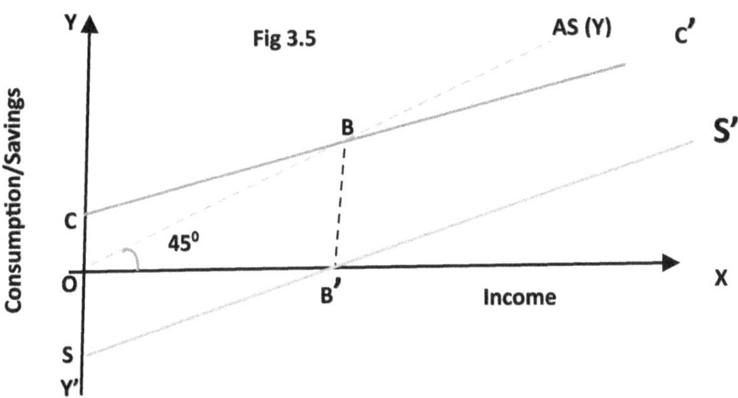

We can derive saving function from consumption function.

- CC is consumption curve. Consumption curve starts from point c not from the origin O, as consumption is never zero, even when income is zero there is some amount of consumption needed for survival.

- 45° line is guide line, point B on this line shows break-even point when consumption is equal to income.

- Draw a perpendicular line from point B to X-axis and mark as B' on X-axis.

- Measure distance OC on Y axis and mark same distance as OS in the negative side of Y axis.

- Now join S and B' and extend it to draw saving function SS'.

3.21 Derive Consumption Function from Saving Function

Straight line consumption curve can be derived from saving curve. Consumption and saving curve are complementary curves. Income = consumption + savings.

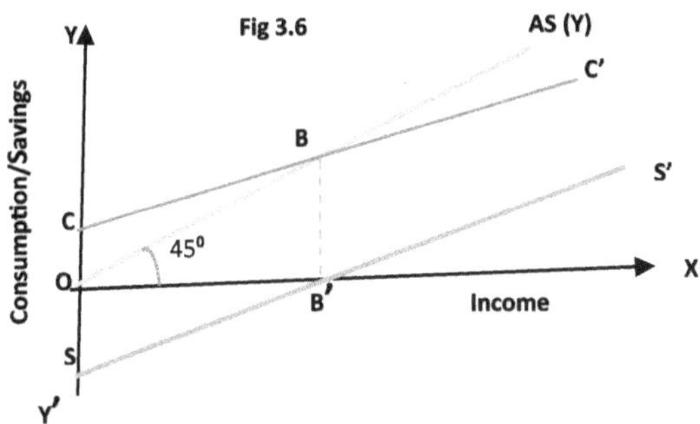

Saving curve SS' start from a point from negative side below origin, it shows at 0 level of income or low level of income there is some dissaving.

Point B' is on X-axis showing zero savings it is break-even point.

Saving curve is upward sloping because as income increases saving also increases.

By measuring vertical distance between saving curve and X-axis at different level of income we can derive consumption curve.

OS distance can be marked as **OC** on Y axis.

Point **B'** can be marked as **B on 45^0** line by drawing a line perpendicular from B' to **45^0** line.

By joining point **C and B** and extending it we can derive consumption curve **CC'**.

3.22 Investment Function

Investment Function: Investment function shows behavior of investment at different level of income.

Investment are expenses made on purchase of capital assets like machine, plants, equipment etc. It is addition in existing physical assets plus change in inventories.

Investment includes anything that adds to the future productive capacity of the economy.

1. Plants and machine

2. Construction

3. Stocks

Factors that determines investment:

According to Keynes investment are determined by two factors.

i. **Marginal efficiency of investment (MEI)** or rate of return: Firms will investment as long as rate of return is more than investment.

ii. **Rate of interest**: Rate of interest on borrowing fund for investment is less than rate of return. The return from investment is more than rate of interest.

3.23 Investment is of Two Types

Induced investment and Autonomous Investment

Induced Investment	Autonomous Investment
Investment which is done with the motive to earn **profit**.	Investment which is done with the motive of **social welfare**.
Induced investment is income elastic.	Autonomous investment is income inelastic.
Induced Investment is **directly** related to the level of income.	Autonomous investment is unrelated to the level of income.
Induced investment curve is positively sloped towards right.	Autonomous investment curve is parallel to X-axis.
Induced investment is normally done by private entrepreneurs.	Autonomous investment is normally done by the government.

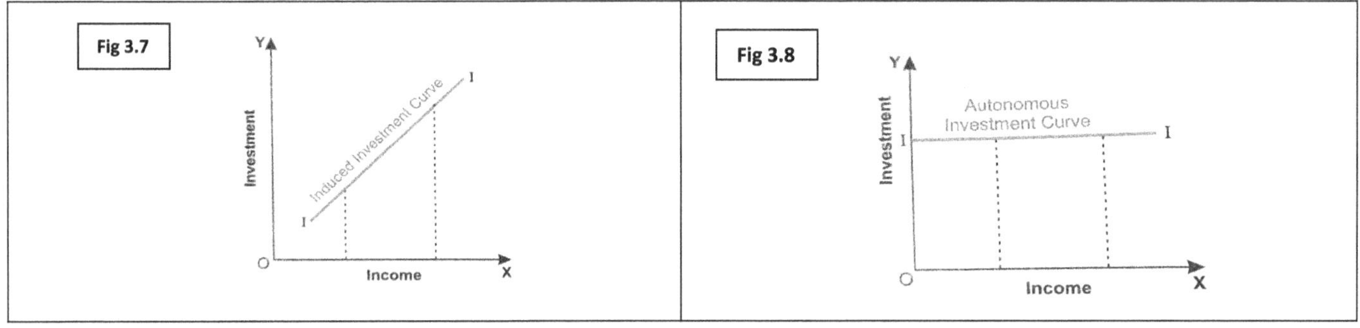

3.24 Planned Savings (Ex-ante Savings) and Planned Investment (Ex-ante Investment)

The economy is in equilibrium when aggregate demand is equal to aggregate supply or when Ex-ante saving = Ex-ante investment.

Planned Savings (Ex-ante Savings): The savings which all the households plan (intend) to make at different level of income during a given period of time is known as planned savings or ex-ante savings. It is desired saving before the given period.

Planned Investment (Ex-ante Investment): The investment which the investors or the entrepreneur's plan (intend) to do at different level of income in an economy during a given period of time is known as Ex-Ante Investment. It is desired investment before the given period.

3.25 Actual Savings (Ex-post Savings) and Actual Investment (Ex-post Investment)

Actual Savings (Ex-post Savings): It is the actual amount of savings done by an economy during a given period of time. It is actual saving done by the households after the specific period.

Actual Investment (Ex-post Investment): It is the actual amount of investment made by all the entrepreneurs in the economy during a given period. It is actual investments done by the firms and entrepreneurs after the specified period.

Actual investment = Planned Investment + Unplanned investment

Note: Actual investment may differ from planned investment because of unplanned addition or reduction in inventories.

3.26 Equilibrium of an Economy

Equilibrium in an economy can be derived by two alternative methods:

1.   Aggregate Demand and Aggregate Supply.

2.   Planned Saving and Planned Investment

Interrelation between two approaches

AD = AS at equilibrium

AD = C + I and AS = C + S

Thus C + I = C + S (C get cancelled as it is common)

Thus, I = S at equilibrium.

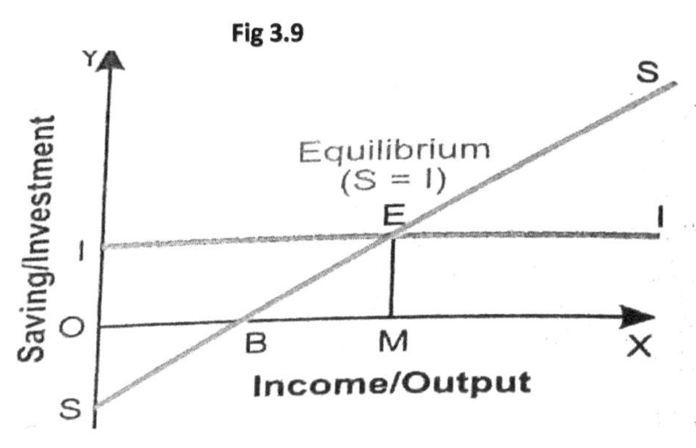

3.27 Determination of Equilibrium Level of Income (S = I)

An economy is in equilibrium at the level of income at which Planned Savings = Planned Investment i.e., S = I

When investment curve intersects saving curve at point E equilibrium. Thus OM is equilibrium level of income. It means the economy invest what it has saved. Such economy is rare as savers and investors are different people and their motive is also different.

When savings and investment are not equal, then production will adjust (increase or decrease) till savings = investments.

(When savings are not equal to investment)

3.28 Adjustment in Output to Achieve Equilibrium

When planned Savings (Ex-ante saving) is more than planned investment (Ex-ante investment): When planned saving is more than planned investment it means aggregate supply is more than aggregate demand. Let us assume savings are ₹20000 crores and investment is just ₹15000 crores. It means aggregate supply in the economy is more than then aggregate demand. There will be unplanned pile up of stock or unintended increase in inventories. AS>AD, excess supply will result into pile of stock unsold, the producers will cut down production as a result people will lose job, income, employment and output will fall. This process of reduction of employment, income and output will continue till planned saving is equal to planned investment.

When planned saving is less than planned investment (Ex-ante savings< Ex-ante investment): When planned saving is less than planned investment it means aggregate supply is less than aggregate demand. This will result in unplanned reduction in inventories because of high aggregate demand. As a result, the producers will increase production to meet increased demand. To increase production more people will be employed, so their income will increase. Thus production, employment and income all will increase. This process of increase in production, employment and income will continue till planned saving = planned investment.

3.29 Determination of National Income Equilibrium through AD and AS Approach

An economy is in equilibrium at that level at which aggregate demand is equal to aggregate supply i.e. AD = AS. When AD = AS implies that whatever is produced in the economy (AS) is either consumed by the households or invested by the firms.

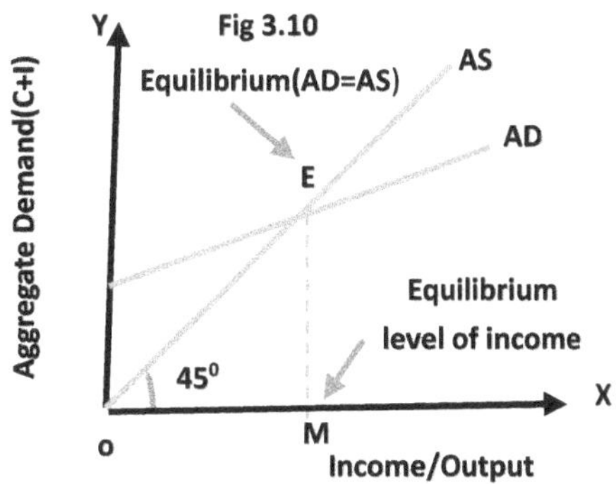

In the figure X axis shows Income/output, Y axis shows aggregate demand. 45⁰ line is AS line. AD line intersects at point E so it is equilibrium point.OM is equilibrium level of income/output.

When AD>AS:

When aggregate demand is more than aggregate supply means people are demanding more than what the producers have produced. To meet increased demand producers will increase supply (output). To increase output more people will be employed so income of people will also increase. Thus the process of increase in output, employment and income will continue till AS = AD.

When AD<AS

When aggregate demand is less than aggregate supply means people are demanding less than goods produced (AS) so some goods will remain unsold. There will be unplanned pile up of stock of goods so the producers will cut down production and people will lose job and their income will fall. As a result, output, income and employment will fall. This process of fall in output, income and employment will continue till AD = AS.

Why is it necessary condition to have AD = AS at equilibrium?

When AD = AS means aggregate demand of the people matches with the aggregate supply, there is no surplus or shortage of supply in respect to demand. Whatever is produced is sold. So it is most stable condition.

3.30 Short Run Equilibrium Level of Output

Under short run fixed prices, equilibrium level of output is exclusively determined by aggregate demand. Aggregate Supply is assumed to be perfectly elastic. According to Keynes in short run technology is constant so output can change only due to change in employment.

1. **Prices are constant**: Prices are assumed to be constant in the short run because economy takes time to respond to the forces of excess demand and excess supply.

2. Supply is perfectly elastic at fixed prices.

3. It is short run analysis: It short run output is solely dependent on employment.

4. The study is in two sectors. AD = C + I

Under these circumstances equilibrium level of output is exclusively depended on Aggregate Demand. This is known as Effective Demand.

3.31 Effective Demand

Aggregate demand which is required to achieve full employment equilibrium is called Effective Demand.

According to Keynes: Under short run fixed run fixed price, it is the level of aggregate demand or effective demand which determine the level of output, income and employment.

3.32 Paradox of Thrift

According to Keynes, as people become thriftier (more saving), they end up saving less.

It is based on the principle of Investment Multiplier $\mathbf{K} = \dfrac{1}{1 - \boldsymbol{MPC}}$

There is direct relationship between multiplier and MPC. When consumption increases National Income will also Increases.

If all the people in an economy increase their savings, consumption demand decreases leading to pile up of unsold items. Producers will cut down production and remove people from job. When people lose their job, they consume from their savings for survival so saving start decreasing. Thus, if all the people in an economy start saving more total savings of the economy will fall or remain save. This is called Paradox of Thrift.

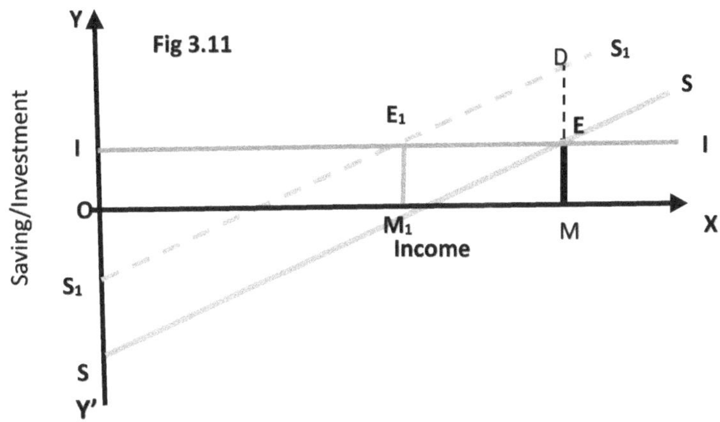

Paradox of thrift can be explained with the help of diagram. X axis shows income/employment/output. Y axis shows savings and investment. SS is saving curve which starts from negative side of Y axis as at zero level or very low level of income there is some amount of dissaving. Investment curve II is parallel to X axis as investment remains constant in short period. E is equilibrium point when Saving is equal to investment.OM is equilibrium level of income/output. When saving increases by ED amount new saving curve will be $S_1 S_1$, New equilibrium point will be E_1 where saving and investment are equal to each other. Equilibrium level of income will decrease from OM to OM_1.Thus when saving increases by ED amount total saving falls by EE_1 amount.

3.33 Deriving the Value of Equilibrium Output and Aggregate Demand at Fixed Price and Rate of Interest

At equilibrium AD = AS

AS = Y Aggregate supply is also called national income (Y).

AD = C + I where C is consumption and I denotes Investment.

$C = \bar{c} + b\,Y$

At equilibrium AS = AD

Or $Y = \bar{c} + b\,Y + I$

(Where $C = \bar{c} + b\,Y$ and I = I[Autonomous Investment in short period according to Keynes])

Sum of Autonomous consumption and autonomous investment = Autonomous Expenditure ($\bar{A}$)

$\mathbf{Y = \bar{A} + b\,Y}$ b = MPC

3.34 Numerical on Equilibrium Level of Income, Consumption and Investment

1. In a two-sector economy the consumption and investment function are; C = 60 + 0.8Y and I = 60 calculate:

    i. Equilibrium level of Income

    ii. Consumption at equilibrium level of Income

    iii. Savings at equilibrium level of Income

    Answer-1: Y = C + I (At equilibrium AS = AD)

    i. Income(Y) = 60 + 0.8Y + 60   Y = 120 + 0.8 Y

    Y-0.8Y = 120   0.2Y = 120 $Y = \dfrac{120}{0.2}$ $Y = \dfrac{1200}{2}$ Y = ₹600

ii.   Consumption (c) = 60 + 0.8   Y = 60 + 0.8 X 600 = 60 + 480

Consumption = ₹540

iii.   Savings(S) = Y-C = 600-540   Savings = 60

2. The saving function of an economy is S = -400 + 0.25 Y and Income = 2,000. Calculate

   a.   Investment expenditure at equilibrium

   b.   Autonomous Consumption.

Solution-2: (a) S = -400 + 0.25x 2000

S = -400 + 500 Savings = 100

At equilibrium Investment = Saving Thus Investment = 100

(b) Autonomous Consumption = Dissaving

Here autonomous Consumption = 400

3. Consumption Function C = $\bar{c}$ + b Y. Calculate consumption, when income level is ₹2000 crore, if autonomous consumption is ₹50 crores and 60% of the additional income is consumed.

Solution 3: Given: Y = ₹ 2000 crores $\bar{c}$ = ₹ 50 crores MPC = 60% = 0.60

C = 50 + 0.60 X 2000 C = 50 + 1200 Consumption = ₹1250 Crore

4. With the help of saving function calculate consumption function with the help of following information **S = -60 + 0.2 Y,** where income is ₹ **4000 crores.**

Solution 4: S = - 60 + 0.2 X 4000 S = -60 + 800 S = Rs.740 crores.

C = 60 + 0.8 X 4000   C = 60 + 3200 **C = ₹3260 crore**

OR

Y = C + S   C = Y-S   C = 4000-740 **C = ₹3260 crore**

5. If MPS is one fourth of MPC and at zero level of income Rs.100 crores. Derive Consumption and Saving, when income is ₹ 8,000 crores.

Solution-5: MPS = 1/4 MPC MPS = 0.25 MPC

MPC + MPS = 1 0.25MPS + MPC = 1 1.25 MPC = 1 MPC = 1/1.25

MPC = 0.8 Then MPS = 0.2

C = 100 + 0.8 X 8000   C = 100 + 6400   Consumption = ₹ 6500 Crores

Y = C + S   S = Y- C   S = 8000 – 6500   Savings = ₹1500 Crores

6. The consumption function for an economy C = 100 + 0.6 Y (crore). determine the level of income when average propensity to consume is 1.

Answer-6: Given APC = 1 and APC = C/Y when C = Y then APC will be 1.

At break -even point C = Y.

We can write Y = 100 + 0.6 Y

Y-0.6 Y = 100   (1-0.6) Y = 100   0.4 Y = 100

Y = 100/0.4   Y = 1000/4   Income = ₹250 crore

7. The break -even level of income for an economy is given to be Rs.6000 crores. If the economy saves 40% additional income, calculate the value of autonomous consumption.

Answer-7: Given: Income = Rs.6000 crore

MPS = 40% = 40/100 MPS = 0.4 MPS + MPC = 1 MPC = 0.6

At Break- Even point Income = Consumption

Income = ₹6000 crores here, Consumption = ₹6000 crore

$C = \bar{c} + 0.6 \times 6000$ $6000 = \bar{c} + 3600$ $\bar{c} = 6000\text{-}3600$

Autonomous Consumption $(\bar{c}) = ₹2400$ crore

8. On the basis of given information, C = 100 + 0.6 Y calculate

   a. Derive Saving Function

   b. Level of income at zero saving.

   c. Saving when income is ₹1000 crore.

   Answer-8: (a) S = - 100 + 0.4 Y (Autonomous consumption is equal to dissaving).

   b) When income = consumption, saving = 0 This is called Break-even point.

   S = -100 + 0.4 Y, then C = 100 + 0.6 Y

   Since C = Y   Y = 100 + 0.6 Y   Y -0.6Y = 100

   0.4 Y = 100   Y = 1000/4   INCOME = ₹250 crore

   c) S = -100 + 0.4 X 1000

   S = -100 + 400 Saving = ₹300 crore

9. In an economy, the ratio of average propensity to consume to average propensity to save is 6:4. The level of Income is ₹8000. How much are the savings? Calculate.

   Answer 9: APC: APS = 6:4.

   APC + APS = 1

   $APC = \dfrac{6}{10} = 0.6$ $APS = \dfrac{4}{10} = 0.4$

   Savings at when income is ₹8000.

   $APS = \dfrac{S}{Y}$ $\dfrac{S}{Y} = \dfrac{4}{10}$

   $\dfrac{S}{8000} = \dfrac{4}{10}$ $\dfrac{S}{Y} = \dfrac{4 \times 8000}{10}$

   Saving = ₹ 3200

10. If an economy plans to increase its income by ₹2,000 crores and marginal propensity to consume is 75%. Estimate the required increase in investment to achieve the targeted increase in income.

    Answer 10: Given: MPC = 0.75

    Change in income $(\Delta Y) = ₹$ 2000 crore

    $K = \dfrac{1}{1-MPC} = \dfrac{1}{1-0.75} = \dfrac{1}{0.25} = \dfrac{100}{25}$ $K = 4$

    $K = \dfrac{\Delta Y}{\Delta I}$ $\Delta I = \dfrac{\Delta Y}{k} = \dfrac{2000}{4}$ $\Delta I = ₹$ 500 crores

3.35 Investment Multiplier (K)

Investment multiplier shows the relationship between initial increase in investment and resultant increase in National Income.

OR

Investment Multiplier (K) shows increase in National Income (ΔY) due to increase in investment (ΔI).

$$K = \frac{\Delta Y}{\Delta I}$$

Investment Multiplier explains multiplying effect of investment on Income.

$$K = \frac{1}{MPS} \quad \text{(Investment multiplier is inversely related to MPS.)}$$

$$K = \frac{1}{1 - MPC} \quad \text{(Investment multiplier is directly related to MPC.)}$$

$$\Delta Y = K \times \Delta I$$

Example: If increase in investment of ₹ 50 crores result in increase in National Income of ₹500 crores, then the value of multiplier will be $\frac{500}{50}$ = 10. The value of Multiplier is 10. This means when there is change in investment, national Income increase 10 times.

WORKING OF MULTIPLIER: The concept of multiplier is based on assumption that expenditure of one person is income of another person. M's expenditure is N's income. N's expenditure is O's income. O's expenditure is P's income and so on till spending become zero.

Example: Suppose Government invests 100 crores in a factory called XYZ. These 100 crores become income of the people working in that factory (XYZ). National Income will increase by 100 crores in first round.

If their MPC is 0.5 it means people are spending 50% of their income on consumption. Thus 50 crores will be spent on consumption goods. This 50 Crores will become income of another group of people in the second round.

If again their MPC is 0.5 it means 50% of their income they will spend which is ₹25 crores. This 25crores will becomes income of third group of people. If again MPC is 0.5, this third group of people will spend ₹12.5 crores which will become income of fourth group of people and this process will continue round after round till spending becomes zero.

The process of income generation has shown in the table:

Round	Increase in Investment	Increase in Income	Increase in consumption
1	₹100 crores	₹100 crores(1st round)	MPC = 0.5 (50 crores)
2		₹50 crores(2nd round)	MPC = 0.5 (25 crores)
3		₹25 crores(3rd round)	12.5 crores
4		12.5 crores(4th round)	6.25 crores
5		6.25 crores(5th round)	3.125 crores

$$K = \frac{1}{1 - MPC} = \frac{1}{1 - 0.5} = \frac{1}{0.5} = \frac{10}{5} = 2$$

Initial investment is 100 crores resultant increase in National Income is 200 crores.

$$K = \frac{\Delta Y}{\Delta I} \quad 2 = \frac{\Delta Y}{100} \quad \Delta Y = ₹200 \text{ crores}$$

Thus, when investment increases by 100 crores National Income increases to 200 Crores due to Multiplier Effect.

3.36 Graphic Presentation of Investment Multiplier

Investment Multiplier explains the relationship between initial increase in investment and resultant increase in National Income. $K = \dfrac{\Delta Y}{\Delta I}$

$$K = \dfrac{\textit{Change in National Income}}{\textit{Change in investment}}$$

The effect of investment multiplier can be explained with the help of Diagram.

In the diagram X axis shows income and Y axis shows Saving/Investment. Investment curve is parallel to X axis as in short period investment remains constant. Saving Curve is starting from negative side showing dissaving at low level of income. Saving curve intersects investment curve at point E when national income is ₹300 crores. When investment increases by 10% National income increases by 50% as new equilibrium point is E'.

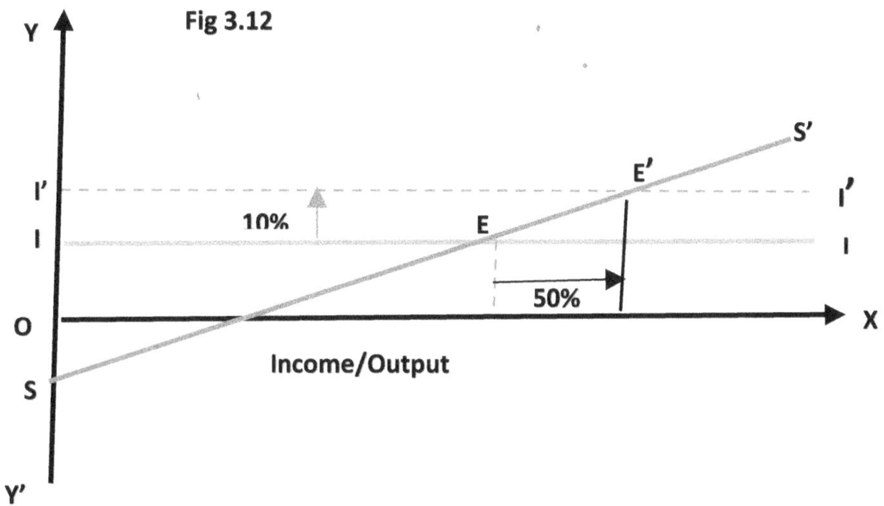

When investment increases by 10 crore National Income increases by 50 crores.

Value of Multiplier is 5 $\left(k = \dfrac{\Delta Y}{\Delta I} = \dfrac{50}{10} = 5\right)$

3.37 Relationship between Multiplier and MPC

There is positive relationship between K and MPC. If MPC is high, K will also be high but if MPC is low, Multiplier value will be low.

Example: When, MPC = 0.8 $K = \dfrac{1}{1-0.8} = \dfrac{1}{0.2}$ K = 5

When, MPC = 0.5 $K = \dfrac{1}{1-0.5} = \dfrac{1}{0.5} = \dfrac{10}{5}$ K = 2

3.38 Relationship between Multiplier and MPS

There is inverse relation between Multiplier and MPS.

If MPS is high Value of Multiplier value will be low and vice versa.

Example: When, MPS is 0.8 $K = \dfrac{1}{MPS} = \dfrac{1}{0.8} = \dfrac{10}{8}$ K = 1.25

When, MPS is 0.5 $K = \dfrac{1}{0.5}$ K = 2

3.39 Minimum and Maximum Value of Multiplier

Range of Investment Multiplier: The range of Investment multiplier lies between

1- ∞ (one to infinity).

- **When MPC is 0, Value of Investment Multiplier is 1** $\left(K = \dfrac{1}{1-MPC} = \dfrac{I}{1} = 1 \right)$

- **When MPC is 1, value of Investment multiplier is** ∞. $\left(K = \dfrac{1}{1-MPC} = \dfrac{I}{0} = \infty \right)$

Value of Multiplier depends on MPC.

3.40 Numerical on Investment Multiplier

1. In an economy the actual level of income is ₹ 500 crores whereas full employment level of income is ₹ 900 crores. The MPC is 0.75. Calculate increase in investment required to achieve full employment level of income.

   Ans-1: $K = \dfrac{1}{1-MPC} = \dfrac{1}{1-0.75} = \dfrac{1}{0.25} = 4$

   Increase in Income = 900-500 ΔY = ₹ 400

   $K = \dfrac{\Delta Y}{\Delta I}$ Increase in Investment $(\Delta I) = \dfrac{400}{4} = ₹ 100$ crore

2. In an economy MPC is 0.5. if investment expenditure increases by ₹800 crores. Calculate increase in income and consumption expenditure.

   Ans-2: $K = \dfrac{1}{1-MPC} = \dfrac{1}{1-0.5} = \dfrac{1}{0.5} = \dfrac{10}{5} = 2$ **K = 2**

   $K = \dfrac{\Delta Y}{\Delta I}$ or, 2 X 800 = ΔY or , ΔY = ₹ **1600**

   Change in Income (ΔC) = MPC X ΔY = 0.5 X 1600 ΔC = ₹ **800**

3. In an economy MPS is 0.2. Investment increases by ₹1000 crore. Calculate total increase in National Income.

   Ans-3: $K = \dfrac{1}{MPS} = \dfrac{1}{0.2} = \dfrac{10}{2}$ **K = 5**

   $K = \dfrac{\Delta Y}{\Delta I}$ $\Delta Y = K \, X \, \Delta I$ = 5x1000 ΔY = ₹ 5000 crore

4. In an economy, investment expenditure increased by ₹700 and MPC 0.9. Calculate total increase in income and consumption expenditure.

   Ans-4: MPC = 0.9 So, MPS = 1-MPC MPS = 1-0.9 = 0.1

   $K = \dfrac{1}{MPS} = \dfrac{1}{0.1} = \dfrac{10}{1}$ **K = 10**

   $K = \dfrac{\Delta Y}{\Delta I}$ $\Delta Y = K \, X \, \Delta I$ = 10x700 = 7000 crore

   Increase in consumption (ΔC) = MPC x ΔY = 0.9 X7000 = ₹ 6300 crores

5. An increase of ₹ 500 crores in investment in an economy results in increase in income of ₹ 2000 crore. Calculate:

(a) MPC (b) Change in saving (c) Change in consumption expenditure (d) Value of Multiplier

Ans-5: (d) $K = \dfrac{\Delta Y}{\Delta I} = \dfrac{2000}{500} = \dfrac{200}{25}$

$K = \dfrac{1}{MPS}$ $4 = \dfrac{1}{MPS}$ $MPS = \dfrac{1}{4}$ **MPS = 0.25**

(a) MPC = 1-MPS = 1-0.25 MPC = 0.75

(b) $\Delta C = MPC \times \Delta Y = 0.75 \times 2000$ $\Delta C = ₹\ 1500$

(b) $\Delta S = MPS \times \Delta Y = 0.25 \times 2000$ $\Delta S = ₹\ 500$

6. In an economy, equilibrium level of income is ₹12,000 crores. The ratio of MPC to MPS is 3:1. Calculate additional investment needed to reach a new equilibrium level of income of ₹ 20,000 crores

Ans-6: $MPC = \dfrac{3}{4} = \mathbf{0.75}$ $MPS = \dfrac{1}{4} = \mathbf{0.25}$

$K = \dfrac{1}{MPS} = \dfrac{1}{0.25}$ **K = 4**

$K = \dfrac{\Delta Y}{\Delta I}$ $\Delta Y = 20,000 - 12,000$ $\Delta Y = ₹\ 8000$ crores

$K = \dfrac{\Delta Y}{\Delta I}$ $\Delta I = \dfrac{\Delta Y}{K} = \dfrac{8000}{4}$ $\Delta I = ₹\ \mathbf{2000}$

7. Increase of ₹ 400 crores in investment in an economy, resulted in total increase in income of ₹ 1,000 crores. Calculate the following:

(a) Value of investment multiplier

(b) Change in savings

(c) Change in consumption expenditure

(d) Marginal propensity to consume

Ans: 7 (a) $K = \dfrac{\Delta Y}{\Delta I} = \dfrac{1000}{400} = 2.5$

(b) $MPS = \dfrac{\Delta S}{\Delta Y}$ $K = \dfrac{1}{MPS}$ $2.5 = \dfrac{1}{MPS}$ $MPS = \dfrac{10}{25}$ $K = 0.4$

$\Delta S = MPS \times \Delta Y$ $\Delta S = 0.4 \times 1000$ $\Delta S = \Delta\ 400$ (c) $\Delta C = MPC \times \Delta Y$

$= 0.6 \times 1000 = ₹\ 600$

(d) MPC = 1-MPS

$= 1\text{-}0.4$ **MPC = 0.6**

8. In an economy S = -50 + 0.5 Y is the saving function (where S = saving and Y = national income) and investment expenditure is ₹7000. Calculate.

(a) Equilibrium level of national income.

(b) Consumption expenditure at equilibrium level

Ans: S = -50 + 0.5 Y (given), investment = ₹7000 (given) of national income.

(a) Equilibrium Level of National Income = $\bar{c}$ + by + I

Y = C + I = 50 + 0.5 Y + 7000

Y-0.5 Y = 7000 + 50

Y-0.5 Y = 7050 $\qquad$ $Y = \dfrac{7050}{0.5}$

Y = ₹ 14,100

(b) Consumption Expenditure at the level of equilibrium = $\bar{c}$ + by

C = 50 + 0.5Y   C = 50 + 0.5 x 14,100   C = ₹ 7,100

OR

Alternatively, Y = C + I

C = Y-I $\qquad$ C = 14,100-7000 $\qquad$ C = ₹ 7,100

3.41 Voluntary Unemployment/Full Employment/Involuntary Unemployment

INVOLUNTARY UNEMPLOYMENT: An involuntary unemployment is a situation when all able person who are willing to work at the given wage rate do not get job.

1. People are Physically and mentally fit to work

2. Willing to work at the given wage rate but not getting job.

Involuntary unemployment is known as unemployment. According to Keynes involuntary unemployment occurs due to lack of effective demand.

VOLUNTARY UNEMPLOYMENT: It refers to a situation when people who are able to work but not willing to work even though job is available in the economy. Such people are not included in the workforce of the country. Example: Housewives.

FULL EMPLOYMENT: It is a situation where those who are able and willing to work at the prevailing wage rate are employed.

Or,when there is no involuntary unemployment.

However frictional, structural and voluntary unemployment can co-exist within the state full employment. Unemployment up to 3% is considered is natural rate of unemployment due to frictional and technological unemployment.

Under Employment (Disguised Unemployment): Under unemployment is a situation when people are engaged in jobs but less than their capacities or qualifications.

According to Keynes full employment indicates that level of employment where increase in aggregate demand does not lead to increase in the level of output or employment but causes prices to go up.

3.42 Full Employment Equilibrium and Under-Employment Equilibrium

Meaning of Equilibrium: The level of income when Aggregate Demand = Aggregate Supply

or Planned saving = Planned Investment

Equilibrium may be at Full Employment or less than Full Employment level.

Full employment Equilibrium: When AD = AS and all the resources are fully employed. There are no unused resources. There is no involuntary unemployment. This is an ideal situation which an economy desires to achieve tries to remain at it. There is neither Deficient Demand nor Excess Demand. Full employment equilibrium is also known as **Effective Demand Equilibrium.**

Underemployment Equilibrium: When Aggregate Demand = Aggregate Supply, at less than full employment (resources are not fully employed) then it is known as underemployment equilibrium. At this situation Aggregate demand is less than Full Employment Aggregate Demand. *It is also known as Deficient Demand and Deflationary Gap.*

3.43 Deficient Demand and Deflationary Gap

When aggregate demand is less than aggregate supply at full employment, the demand is said to be deficient demand and the gap is called deflationary gap.

This situation is caused not by low level of output but by lack of demand.

Example: By employing all the resources an economy can produce 10,000 quintals of rice whereas demand for rice is 7,000 quintals. Here aggregate supply at full employment is 10,000 quintals but aggregate demand is only 7000 quintals. This is a situation of deficient demand. The demand is deficient by 3000.

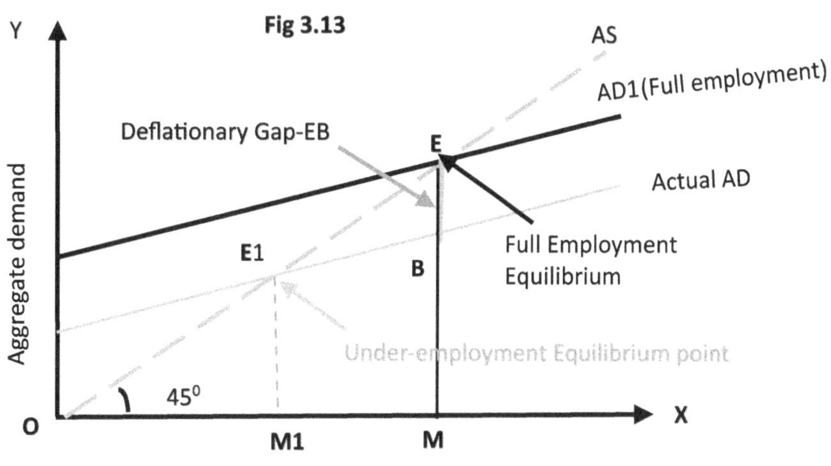

National Income/Aggregate Supply

This gap between actual aggregate Demand and full employment aggregate demand is Known as deficient Demand and the gap is known as deflationary gap. This situation is known as deficient Demand and deflationary gap or underemployment equilibrium.

In the figure point **E** shows full employment equilibrium. E_1 shows under employment equilibrium.

AD$_1$ is actual aggregate Demand which is less than full employment demand. At E_1 actual AD intersect with AS, so it is point of underemployment equilibrium, **OM**$_1$ is underemployment equilibrium.OM is full employment equilibrium whereas EB shows amount of deficient Demand or Deflationary Gap.

To reach full employment, additional investment equal to EB is required.

CAUSES OF DEFICIENT DEMAND:

1. Fall in public expenditure.
2. Fall in money supply.
3. Fall in investment demand.

4. Fall in Private consumption demand due to fall in MPC.

5. Increase in MPS. People are saving more and spending less.

IMPACT OF DEFICIENT DEMAND:

1. Fall in prices of the commodities.

2. Fall in Income, employment and output.

3. Leads to recession and depression marked by over production.

MEASURES TO CONTROL THE SITUATION OF DEFICIENT DEMAND

FISCAL POLICY: Revenue and Expenditure policy of the government is known as Fiscal Policy.

a. **Public Expenditure (Increase):** Government should make huge investment in public work like construction of roads, railways, bridges, buildings canals, and provide free health and education facilities. It will pump money in the economy. People will get income and they will increase their demand. **Keynes advocates deficit Budget to increase aggregate Demand.**

b. **Revenue Policy (Reduce):** Taxes on personal income and Corporate income should be reduced to encourage consumption and investment as when more money is left with people consumption demand and investment will increase leading to increase in Aggregate Demand.

c. **Deficit Financing(increase):** (Printing one rupee note): Deficit financing helps in generating demand as more money in the hand of people will increase consumption demand and investment demand.

d. **Public Borrowing (Decrease):** Government should not borrow money from the public which will result into more money in the hands of pubic leading to increase in demand and investment.

MONETARY POLICY: It is the policy of Central Bank of a country to control credit and money supply.

The aim of monetary policy in the time depression is to cause an increase in the investment expenditure by the firms. The credit is made cheap and easy.

Quantitative Measures

1. **Repo Rate (Reduce):** Repo rate is the rate of interest at which central bank lends to commercial bank for short period. At the time of deficient demand, the central bank reduces lending rate (Bank rate and repo rate) to the commercial banks. Commercial bank in turn reduces rate of interest which make credit cheap and people can take loan at low interest and investment.

2. **Open Market Operation (Buy Security):** The Central bank should buy government bonds and security from commercial banks by paying them cash to increase their cash stock and lending capacity. The commercial banks lend money at low interest rate which increases borrowing capacity of the people. This will help to increase aggregate demand and reduce deflation.

3. **Cash Reserve Ratio (Reduce):** When Central Bank reduces Cash Reserve Ratio(CRR) more cash is left with commercial banks increasing bank's capacity to give credit during depression. Central Bank increase Cash Reserve Ratio(CRR) to decrease bank's credit creation capacity (to curtail credit).

4. **Statutory Liquidity ratio (Reduce):** SLR is reduce so that banks are supposed to keep less proportion as cash with them and can give more loan.

Qualitative Measures

These are the qualitative measures to regulate and channelize credit for specific purpose.

1. **Margin requirement** (Reduce): To check depression, Central bank reduces margin requirement (Security) of loan which increases borrowing capacity. To check inflation, Central Bank increases margin requirement

of loan which reduces borrowing capacity. Margin requirement is excess amount of security deposit in respect to loan amount. (The difference between loan amount and security amount is called margin requirement).

2. **Moral Suasion:** The Central bank request, advises, appeals, admonish and persuades commercial banks to be liberal in lending and giving credit during depression and be strict during inflation.

3. **Direct Action:** The Central Bank may take direct action against those banks which do not comply with its direction.

4. **Rationing of credit**: This means fixation of quotas for loan to be given for different business activities.

Export Promotion: To increase Aggregate Demand export should be increased. It will help to reduce deflation.

3.44 Excess Demand and Inflationary Gap

In an economy when aggregate demand is more than aggregate supply at full employment the demand is said to Excess Demand and the gap is called Inflationary gap.

We can say Excess Demand is the amount by which aggregate demand is more than aggregate supply at full employment.

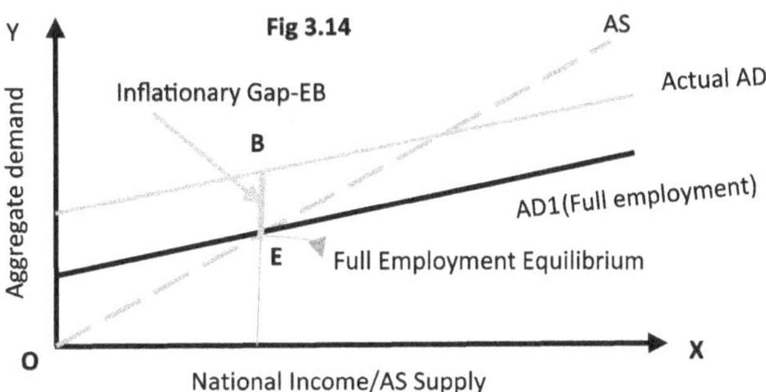

It is called inflationary gap because in this situation even though aggregate demand is more supply cannot increase as the economy is already at full employment. In this situation only prices will increase as a result of excess demand.

In the figure point E on $45°$ shows Full employment equilibrium. This is an ideal situation. But if Actual Aggregate Demand (BM) is more than Full Employment Aggregate (EM) Demand by EB. This EB is known as excess Demand or Inflationary Gap.

Reasons for Excess Demand:

1. Increase in consumption demand due to increase in MPC.

2. Increase in Investment Demand.

3. Increase in Public Expenditure.

4. Increase in Money supply.

5. Increase in Export demand.

6. Deficit Financing

Impact of Excess Demand

1)Rise in Prices.

2) Social unrest

3) Inequality of income and wealth will rise.

MEASURES TO CONTROL EXCESS DEMAND

FISCAL POLICY:

a. **Public Expenditure (Decrease):** Government should reduce expenditure on public work like construction of roads, railways, bridges, buildings canals, and provide free health and education facilities. It will reduce money supply in the economy. People will have less income and they will decrease their demand.

b. **Deficit Financing (Decrease):** (Printing one rupee note): Deficit financing should be curtailed. It will reduce money in the hand of people leading to decrease Consumption demand and Investment Demand.

c. **Revenue Policy (Increase):** Taxes on personal income and Corporate income should be increased to discourage consumption and investment as less money is left with people to demand for consumption and investment. It will decrease in Aggregate Demand.

d. **Public Borrowing (Increase):** Government should borrow money from the public leading to decrease in money (supply less money in the hands of pubic). It will decrease consumption and investment demand.

Monetary Policy: It is the policy of Central Bank to control money supply and credit in the economy.

Quantitative Measures

1. **Repo Rate (Increase):** Repo rate is the rate of interest at which central bank lends to commercial bank for short period. At the time of Inflation, the central bank should increase lending rate to the commercial banks. Commercial bank in turn will increase rate of interest which make loan costlier and people will be discouraged to take loan at high interest rate.

2. **Open Market Operation (Sell Security):** The Central bank should sell government bonds and security to commercial banks, to decrease their cash stock and lending capacity. The commercial banks will lend money at high interest rate to the public which will decrease borrowing capacity of the people. This will help to decrease aggregate demand and reduce inflation.

3. **Cash Reserve Ratio (Increase):** Central bank should increase cash Reserve ratio which in turn reduce bank's capacity to give more credit.

4. **Statutory Liquidity Ratio (Increase):** SLR is increased so that banks are supposed to keep more proportion as cash with them and can give less loan to people and investors.

Qualitative Measures

These are the qualitative measures to regulate and channelize credit for specific purpose.

1. **Margin requirement** (Increase): To check inflation, Central bank increases margin requirement (Security) of loan which decreases borrowing capacity.

2. **Moral Suasion:** The Central bank request, advises, appeals, admonish and persuades commercial banks to give less credit.

3. **Direct Action:** The Central Bank may take direct action against those banks which do not comply with its direction.

4. **Rationing of credit:** This means fixation of quotas for different business activities.

3.45 NOTE: Bank Rate / Marginal Standing Facility

Bank Rate is now called Marginal Standing Facility is a special window for the banks to borrow in an emergency situation. MSF rate is higher than Repo Rate.

Bank Rate: When Central bank lends to commercial banks for long term (and emergency) it is called Bank Rate.

Repo Rate: When central bank lends to commercial Banks for short period it is called Repo rate.

Reverse Repo Rate: It is the rate of interest when commercial Banks park their surplus money in Central Bank and earn interest on it.

3.46 Distinguish Between Inflationary Gap and Deflationary Gap

Inflationary Gap & Excess Demand	Deflationary Gap& Deficient Demand
AD > AS at full employment, it is situation of excess Demand and inflationary Gap	AD<AS then it is deficient Demand and Deflationary gap
MPC is high	MPC is low
Money supply is high	Money Supply is low
MPS is low	MPS is high
Repo Rate should be increased to control excess demand	Repo Rate should be decreased to control the situation of deficient demand
Deficit Financing should be discouraged	Increase in deficit financing
Tax should be increased to reduce Aggregate Demand	Tax should be decreased to in Aggregate Demand

3.47 Points to remember

1. Aggregate Demand (AD) = Consumption Demand + Investment Demand(C + I)

2. Aggregate Supply(AS) = Consumption + Savings (C + S).AS is also called National Income(Y) or aggregate output.

3. Consumption = $\bar{c}$ + bY (autonomous consumption + induced consumption)

4. $\bar{c}$ is autonomous consumption which means consumption at zero level of income which is needed for survival. Autonomous consumption is independent of level of income.

5. *bY is induced consumption* which means as income increases consumption also increases. B is MPC and Y is Income.

6. *Change in consumption is dependent on change in income.*

   Consumption is never zero.

7. Slope of consumption curve is MPC.

8. *When income = consumption ,it is called break* −even point. APC = 1 at break-even point.

9. *Saving is zero at break* −even point. So APS = 0.

10. The value of APC can be more than one, less than one or equal to 1.

11. The value of APS cannot be equal to 1 or more than 1. It is always less than one. As savings cannot be equal to income or more than income

12. APC is never zero as consumption is never zero.

13. The value of APS can be negative when consumption is more than income. (There is some amount of dissaving).

14. The value of MPC lies between 0 to 1. **0< MPC <1**

15. The value of MPS lies between zero to one. **0<MPS<1.**

16. APC + APS = 1

17. MPC + MPS = 1

18. Effective demand is the amount of aggregate demand required for full employment equilibrium.

19. When planned saving is more than planned investment, aggregate demand is less than aggregate supply, so there will be unplanned increase in inventory, producers will cut down production, income output and employment will start falling till planned saving is equal planned investment.

20. Investment Multiplier is directly related to MPC. Higher the value of MPC is higher the value of Multiplier.

21. Investment Multiplier is inversely related to MPS. Higher the value of MPS, lower the value of Investment Multiplier.

22. Minimum value of multiplier is 1, when MPC is 0.

23. Maximum value of multiplier is infinity, when MPC is 1.

24. Investment Multiplier is never zero.

25. Equilibrium condition for an economy is when AD = AS Or Planned saving = Planned Investment.

26. Paradox of thrift: When all the people in an economy start saving more total savings of the economy will either fall or remain same.

3.48 Important Formulae and Concepts

1. $AD = C + I$

2. $AS = Y = C + S$

3. $C = Y-S$

4. $S = Y-C$

5. At Equilibrium $Y = C + I$ (AS = AD)

6. At equilibrium: AD = AS or S = I or, $Y = \bar{c} + bY + I$

7. APC + APS = 1 So, (APC = 1-APS) (APS = 1-APC)

8. MPC + MPS = 1 so, (MPC = 1-MPS) (MPS = 1-MPC)

9. Investment Multiplier $(K) = \dfrac{\ddot{A}Y}{\ddot{A}I}$ or, $K = \dfrac{1}{MPS}$ or, $K = \dfrac{1}{1-MPC}$

10. $C = \bar{c} + bY$ where $\bar{c}$ is autonomous consumption, b = MPC Y = Income

11. $S = -\bar{c} + (1-b)Y$ where $-\bar{c}$ is dissavings (dissaving are always equal to autonomous consumption) (1-b) is MPS)

12. $MPC = \dfrac{\Delta C}{\Delta Y}$ $\Delta C = MPC \times \Delta Y$ where ΔC is change in consumption.

13. $MPS = \dfrac{\Delta S}{\Delta Y}$ $\Delta C = MPS \times \Delta Y$ where ΔS is change in Saving.

14. Full employment equilibrium: When AD = AS at full employment.

15. Investment Multiplier: Change in national income due to change in investment.

16. Investment Multiplier is directly related to MPC.$K = \dfrac{1}{1-\mathbf{MPC}}$

17. Investment Multiplier is inversely related to MPS.$K = \dfrac{1}{\mathbf{MPS}}$

18. Minimum value of multiplier is 1, when MPC is 0

19. Maximum value of multiplier is infinity, when MPC is 1.

20. Multiplier works in forward as well as in backward direction.

21. Underemployment equilibrium refers to a situation when aggregate demand is less than the aggregate supply at a level full employment. It is also known as deficient demand.

22. Excess demand and inflationary gap is a situation when aggregate demand is more than aggregate supply at full employment.

3.49 Practice Question Answer

QUESTIONS AND ANSWERS:

1. When MPC is 0, the value of investment multiplier is:

   a. One

   b. Zero

   c. Infinity

   d. None.

   Ans.(a) one

2. Aggregate demand can be increased by: [Delhi 2017]

   a. Increasing bank rate

   b. Selling government securities by Reserve Bank of India

   c. Increasing cash reserve ratio

d. None of the above

Ans.(d)

3. Which of the following are the components of aggregate demand?

   a. Household Consumption Expenditure and Investment Expenditure

   b. Government Consumption Expenditure and Net Export.

   c. Both (a) and (b)

   d. Neither (a) nor (b)

   Ans. (c)

4. Value of National Income is equals:

   a. Aggregate Demand

   b. Aggregate Supply

   c. Personal Income

   d. Disposable Income

   Ans.(b)

5. Consumption function is a functional relationship between:

   a. Income and Saving

   b. Price and Consumption

   c. Income and Consumption

   d. Income, Consumption and Saving

   Ans. (c)

6. Value of APC at Break-even point is:

   a. Zero

   b. One

   c. Infinity

   d. None

   Ans. (B) One

7. Among the following, whose value can be greater than one:

   a. APC

   b. APS

   c. MPC

   d. MPS

   Ans. (a) APC

8. When MPS = 0, then K is:

   a. 1

   b. 0

c. α

d. None of these.

Ans.(c) α

9. The concept that under employment equilibrium was given by:

   a. Adam Smith

   b. Malthus

   c. JM Keynes

   d. None of these

   Ans. J M Keynes

10. Full employment means absence of:

    a. Voluntary unemployment

    b. Involuntary unemployment

    c. Unemployment

    d. None of these

    Ans. (b) Involuntary Unemployment.

11. The value of investment Multiplier is: [All India 2015]

    a. $\dfrac{1}{MPC}$

    b. $\dfrac{1}{MPS}$

    c. $\dfrac{1}{1-MPS}$

    d. $\dfrac{1}{MPC-1}$

    Ans. (b) $\dfrac{1}{MPS}$

12. Suppose in a hypothetical economy, the income rises from ₹5,000 crores to ₹6,000 crores. As a result, the consumption expenditure rises from ₹4,000 to ₹4,600 crores. Marginal propensity to Consume in such case would be: [Delhi 2019]

    a. 0.8

    b. 0.4

    c. 0.2

    d. 0.6

    Ans.(d) 0.6

13. In case of underemployment equilibrium, which of the following alternative is not true: [CBSE 2020].

    a. Aggregate demand is equal to aggregate supply.

    b. There exists excess production capacity in the economy.

c. Resources are not fully and efficiently utilized.

d. Resources are fully and efficiently utilized.

Ans. (d)Resources are fully and efficiently utilized

14. In a situation of excess demand, Bank rate should be:

a. Increase

b. Decrease

c. Constant

d. None

Ans.(a) Increase

15. The Central Bank appeals to the commercial Bank through:

a. Open market operation

b. Bank Rate

c. Moral Suasion

d. Reserve Ratio

Ans. (c) Moral Suasion

16. Which monetary measure is the affective method to control deficient demand:

a. Increase in Public expenditure.

b. Decrease in public Expenditure.

c. Increase in deficit financing

d. Decrease Margin Requirement.

Ans.(d) Decrease Margin Requirement.

17. In an equilibrium, break- even point and equilibrium point may lie in the same of income, if ex-ante investment is:

a. Zero

b. One

c. Infinity

d. None

Ans. (a) Zero

18. When consumption Expenditure is more than the income, the value of APS

a. One

b. Zero

c. Positive

d. Negative

Ans. (d) Negative

19. At break-even point the value of APS is

   a.   One

   b.   Zero

   c.   Infinity

   d.   None

   Ans.(b) Zero

20. Value of APS is negative when:

   a. $Y = C$

   b. $Y > C$

   c. $Y < C$

   d. $Y > S$

   Ans. (C) $Y < C$

21. When MPC = MPS, the value of K will be:

   a.   1

   b.   0

   c.   2

   d.   4

   Ans.21: (c) 2

22. When consumption function is $C = 50 + 0.8\ Y$, the value of investment Multiplier will be:

   a.   1

   b.   5

   c.   4

   d.   2

   Ans.22: (b) 5

True/False Questions:

1.   Consumption depends on investment in the economy. (True/False)

     Answer: False. Consumption depends on income not on investment.

2.   In macroeconomics, aggregate demand refers to planned purchase of goods and serviced during a year. (True/False).

     Answer: True

3.   The minimum level of expenditure depends on income in the economy. (True/False)

     Answer: False

4.   When Consumption function is $C = 50 + 0.5\ Y$, saving is -20 and Income is 0. (True /False)

     Answer: False, When $Y = 0$, autonomous consumption is equal to dissaving.

5. When Ex-Ante Investment >Ex-Ante saving, Income, employment and output will increase. (True/False)

   Answer: True

6. MPC of a poor is more than that of a rich. (True/False). Give reason.

   Answer: True, Poor spends greater portion of their increased income on consumption expenditure as most of their basic requirements are not fulfilled with their low income. Whereas a rich spends less amount of their increased income on consumption expenditure as their basic needs are already satisfied.

7. APC falls with increase in income. (True/False).

   Answer: True, APC falls with increase in income because when income is more, less proportion will be spent on consumption.

8. Aggregate demand beyond full employment equilibrium does not lead to rise in output. (True/False).

   Answer: True, the level of output cannot rise as the economy is already at full employment and there is no resource idle.

9. Deflationary demand decreases national income of the economy. (True/False).

   Answer: True, deficient demand will lead to decrease in income and output and thus national income will fall.

10. An increase in the bank rate makes borrowing costlier for the general public. (True/False)

    Answer: True, Increase in the bank rate forces the commercial banks to increase their lending rates, which makes borrowings costlier for the general public.

IDENTIFY THE CORRECT MATCH:

1. Identify the correct pair from the following Column I and Column II:

Column I	Column II
A. Break Even Point	i. $C = Y$
B. Value of aggregate supply	ii. Equals to domestic Income
C. MPS	iii. $\dfrac{\Delta Y}{\Delta C}$
D. Saving function	iv. Starts from the origin

   Alternatives: (a) A-(i) (b) B-(ii) (c) C-(iii) (d) D-(iv)

   Answer: (a) A-(i)

3. Identify the correct pair from the following Column I and Column II:

Column I	Column II
A. MPC	i. Ratio of consumption to income.
B. MPS	ii. Slope of saving curve
C. Induced Consumption	iii. $\overline{C}$
D. Investment Multiplier	iv. $\dfrac{\Delta I}{\Delta Y}$

Alternatives: (a) A-(i) (b) B-(ii) (c) C-(iii) (d) D-(iv)

Answer:-(b) B-(ii)

5. Identify the correct pair from the following Column I and Column II.

Column I	Column II
A. Excess Demand	i. When AD< AS at full employment level of income
B. Deflationary gap	ii. $\dfrac{\Delta C}{\Delta Y}$
C. Autonomous consumption	
D. Break-even Point	iii. Consumption at zero level of income.
	iv. When consumption = saving

Alternatives:

(a) A-(i) (b) B-(ii) (c) C-(iii) (d) D- (iv)

Answer: (c) C-(iii)

7. Identify the correct pair from the following Column I and Column II.

Column I	Column II
A. Involuntary unemployment	i. When able people are not willing to work.
B. Margin requirement	ii. Quantitative Measure to control credit.
C. 45^0 line	iii. Aggregate demand curve.
D. Rationing of credit	iv. Qualitative Measure to control credit .

Alternatives:

A-(i) (b) B-(ii) (c) C-(iii) (d) D- (iv)

Answer: (d) D- (iv)

9. Identify the correct pair from the following Column I and Column II.

Column I	Column II
A. Components of Aggregate Demand	i. C + S
B. Determinants of investment	ii. Rate of interest and MEI.
C. Ex-ante investment	iii. The actual amount of investment.
D. Aggregate supply	iv. C + I

Alternatives:

A-(i) (b) B-(ii) (c) C-(iii) (d) D- (iv)

Answer: (b) B-(ii)

ASSERTION –REASON QUESTIONS:

1. Read the following statement -Assertion (A) and Reason (R). Choose one of the correct alternatives given below:

    Assertion (A): Consumption and savings are two component of an aggregate demand of an economy.

    Reason (R): Consumption curve starts from a point above origin, which is equal to autonomous consumption.

Alternatives:

a. Both Assertion (A) and Reason (R) are true and Reason (R) is the correct explanation of Assertion (A).

b. Both Assertion (A) and Reason (R) are true and Reason (R) is not the correct explanation of Assertion (A).

c. Assertion (A) is true but Reason (R) is false.

d. Assertion (A) is false but Reason (R) is true.

Answer: (d) Assertion (A) is false but Reason (R) is true.

2. **Assertion (A):** APC is never zero.

    Reason (R): Some amount of consumption is needed for survival even at zero level of income.

    Answer: a) Both Assertion (A) and Reason (R) are true and Reason (R) is the correct explanation of Assertion (A).

3. **Assertion (A):** Savings curve starts from the origin.

    Reason (R): When consumption is more than income there is some amount of dissaving.

    Answer:(d) Assertion (A) is false but Reason (R) is true.

4. **Assertion (A):** Consumption and savings are complementary.

    Reason (R): Consumption is equal to saving at break- even point.

    Answer: (c) Assertion (A) is true but Reason (R) is false.

5. **Assertion (A):** Investment Multiplier is directly related to consumption.

    Reason (R): Higher the consumption expenditure more the income will be generated.

    Answer: a) Both Assertion (A) and Reason (R) are true and Reason (R) is the correct explanation of Assertion (A).

6. **Assertion (A):** Slope of consumption cure is marginal propensity to consume.

    Reason (R): Slope of consumption curve is constant.

    Answer:(a) Both Assertion (A) and Reason (R) are true and Reason (R) is the correct explanation of Assertion (A).

7. **Assertion (A):** The value of APC and APS lies between zero to one.

    Reason (R): Consumption can be more than income at low level of income.

    Answer: (d) Assertion (A) is false but Reason (R) is true.

8. **Assertion (A):** MPC of poor is more that of rich.

    Reason (R): MPC falls with increase in income.

    Answer:(a) Both Assertion (A) and Reason (R) are true and Reason (R) is the correct explanation of Assertion (A).

9. **Assertion (A):** APS can never be one or more than one.

    Reason (R): APC increases with an increase in income.

    Answer: (c) Assertion (A) is true but Reason (R) is false.

10. **Assertion (A):** When 45^0 line coincides with consumption curve, it is called break-even point.

Reason (R): Value of investment multiplier lies between 1 and infinity.

Answer: b) Both Assertion (A) and Reason (R) are true and Reason (R) is not the correct explanation of Assertion (A).

Statement Questions:

1. **Read the statements carefully and choose the correct option.**

   Statement 1: The investment curve is straight line parallel to X-axis because investment cannot change in short period.

   Statement 2: Investment is a part of aggregate demand.

   a. Statement 1 is true and statement 2 is false.

   b. Statement 1 is false and statement 2 is true.

   c. Both statement 1 and statement 2 are true.

   d. Both statement 1 and statement 2 are false.

   Answer: (c)Both statement 1 and statement 2 are true.

2. **Read the statements carefully and choose the correct option.**

   Statement 1: The Aggregate demand curve is parallel to Consumption curve.

   Statement 2: Consumption curve starts from origin and it is upward sloping.

   a. Statement 1 is true and statement 2 is false.

   b. Statement 1 is false and statement 2 is true.

   c. Both statement 1 and statement 2 are true.

   d. Both statement 1 and statement 2 are false.

   Answer: (a) Statement 1 is true and statement 2 is false.

3. **Read the following statements carefully and answer:**

   Statement 1: The consumption curve is an upward sloping straight line curve due to the direct relationship between investment and consumption and the assumption of constant Marginal Propensity to Consume.

   Statement 2: Aggregate Demand curve and Consumption curve are parallel to each other.

   Answer. b) Statement 1 is false and statement 2 is true.

4. **Statement 1:** When MPC is zero, value of multiplier is one.

   Statement 2: Investment Multiplier is directly related to MPS.

   Answer. a) Statement 1 is true and statement 2 is false.

5. **Statement 1:** Unemployment is also called involuntary unemployment.

   Statement 2: According to Keynes demand creates its own supply.

   Answer: (c) Both statement 1 and statement 2 are true.

6. An economy is in equilibrium. Its consumption function is C = 300 + 0.8Y where C is consumption expenditure and Y is income and investment is ₹700. Find national income. [Foreign 2011 Set-1]

   Answer: At equilibrium AS = AD or Y = C + I

   Y = 300 + 0.8 Y + 700   Y-0.8Y = 1000 0.2Y = 1000 $Y = \dfrac{1000}{0.2}$ Y = 5000

   National Income = ₹ 5000

7. Find investment from the following: National income = ₹ 800

   Autonomous Consumption = ₹ 50

   Marginal Propensity to consume = 0.8 [Foreign 2012 C Set-1]

   Answer: AS = AD at equilibrium or Y = C + I

   800 = 50 + 0.8 X 800 + I

   800 = 690 + I or I = 800- 690 = 110

   Investment = ₹110

8. Find consumption expenditure from the following:

   Autonomous Consumption = ₹ 150

   Marginal Propensity to consume = 0.75

   National Income = 1000 [Foreign 2012 C Set-2]

   Answer: C = 150 + 0.75 X 1000

   C = 150 + 750 Consumption Expenditure = ₹900

9. An economy is in equilibrium. Calculate Marginal Propensity to save from the following:

   National Income = ₹1,000 crores

   Autonomous consumption = ₹100 crores

   Investment Expenditure = ₹ 200 crores

   Answer: AS = AD at equilibrium

   Y = C + I

   Y = c + MPC X Y + I

   1000 = 100 + MPC (1000) + 200

   1000 = 300 + MPC x 1000

   1000-300 = MPC x 1000

   $\dfrac{700}{1000}$ = MPC MPC = 0.7 MPS = 0.3

10. Given consumption function is C = 80 + 0.75 Y (C = consumption function, Y = National Income) and investment expenditure is ₹200.

    a. What will be equilibrium level of income.

    b. What will be new equilibrium level of income if investment increases by ₹25 crores?

Answer:

a. $Y = 80 + 0.75Y + 200$ $Y = \dfrac{280}{0.25}$ $Y = ₹1120$

b. $Y = 80 + 0.75Y + 225$ $Y = \dfrac{305}{0.25}$ $Y = ₹1220$

11. In an economy investment expenditure is increased by ₹400 crores. Marginal Propensity is Consume is 0.75. Calculate total increase in consumption and saving.

Answer: $K = \dfrac{I}{1-MPC}$ $K = \dfrac{I}{1-0.75}$ $K = \dfrac{I}{0.25}$ $K = 4$

$K = \dfrac{\Delta Y}{\Delta I}$ $4 = \dfrac{\Delta Y}{400}$ $\Delta Y = 4 \times 400$ $\Delta Y = 1600$

Increase in consumption = $\Delta Y \times MPC = 1600 \times 0.75$ **ΔC = ₹1,200 Crores.**

Increase in saving = $\Delta Y \times MPS = 1600 \times 0.25$ **ΔS = ₹ 400 crores**

12. Complete the following table:

Consumption Expenditure(₹)	Savings(₹)	Income(₹)	MPC
100	50	150	
175	75		
250	100		
325	125		

Answer:

Consumption (₹)	Savings(₹)	Income(₹)	$MPC = \dfrac{\Delta C}{\Delta Y}$	ΔC	ΔY
100	50	150	-	-	-
175	75	250	0.75	75	100
250	100	350	0.75	75	100
325	125	450	0.75	5	100

14. The saving function of an economy is S = -200 + 0.25 Y. The economy is in equilibrium when income is equal to 2000. Calculate(a) Investment expenditure at equilibrium level of income. (b) Autonomous consumption. [Board sample Paper 2009].

Answer: (a) At equilibrium Panned saving = Planned Investment

S = -200 + 0.25 x 2000

Savings = -200 + 500 = 300 **At equilibrium**, Saving = Investment **so Investment = 300**

Autonomous consumption = Dissaving

Dissaving = -200, so Autonomous consumption = 200

OR

Y = C + S

2000 = C + 300 C = 2000-300 C = 1700

C = c + by

1700 = c + 0.75 x2000

1700 = c + 1500 c = 1700-1500 autonomous Consumption = 200

Question- Answer (3marks, 4marks,6marks)

1. **Derive two alternative conditions of expressing national income equilibrium. Show these equilibrium condition in a single diagram. [Foreign2016]**

   Answer: An economy is in equilibrium when AS = AD

   Or when Ex-Ante Saving = Ex-Ante Investment

   So, C + S = C + I i.e., S = I

   When aggregate supply = aggregate demand the economy will be in equilibrium. Or when planned saving = planned investment the economy will be in equilibrium.

   In the diagram, X axis shows National Income, Y axis show Aggregate demand/ Saving/ Investment. AS is a 45^0 line and AD is not starting from origin as AD is sum of consumption and investment and consumption is never zero.AS = AD at point E, so E is equilibrium point and OM is equilibrium level of income /output or employment

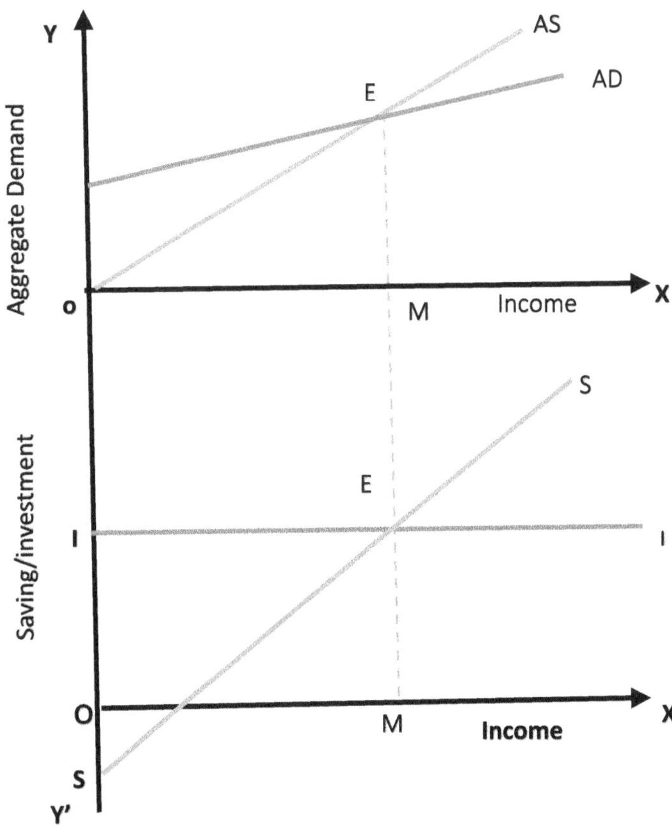

   II is investment curve which is constant in short period thus investment curve is parallel to X axis. Saving curve stats from negative side as at zero level and very low level of income, there is some amount of dissaving as consumption is more than income. Saving and investment Curve are equal at point E_1. E_1 is equilibrium point. Thus the economy will be equilibrium when income is OM.

2. **Discuss the working of adjustment mechanism in the following situations with diagram:**

   a. **Aggregate Demand is greater than Aggregate Supply.**

   b. **Ex-Ante Investment is lesser than Ex-Ante Savings.**

Answer: a) When AD>AS, buyers are demanding more goods and services then what the producers planned to produce. It will lead to unintended decrease in the inventories. Because of high demand resulting in unexpected profit, producers will be induced to produce more. Producers will increase production of goods and services, more people will get employment, which will increase income and output(AS). This process of increase in employment, income and output will continue to increase till AD becomes equal to AS.

(b)When Ex-Ante Investment is less than Ex-Ante Savings(I<S) which means aggregate demand is less than aggregate supply. Buyers will buy less than what the producers are intended to produce. It will lead to rise in unplanned inventories, producers will incur lose so they will cut down production. People will be removed from the job. Income, employment, output will fall. This process of fall in employment, income and output will continue till Ex-Saving becomes equal to Ex- Investment.

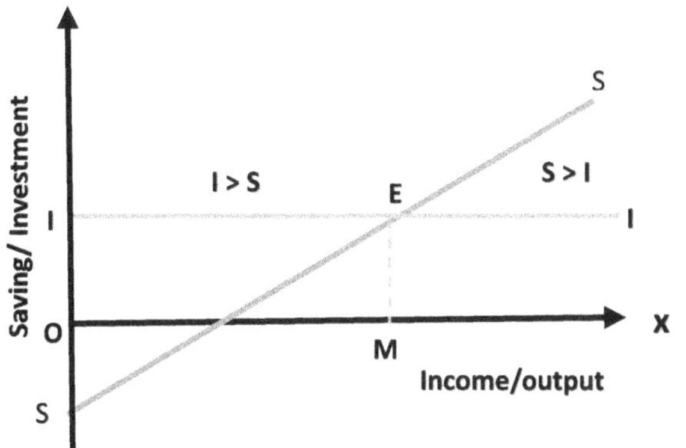

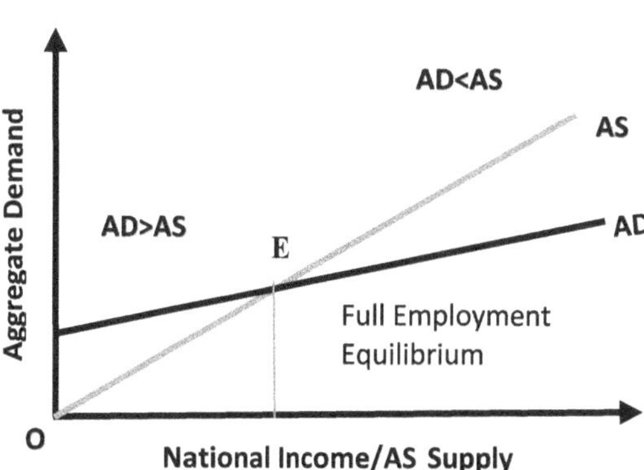

3. **(i) Giving reasons, state whether the following statements are true or false:**

   a. There is a direct relationship between value of marginal propensity to consume and investment multiplier.

   b. When the value of average propensity to save is negative, the value of marginal propensity to save will also be negative.

   c. Investment Multiplier is 1, when the value of APC is 0.

(ii). Aggregate demand required for full employment is called ______________.

Answer: 3-(i) (a) True, When MPC rises it mean consumption expenditure increases, income of the people also will increase as expenditure of one person is the income of the others.

(b) False, When APS is negative, the value of MPS will not be negative because value of MPS lies between 0 to 1.

(c)False, Investment multiplier is 1 when MPC is 0. **(ii).** Effective Demand

4. **What is meant by the "Effective Demand Principle" in Keynesian theory of employment? Discuss using schedule and diagram**

Answer: "Effective Demand Principle" in Keynesian theory means aggregate demand required to achieve full employment. Effective Demand equilibrium is that level of equilibrium when aggregate demand is at full employment. When aggregate demand is equal to aggregate supply and the economy is at full employment le This can be explained with the help of following example:

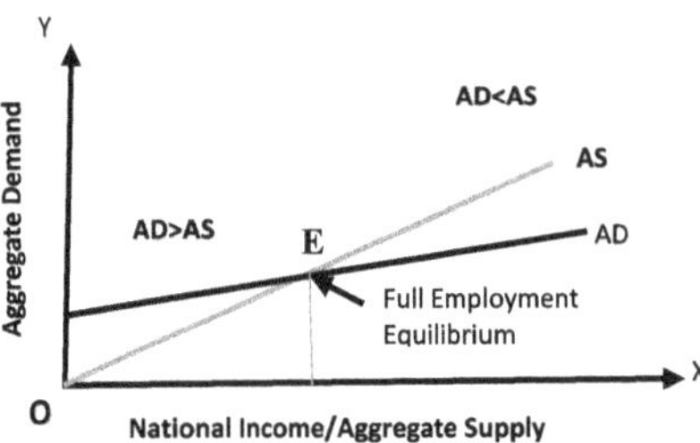

AS	C	I	AD
0	50	100	150
100	80	100	180
200	150	100	250
300	200	100	300
400	320	100	420
500	410	100	510
600	520	100	620

5. **What is repo rate? How the change in repo rate controls demand for credit in an economy?**

Answer: Central bank controls money supply and credit by changing repo rate.

Repo rate is the rate at which central bank of the country lends money to the commercial banks for short period when the banks fall short of funds. Repo rate helps to regulate liquidity in the economy.

When central bank increases repo rate, borrowing becomes costlier and it discourages commercial banks to borrow from central bank. As a chain action commercial banks also increases their lending rate of interest to the customers and investors. Demand for loan/credit falls due to increased lending rate. Thus credit creation by the banks will decrease. This is done to reduce money supply in the economy during **inflation.**

If repo-rate is decreased by central bank, commercial bank will borrow more money at lower rate of interest. Lending rate of interest of commercial bank will also fall and taking loan will become cheaper for the customers and investors. Thus at decreased Repo-rate, demand for credit/loan will increase. This is normally done during **recession or deflation.**

6. **What happens when aggregate demand increases beyond full employment?**

Answer: When aggregate demand increases beyond full employment, output remains constant as all the resources are fully employed and further increase in resources is not possible. Because of the increased demand without subsequent increase in supply, prices of the commodities will rise and economy will face inflation.

7. **What is the difference between full employment equilibrium and under employment equilibrium?**

Answer: Full employment equilibrium is a situation when AD = AS and all the resources are fully employed and utilized. There are no unused or underutilized resources.

Underemployment equilibrium is a situation when AD = AS, but some resource remains unused or people are unemployed. This is due to lack of aggregate demand. This situation is also known as deflationary situation.

8. **Distinguish between voluntary and involuntary unemployment.**

Answer: Involuntary unemployment: In an economy when people are able and willing to work at the given wage rate but they are not getting job, then it is called involuntary unemployment or unemployment. In this situation people willing to work at the prevailing wage rate but they are not getting job. They are included in the unemployed people of the country; they are actually the workforce of the country without job.

Voluntary Unemployment: People who are able but not willing to work even when job is available in the market, they are called voluntary unemployed. They are not included in the workforce (labour force) of the country. They are not included in the unemployment list of the country.

1. **Read the following and answer the questions on the basis of the same.**

   Keeping in the view the continuing hardship faced by the banks in terms of social distancing of staff and consequent strain on reporting requirements, the reserve bank of India has extended relaxation of the minimum daily maintenance of the CRR of 80% for up to 25th September 2020. Currently CRR is 3% and SLR is 18.5%.

   An announcement in the statement of development and regulatory policies of 27th March 2020, the minimum daily maintenance of CRR was reduced from 90% to the prescribed CRR of 80% effective from the fortnight beginning from 28th March 2020 till 26th June 2020, that was now extended up to 25th September 2020, said RBI.

   a. **What will be the value of money multiplier?**

      i.   3.33

      ii. 5.4

      iii. 4.65

      iv. None of these.

   b. **Decrease in CRR will lead to:**

      i.   A fall in aggregate demand

      ii. A rise in aggregate demand

      iii. No change in aggregate demand

      iv. A fall in general price level

   c. **SLR implies:**

      i.   Certain percentage of total bank deposit to be kept with current account of RBI.

      ii. The minimum percentage of deposits that a commercial bank has to maintain in the form of liquid cash, gold or other securities.

      iii. Certain percentage of net demand deposit to be kept with the RBI.

      iv. None of the above.

      Answer:

   a. (c) 4.65

   b. (b) A rise in aggregate demand

   c. (b) The minimum percentage of deposits that a commercial bank has to maintain in the form of liquid cash, gold or other securities.

2. Read the following and answer the questions on the basis of the same.

   The notable English economist Prof. J.M. Keynes gave an important theory of investment Multiplier. An increase in the investment whether it is Government Investment, Private investment, Foreign Investment, Community investment will lead to increase in National Income by multiple folds. It is based on the concept that expenditure of one person is the income of another person and trickle-down effect of income. Increase in investment leads to increase in income and increase in income has chain effect. When a person spends money on buying goods from shop, his expenditure becomes income of the shopkeeper. Shopkeeper purchases goods from the whole sellers, so his expenditure becomes income of the whole seller. Whole-seller purchases goods from the factory, so his spending becomes income of factory owner. Thus it is noted that an economy grows multiple times due to increase in investment.

The size of investment multiplier depends on marginal propensity to consume or tendency of the people to spend their income. Higher the value of MPC more will be Multiplier and vice –versa. Marginal propensity to save has inverse relation with Investment Multiplier.

i. **Which factor effects Investment Multiplier?**

   a. MPC

   b. MPS

   c. Both i. and ii.

   d. None

ii. **Investment Multiplier is the ratio between:**

   a. Change in saving due to change in income.

   b. Change in income due to change in investment.

   c. Both i. and ii

   d. None

iii. **Keynesian multiplier shows relation between:**

   a. Income and Investment

   b. Income and Savings

   c. Investment and savings

   d. None

iv. **Investment Multiplier has direct relation with:**

   a. MPC

   b. MPS

   c. APC

   d. APS

   Answers:

   i. (c)Both i and ii

   ii. (b) Change in income due to change in investment.

   iii. (a) Income and Investment.

   iv. (a) MPC

3. Read the following and answer the questions on the basis of the same.

   J. M. Keynes who is also known as father of modern macroeconomics discarded a lot of concepts given by classical and neo-classical economist. He gave new concepts of macroeconomics known as Keynesian revolution. He propounded that in an economy determination of income, employment or output is mainly depends upon aggregate demand of the economy in short period. Aggregate demand depend on final demand for goods and services in the economy. Aggregate demand is total expenditure done by the households, firms and the government on purchase of goods and services. Aggregate demand and aggregate expenditure are same concept.

If ex-ante expenditure has increased or we can say planned expenditure has increased, then it means that aggregate demand has increased. If planned expenditure has decreased means aggregate demand has decreased. National income or total output of a country mainly depends on aggregate demand. Higher the aggregate demand, higher the national income and vice-versa.

1. **When the price level is high aggregate demand will be**:

    a. Low

    b. High

    c. Unchanged

    d. None

2. **What is total intended expenditure called:**

    a. Ex-post expenditure

    b. Ex- ante expenditure

    c. Ex-expenditure

    d. None

3. **Aggregate demand does not include**:

    a. Consumers

    b. Producers

    c. Foreigners

    d. Government

4. **The Keynesian framework of output and employment depends upon**:

    a. Aggregate demand in long term.

    b. Aggregate demand in short term.

    c. Aggregate supply in long term.

    d. Aggregate supply in short term.

Answers:

1. a) Low

2. b) Ex-ante expenditure

3. c) Foreigners

4. b) Aggregate demand in short term.

X--X

UNIT: 4

GOVERNMENT BUDGET AND THE ECONOMY

4.1 Government Budget

Government Budget is an annual financial statement showing item wise estimate of expected revenue and expected expenditure in a fiscal year.

It is not actual income and expenditure of the government but the estimated income and expenditure of the government in a financial year.

It is estimated in the beginning of the financial year and presented in the Lok Sabha by the Finance minister. The government plans expenditure according to its objectives and tries to get income from different sources to meet its planned expenditures.

Government gets revenue from taxes, fees, fines, interest on loans, dividend given to states and dividend from Public sector enterprises.

Government spends on maintaining law and orders, administration, salary to government employees, pension, defence, Police, other goods & services to citizens.

The Finance minister presents budget every year in the Lok Sabha on the last working day of February. This budget is proposed before the beginning of financial year. A financial year is from 1st April to 31st March. Budget shows financial performance of the government in the previous year and financial plans and programme of coming year and next year.

4.2 Element of Budget

1. It is a statement which includes estimates if government receipt and expenditure.

2. Budget is made for one year.

3. Expenditure are planned according to revenue expected by the Government.

4. Budget requires approval of assembly or Parliament or competent Authority before implementation.

4.3 Objectives of Government Budget

1. **Reallocation of resources:** Rapid and balance economic growth with equality and social justice was the objective of all our policies and plans.

   Private sector allocates the resources in those areas which gives high profit. Private sector may produce those goods which are harmful for the society like Alcohol, cigarette, tobacco etc. for their personal profit. Government Budget of the country directs to allocate the resources in such a way that there is balance between profit maximisation and social welfare. Production of goods which are injurious to health (like cigarettes, tobacco and alcohol) is discouraged through heavy taxation. Goods which are socially useful goods (handicrafts, compost, fertilisers) is promoted through subsidies.

2. **Reduction in inequalities in income and wealth**: Government can reduce inequalities of income and wealth through its tax and expenditure policy. The government should charge high tax from high income people and tax on the goods which is consumed by rich people to withdraw money from them. Government

should provide subsidies, tax rebate and other amenities to low-income people. Through tax and subsidies inequality in income and wealth can be reduced.

3. **Redistribution of Income:** Money collected from tax on rich people should be utilised to benefit poor section of the society. Basic requirement like food, cloth, house, education and health facilities should be given free of cost to all the people of the country especially the unprivileged section. Government should take measure to provide free amenities to poor people like Food grains, LPG, clothes, house, education.

4. **Increase in Economic growth (GDP):** Sustainable increase in production of goods and services is known as economic growth. One of the important objectives of government budget is to increase production of goods and services so that people of the country get more goods to consume and their standard of living will increase.

5. **Providing employment and alleviating poverty:** Government objective is to provide employment opportunities through various measures like industrialising the country or construction of roads, dams, electrification and railways. Promotion of cottage and small-scale industries. Providing employment will reduce poverty. Various employment generation programmes can help in reducing poverty and increasing employment.

6. **Price Stability/ Economic Stability:** Government objective is to keep the prices of the commodity stable and control fluctuation of prices through taxes, subsidies and expenditure. For example, during recession, government should increase its expenditure through public work like construction of dams, bridges etc. reduce tax and grant subsidies. It will increase the purchasing capacity of people. During inflation government should cut down its expenditure to control money supply in the economy and impose on rich people. It will reduce the purchasing capacity of the people. Benefit of economic growth should reach to all the people especially weaker section of the society.

7. **Management of public enterprises:** The government has to finances and manages public sector enterprises for the welfare and development of the country. Example: Railways, power generation, steel production (SAIL).

4.4 Importance of Budget

1. Every country wants to improve standard of living of its people. Economic growth, self- reliance, reduction of poverty, unemployment and unequal distribution of wealth. Hence government makes its budget accordingly.

2. Budget shows fiscal policy of the government which means revenue and expenditure of the government. Item-wise detail of revenue and expenditure is shown in the budget.

4.5 Types of Budget

1. **BALANCE BUDGET:** When Government revenue is equal to government expenditure, then it is called Balance Budget.

   Balanced Budget = Estimated Government Receipt = Estimated government Expenditure.

2. **UNBALANCE BUDGET:** When government revenue is not equal to government expenditure. Either government revenue is more or less then government expenditure.

   (i) Surplus Budget: When government revenue is more than government expenditure, it is called Surplus Budget.

   Surplus Budget = Estimated Government Receipt>Estimated government Expenditure.

(ii) Deficit Budget: When government revenue is less than government expenditure, it is called Deficit Budget.

Deficit Budget = Estimated Government Receipt < Estimated government Expenditure.

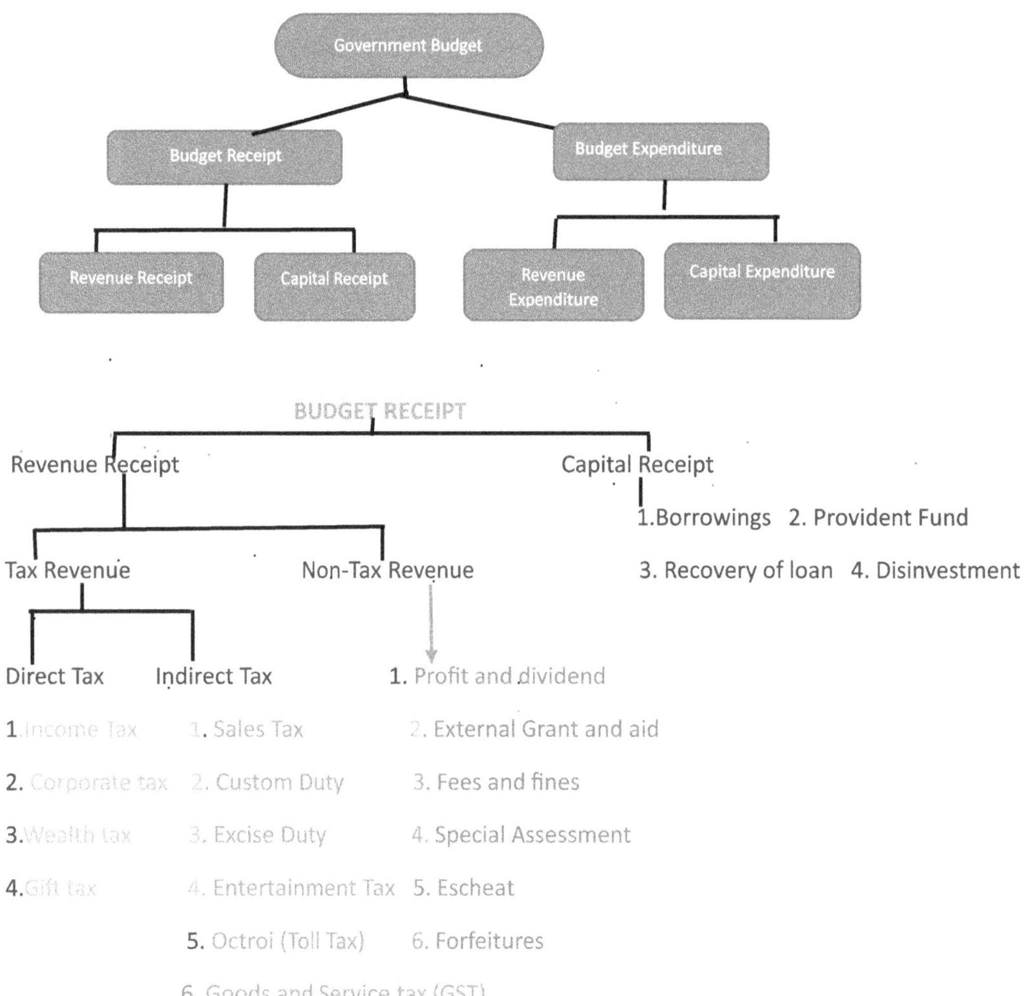

4.6 Components of Budget

Government Budget has two components Revenue Budget and Capital Budget

1. Revenue Budget: It includes both revenue receipts like tax and non-tax revenue and revenue expenditure like salaries to government employees, pension, expenses on police and judiciary.

2. **Capital Budget**: It includes both capital receipts (borrowings, disinvestment, recovery of loan) and capital expenditure (Construction of building, hospitals, Dams, bridges).

i) **Revenue Receipt**: Those income of the government which neither creates liabilities nor reduces assets of the government is called revenue receipt. Government had no liability to return such income. Government assets is also not reduced.

Example: Tax Revenue and Non-Tax Revenue.

Tax revenue: Income of government from tax is called tax revenue. Tax revenue is of two types Direct Tax and Indirect tax.

Tax: Tax is legally compulsory transfer payment to the government.

Direct Tax: Those taxes where the liability to pay the tax and burden of the tax falls on the same person. Burden of tax cannot be shifted on others. Example Income tax, corporate tax

Income Tax: Tax on the personal income of an individual is called Income tax.

Corporate Tax or profit Tax: Tax imposed on the profit of a company is called corporate tax or profit tax.

Wealth Tax: Tax imposed on the wealth of a person is called wealth tax.

Gift Tax: Tax imposed on the gift is called gift tax.

Indirect Tax: Those taxes where the liability to pay the tax falls on someone and burden is shifted to others. Example: Sales Tax. Custom Duty, Excise Tax.

Sales Tax: Tax imposed on sales of the commodity (imposed on shopkeeper) is called sales tax. The shopkeeper shifts the tax amount on price of the commodity so the burden is shifted on the consumers.

Excise Duty: Tax imposed on the production of the commodity is called excise duty. In India maximum revenue is collected from excise duty.

Entertainment tax: Tax imposed on cinema, theatre, Circus, amusement park etc. is called entertainment tax. It is charged on tickets of these entertainment. Thus the tax is shifted on customer.

Goods and service Tax: Single Tax imposed on goods and services is known as GST, it's burden is shifted on the consumers.

NOTE: *GST was introduced in India on 1ˢᵗ July 2017 as a major reform in the taxation system as a single uniform tax for entire nation based on the principle One Nation One Tax. Presently four slabs of GST are there-55%, 12%, 18% and 28%. Some essential goods are exempted from GST.*

Value added Tax: It is imposed on value added at different stage of production.

Service Tax: It is imposed on services provided by hotels, restaurants, banks etc.

Non -Tax Revenue: Income of the government received from non- tax components. Example: Income from profit of Public sector undertaking, dividend from government investment, Fees and Fines, Special assessment, External grant and aid.

Commercial Revenue: Profit, Dividend, Interest.: Revenue earned by the Government from the profit of PSUs or interest on the loans given by the central government to state government or union territory is commercial revenue. Dividends on share purchased by the government.

Administrative Revenue: Revenue earned from administrative functions of the government:

Fee: Licence fee, passport fee, registration fee, court fee, OPD fee, Government School fee, College fee etc. are sources of revenue for the government. It is charged on the ground of services provided to the people.

Fines and Penalties: It is imposed on those people who break the rules and regulations of the government. Example Crossing Red Light, driving without licence, travelling without ticket etc.

Forfeitures: It is type of penalty imposed by the court for failing to comply with the order of the court.

Escheat: When government acquires property of a person who dies without any legal heir or without leaving a legal will.

Special Assessment: Price of property of certain area increases due the development work done by the government like areas facing park or two side road, sea shore area, near metro station etc. value of the property in such areas are appreciated but government recovers revenue from the property holders.

ii) **Capital Receipt:** Receipt of the government which either creates liabilities or reduces assets are called capital receipt. Capital receipts are non-repetitive and non-routine in nature.

1. **Borrowing [creates liability] (Domestic and External):** Borrowings are made to meet the financial requirement of the country.

   Domestic Borrowings: Government issues bonds in the open market which is purchased by the public in this way government get money from public. But it creates liability for the government to return their money with interest.

   External Borrowings: When government borrows money from World Bank or International Monetary Fund or any other foreign financial institution, it creates liability to return the loan and interest on it.

2. **Disinvestment [reduced assets]:** Government raises funds from disinvestment. Disinvestment means selling of the shares of government sector to general public. Fund is raised but asset of government is reduced.

3. **Recovery of loans and advances [Reduces Assets]:** Loan offered by the central government to other states and union territory and local bodies are assets of the government. It is capital receipt as it reduces government assets. Example: Government of India gives loan to Bihar Government ₹500 crores, here ₹500 crores is asset of the Government of India. When Bihar Government returns ₹100 crores to central government of India's asset is reduced to ₹400 crores.

4. **Small Savings and provident Fund [Reduces Assets]:** Small saving like Kisan Vikas Patra, Provident fund, National Saving Certificate etc. Government has to pay interest on such funds so it creates liability.

4.7 Debt Creating and Non-Debt Creating Capital Receipt

DEBT CREATING CAPITAL RECEIPT	NON-DEBT CREATING CAPITAL RECEIPT
The capital receipt which creates liability to return is called debt creating Capital Receipt.	The capital receipt which does not create liability to return is called Non-Debt Creating Capital Receipt.
Borrowing, loans received from foreign Government, IMF and RBI etc.	Disinvestment, Recovery of Loan It reduces assets but no liability is created.

4.8 Difference Between Direct and Indirect Tax

DIRECT TAX	INDIRECT TAX
Those taxes where the liability to pay the tax and burden of the tax falls on the same person.	Those taxes where the liability to pay the tax falls on someone but burden can be shifted on others.
It is progressive in nature.	It is regressive in nature.
Imposed on personal income, wealth, profit or gift.	It is generally imposed on production and sale of goods and services.
Tax Burden cannot be shifted on others.	Tax burden can be shifted on others.
Income tax, Corporate Tax, Wealth Tax, Gift Tax	Sales tax, Excise Duty, Custom Duty, Entertainment Tax, Octroi

4.9 Difference Between Revenue and Capital Receipt

Revenue Receipt	Capital Receipt
Revenue Receipt does not create any liability on the Government to return the amount. Eg: Tax receipt	Capital Receipt create liability on the Government to return. Example: Borrowings

Revenue Receipt does not reduce asset of the Government.	Capital Receipt may reduce asset of the government. Example: Disinvestment, recovery of loan.
Eg: Fees and Fines, Profit and dividend	

4.10 Distinguish between Tax and Non-Tax Revenue

Tax Revenue	Non-tax Revenue
It is revenue collected through tax imposed by the government.	It is the revenue collected by government through other sources other than tax.
It is the main source of income of the government.	Revenue collected from administrative function of the government.
Income tax, Custom duty, Sales Tax, Excise Duty	Fees, Fines, Profits and dividends

4.11

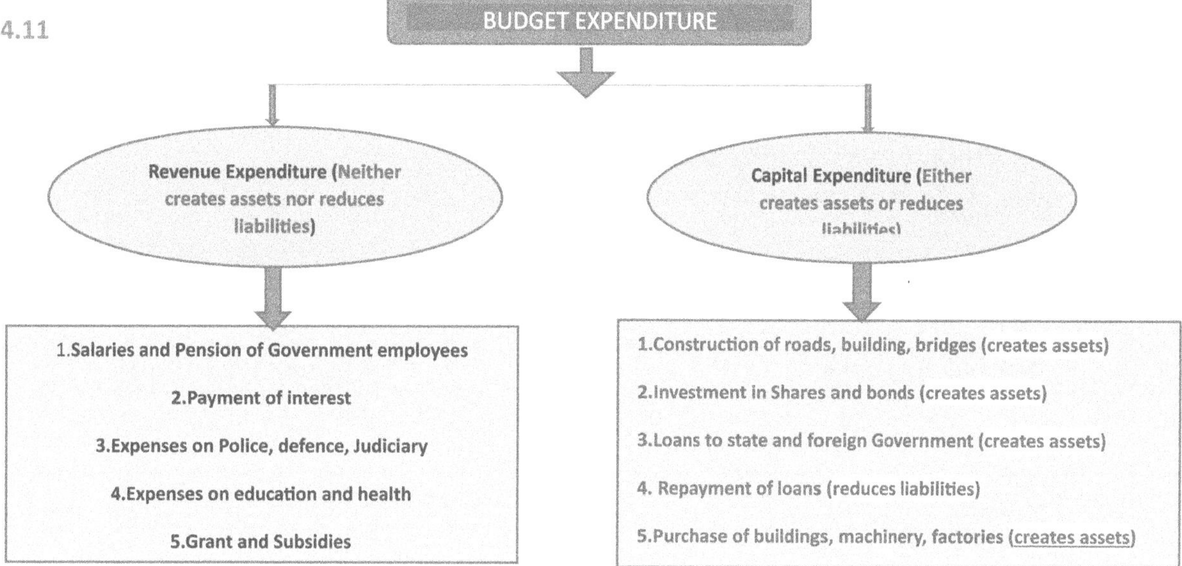

4.12 Budget Expenditure

It is estimated expenditure of the government to be done on different sectors and various programmes in a fiscal year.

Government spends for the welfare of the people, economic development of the country, reduce inequality of wealth and income, to remove poverty and unemployment, to control general price level, development of infrastructure, reducing regional disparities, controlling business cycle etc. Government also spent for routine functioning of the system like on Administration, Police, Judiciary, Defence etc.

4.13 Revenue Expenditure

It is the expenditure of the government which neither creates assets nor reduces liabilities of the government.

These are short term expenditure and recurring in nature.

1. Expenditure on the salaries and pension of government employees.
2. Expenditure on giving grants and subsidies.

3. Expenses on Education and health.

4. Expenditure on collection of taxes.

5. Expenses on payment of interest on previous loan.

The objective of revenue expenditure is smooth functioning of the government with rapid and balanced economic development and welfare of the people.

4.14 Capital Expenditure

Government expenditure which either creates assets or reduced liabilities are called capital expenditure.

These expenditures are long term expenditure and non-recurring in nature.

Capital expenditure which creates assets are:

1. Construction of roads, building, bridges, dams, canal etc.

2. Investment in shares and bonds.

3. Purchase of land, building, factories, machinery, plants etc.

4. Loans to state government, union territory and foreign government.

Capital expenditure which reduces liability are:

1. Repayment of Loan.

4.15 Distinguish between Revenue Expenditure and Capital Expenditure

Revenue Expenditure	Capital Expenditure
Expenditure incurred on routine functioning of the government.	Expenditure incurred on creating assets or reducing liabilities.
It does not create assets.	It creates assets.
It is done for the welfare of the people.	It is done for creating base for economic development of the country.
4.It is short term expenditure	4.It is long term expenditure
5. It is recurring in nature.	It is non-recurring in nature.
Example: Salaries and pension of government employees, grants and subsidies, maintaining law and order in the country.	Example: Construction of Dam, building, bridges, factories. Repayment of loan.

4.16 Balanced Budget: Surplus Budget: Deficit Budget

BALANCED BUDGET: Estimated Government Receipt = Estimated Government Expenditure

Balance Budget is that type of Government Budget where estimated receipt is equal to estimated expenditure.

Merits of Balanced Budget:

1. It ensures financial stability.

2. It avoids wasteful expenditure.

Demerits of Balanced Budget:

1. Limited economic growth.

2. Limited welfare

4.17 Surplus Budget

Estimated Government Receipt >Estimated Government Expenditure

Surplus Budget is the budget in which Estimated Government Receipt is more than Estimated Government Expenditure.

Surplus budget is situation when government take more money from the public and spends less on public. At the time of inflation, when demand increases, government should increase tax to decreases purchasing capacity of the people. Thus, Demand will decrease and inflation can be controlled.

Merits of Surplus Budget:

1. It helps in controlling inflationary situation.

2. It helps to reduce prices of the commodity.

Demerit of Surplus Budget:

1. Purchasing capacity of the people reduces.

2. Leads to recession.

3. Welfare and developmental work is limited.

4.18 Deficit Budget

Estimated Government Receipt < Estimated Government Expenditure

When estimated Government receipt is less than expected Government Expenditure, it is called deficit budget.

Most of the developing countries has deficit budget because of high expenditure on welfare and developmental work of the economy.

The famous English economist J.M. Keynes has recommended deficit budget as a measure to solve the situation of recession and depression. Deficit budget helps to solve the problem of unemployment.

The gap between government expenditure and income is covered either by borrowing from domestic and external sources or by withdrawing from reserve or deficit financing.

Merits of Deficit Budget:

Deficit budget is common in developing country where government expenditure for developmental requirement is more than its revenue.

1. Accelerates economic growth.

2. Accelerates welfare work.

3. It is measure to control recession and depression as it increases money supply.

4. It helps to generate employment.

Demerits of Deficit Budget:

1. Wasteful expenditure of government.

2. Discourages foreign investors to invest in the country.

3. It may create financial and political instability in the country.

4.19 Types of Deficit Budget

Budget Deficit: Budget Deficit is excess of total expenditure (revenue + capital) over total receipt (revenue + capital).

There are three types of deficit budget.

1. Revenue Deficit

2. Fiscal Deficit

3. Primary deficit

4.20 Revenue Deficit

When revenue expenditure is more than revenue receipt, it is called revenue receipt.

Revenue Deficit = Revenue expenditure>Revenue receipt

Implications of revenue deficit:

1. Revenue deficit includes only transactions that effects current income and current expenditure of the government.

2. Revenue deficit is a situation when government's own earning is not sufficient to meet its expenses for regular functioning.

3. **Borrowing:** Government has to borrow money (capital receipt) or sell its asset to cover the gap between income and expenditure.

4. **Inflationary Situation:** It leads to inflationary situation as government expenditure is high on routine functioning of the government. Consumption demand rises leading to high price.

5. **Debt Trap.** As borrowing will lead to interest payment, return of loan, many times other loan is taken to pay previous loan.

6. **Reduction of assets:** Revenue deficit indicates dissaving on government account as government has to cover the gap of deficit either through borrowings or by selling its assets.

7. **Burden of increased Tax:** To overcome revenue deficit, government increases tax which reduces purchasing of the people.

Measures to control Revenue Deficit:

1. The government should reduce its expenditure and avoid unnecessary expenditure.

2. The government should levy high rate of tax on rich people and luxuries goods, moderate tax on other items.

4.21 Fiscal Deficit

Fiscal Deficit = Total expenditure-total receipt (net of borrowing)

Fiscal Deficit = Borrowing

Fiscal Deficit = Total Expenditure (Revenue + Capital)-Revenue Receipt (Tax and Non-Tax Revenue)-Non Dept Capital Receipt (Recovery of loans + Disinvestment

Fiscal deficit is always equal to borrowings.

If fiscal deficit is 3-5% of GDP is considered safe.

Implication of Fiscal deficit:

1. **Inflation:** To meet fiscal deficit government borrows from RBI or other sources. Sometime government prints one rupee note which is put to circulation. This leads to inflationary pressure in the economy.

2. **Debt Trap:** As borrowing will lead to interest payment. Sometimes to return the previous loan other loan is taken. This process of taking loan one after another to repay previous loan is called Debt Trap.

3. **Wasteful Expenditure:** High fiscal deficit is generally due to wasteful and unnecessary expenditure by the government creating inflation.

4. **Retards Future Growth and burden of future generation:** Borrowing creates financial burden on future generation which limits economic growth and development of the country.

5. **Partial use of Borrowings**: When the government borrows money, the whole amount is not used for developmental purpose rather a part of it is used for paying interest on the previous loan. **Only primary deficit is used for financial or developmental expenditure**. (Primary Deficit = Fiscal Deficit-Interest Payment).

6. **Foreign Dependence**: To overcome fiscal deficit, sometimes government borrows from other countries. Financial dependence leads to political and economic interference in the internal matter of the country.

MEASURES TO CONTROL FISCAL DEFICIT:

1. By reducing Government expenditure:

    i. Reduction in subsidies, scholarship and other facilities.

    ii. Check on LTC, Bonus, leave encashment etc.

    iii. Check on unnecessary government expenditure by government officials on tour and travelling.

2. By increase in revenue:

    i. Increase in tax rate on rich people

    ii. Increase in tax on luxury goods.

    iii. Check and control on tax evasion.

    iv. Spectrum sales and sale of coal blocks.

    v. Disinvestment.

METHODS TO MEET FISCAL DEFICIT:

Borrowing is the only method to finance fiscal deficit.

1. **Borrowing from domestic sources**: Government can borrow from RBI, Public, commercial banks or through open market operation. This will not increase money supply.

2. **Borrowing from external sources**: Borrowing from IMF, World Bank and Foreign Banks. This will increase liability of the government.

3. **Deficit Financing**: Printing of one rupee note to overcome budget deficit is called deficit financing. It increases money supply and leads to inflation.

4. **Disinvestment**: Sale of shares of Public Sector Undertakings to generate income. It will decrease money supply.

> **Question: Can there be fiscal deficit without a revenue deficit?**
>
> **Answer: Yes, it is possible**
>
> **1.When revenue budget is balance but capital budget is in deficit.**
>
> **2.When revenue budget is in surplus but capital budget is in deficit higher than surplus.**

4.22 Primary Deficit

Fiscal Deficit minus interest payment is called primary deficit.

Primary Deficit = Fiscal Deficit-Interest Payment.

When interest payment is zero then Primary Deficit = Fiscal Deficit.

Primary Deficit is Zero, when interest payment = fiscal deficit. **It means borrowing is done only to pay the interest on previous loan.**

Implications of Primary Deficit:

Primary deficit shows borrowing requirement of the government for meeting its expenditures excluding interest payment. Thus, primary deficit shows that amount of borrowing which government uses for development or routine functioning.

4.23 Goods and Service Tax

GST is a single comprehensive indirect tax on manufacture, sale and consumption of goods and services throughout India, to replace taxes levied at central and state level. It has replaced multiple tax system. It was introduced in the year 2017.

Under the Indian GST, goods and services are categorized into different tax slabs, including 5%, 12%, 18%, and 28%. Some essential commodities are exempted from GST, Gold and job work for diamond attract low rate of taxation. Compensation cess is being levied on demerit goods and certain luxury items.

The main objectives of GST are to create a common market in India with a uniform taxation system, remove the cascading effect of indirect taxes, reduce the need for multiple documentation, subsume most indirect taxes into a single taxation system, and widen the tax base in India.

The two GST are **CGST** and **SGST**.

It has created common market in the country.

It has facilitated the free movement of goods and services across the country.

Standardised laws, procedure and rate of tax across the country.

4.24 Practice Question Answer

NUMERICALS

Question:1 From the following data calculate

(i) Fiscal Deficit (ii) Revenue Deficit (iii) Primary Deficit

Particulars	₹ in Arab
Capital Expenditure	200
Revenue Receipts	100
Revenue Expenditure	200
Interest Payment	50
Capital Receipts net of borrowings	110

Solution:1

i. Fiscal deficit = Total expenditure (Revenue Expenditure + Capital Expenditure) -Revenue Receipts-Capital Receipts net of borrowings.

   FD = (200 + 200)-100 -110   FD = 400-210   Fiscal Deficit = 190 Arab

ii. Revenue Deficit = Revenue Expenditure- Revenue Receipt

   RD = 200-100   Revenue Deficit = ₹ 100 Arab

iii. Primary Deficit = Fiscal Deficit - Interest Payment

   PD = 190 -50 Primary Deficit = ₹ 140 Arab

Question:2: From the budget estimates of Government of India for the year 2000-2001.Calculate (a) Revenue Deficit (b) Fiscal Deficit (c) Primary Deficit

Particulars	Crore (₹)
Revenue Receipts	2,035
Revenue Expenditure	2811
Capital Receipts	1343
Capital Expenditure	574
Recoveries of loans and others receipts	230
Borrowing and other liabilities	1113
Interest Payment	1000

Answer-2: (a) Revenue Deficit = Revenue Expenditure – Revenue Receipts

= 2811-2035

R D = ₹ 776 crores

(b) Fiscal Deficit = Total Expenditure- Revenue Receipt- Recoveries of loan and other receipts

= (2811 + 574) -2,035-230 = 3385-2,035-230

F D = ₹ 1,120 crores

(c) Primary Deficit = Fiscal Deficit – interest payment

PD = 1,120 -1000 Primary Deficit = ₹ 120 Crores.

1. Identify direct tax from the following:

   a. Wealth Tax

   b. Gift Tax

   c. Corporate Tax

   d. All of them

   Answer:(d) All of them

2. Free distribution of LPG connection to the poor people is a sign of social justice. Identify the objective of 'Government Budget' from the above mentioned statement. [CBSE 2021].

   a. Promote economic growth.

   b. Management of public enterprise.

   c. Create equitable distribution of income

   d. Create fluctuation in the revenue of the Government.

   Answer:(c) Create equitable distribution of income.

3. Which of the following is Capital Receipt of the government. [KVS]

   a. Recovery of loan.

   b. Borrowing.

   c. Disinvestment.

   d. All of these

   Answer: (d) All of these

4. Primary deficit in a government budget is: [All India 2015]

   a. Revenue Expenditure-Revenue Receipt

   b. Total Expenditure- Total Receipt

   c. Revenue Receipt- Interest Payment

   d. Fiscal Deficit-Interest Payment

   Answer:(d) Fiscal Deficit-Interest Payment

5. Primary deficit in a government budget will be zero. [All India 2019]

   a. Revenue deficit is zero.

   b. Net Interest Payment is zero.

   c. Fiscal deficit is zero

   d. Fiscal deficit is equal to interest payment.

   Answer: (d) Fiscal deficit is equal to interest payment.

6. Fiscal Deficit equals: [**Delhi 2017 C**}

   a. Primary Deficit Minus Interest Payment

   b. Primary Deficit plus Interest Payment

c. Total budget expenditure minus total; budget receipts.

d. None of these

Answer: (b) Primary Deficit plus Interest Payment

7. Which of the following is non-tax Receipt of the government?

a. Death duty

b. Escheat

c. Octrai

d. None of these

Answer: (b) Escheat

8. Pension is an example of:

a. Capital Expenditure

b. Plan Expenditure

c. Revenue Expenditure

d. All of these.

Answer:(c) Revenue Expenditure

9. When fiscal deficit is equal to interest payment:

a. Revenue deficit is zero

b. Zero Profit

c. Primary deficit is zero

d. None of these

Answer: (c) Primary deficit is zero

10. Borrowing in government budget is:

a. Revenue deficit

b. Fiscal Deficit

c. Primary Deficit

d. Budget Deficit

Answer: (b) Fiscal Deficit.

11. Repayment of loan is an example of:

a. Capital Expenditure

b. Revenue Expenditure

c. Total Expenditure

d. Plan Expenditure

Answer: (a) Capital Expenditure

12. The incidence of tax implies:

    a. Rate of tax

    b. Ultimate bearer of tax burden

    c. Amount of tax

    d. Methods of tax collection

    Answer:(b) Ultimate bearer of tax burden

13. Printing of one-rupee note done to overcome budget deficit is known as:

    a. Financial Aid

    b. Revenue deficit

    c. Government loan

    d. Deficit Financing

    Answer: (d) Deficit financing

14. Which of the following is an indirect tax: [All India C 2017]

    a. Profit Tax

    b. Wealth Tax

    c. Custom Duty

    d. Gift Tax

    Answer:(c) Custom duty

15. Which of the following is non-tax revenue receipt:

    a. Estate duty

    b. Education cess

    c. Forfeiture

    d. VAT

    Answer: (c)Forfeiture

16. Which of the following are the objective of government budget? [KVS]

    a. Redistribution of income and wealth

    b. Economic stability

    c. Both (a) and (b)

    d. None of these

    Answer:(c) Both (a) and (b)

17. Monetisation of budget deficit is known as:

    a. Deficit Financing

    b. Fiscal deficit

    c. Primary Deficit

d. None

Answer: (a) Deficit financing

18. Direct tax is called direct because it is collected directly from:

    a. The producers on the goods produced

    b. The sellers of the goods sold

    c. Buyers of the goods

    d. The income earners

    Answer. (d) The income earners.

19. Which of the following is not a Capital receipt:

    a. Recovery of loan

    b. Provident funds

    c. Disinvestment

    d. Special assessment

    Answer:(d) Special assessment

20. Calculate primary deficit when fiscal deficit is ₹6000 crores and interest payment is ₹ 5,000 crores.

    a. ₹ 6,000

    b. ₹ 11,000

    c. ₹ 1000

    d. ₹5,000

    Answer:(C) ₹1000

21. If borrowing of the government is ₹1200 crores and interest payment is ₹ 1,000 crores. How much will be the fiscal deficit?

    a. ₹ 200 crores

    b. ₹ 1200 crores

    c. ₹ 1000 crores

    d. ₹ 500 Crores

    Answer: (b) ₹1,200 crores

22. A budget shows____________ policy of the government.

    a. Monetary

    b. Fiscal

    c. Both (a) and (b)

    d. None

    Answer: (b) Fiscal

23. The receipt which neither creates liabilities nor reduces assets are:

    a. Revenue Receipt

    b. Capital Receipt

    c. Government Receipt

    d. None of the above

    Answer: (a) Revenue Receipt.

24. Observe the given figure carefully and choose the correct option from the alternatives given: These are the objectives of_____________.

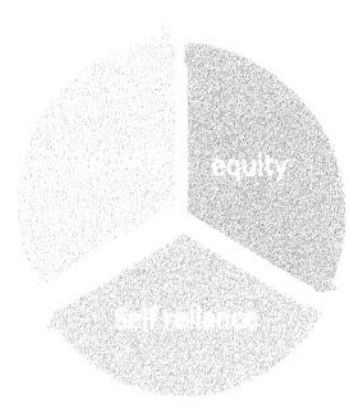

    a. Fiscal Policy

    b. Monetary Policy

    c. Foreign policy

    d. All of the above

    Answer: (a) Fiscal Policy

25. Identify which of the following statement is true?

    a. Fiscal deficit is the sum of primary deficit and interest payments.

    b. Primary deficit is the difference between total receipt and interest payment.

    c. Fiscal deficit is the sum of revenue receipt and capital receipt.

    d. Fiscal deficit is the difference between planned savings and planned expenditure.

    Answer:(a) Fiscal deficit is the sum of primary deficit and interest payments.

26. To get primary deficit interest payment is subtracted from which of the following:

    a. Revenue Deficit

    b. Fiscal Deficit

    c. Capital Deficit

    d. None of the above

    Answer:(b) Fiscal Deficit

True/False-Questions:

1. Borrowing from the general public leads to an increase in revenue deficit. (True/False)

    Answer: False. It leads to decrease in revenue deficit.

2. Recovery of loan is a revenue expenditure. (True/False).

   Answer: False (it is capital expenditure)

3. Expenditure on interest payment is a capital expenditure. (True/False)

   Answer: False (it is revenue expenditure).

4. RBI acts as a banker to the government and commercial bank is the banker to the state government. (True/False)

   Answer: False.

5. Escheat is an example of non-tax revenue. (True/False)

   Answer: True

6. Disinvestment is an example of revenue receipt.

   Answer. False (It is capital receipt)

7. Burden to pay the tax cannot be shifted in direct tax. (True/False).

   Answer: True.

8. Burden of indirect tax is more on poor people then rich. (True/False)

   Answer: True (poor pay more proportion of their income on tax then rich people).

9. Deficit budget does not create inflation. (True/False).

   Answer: False

10. Wealth tax is direct tax. (True/False)

    Answer: True

Identify the correct match:

1. Identify the correct pair from the following Column I and Column II:

Column I	Column II
A. Fiscal Deficit	i. Total Expenditure-Total Receipt
B. Primary Deficit	ii. Fiscal Deficit + Interest
C. Revenue Receipt	iii. Fines
D. Capital Expenditure	iv. Scholarship

   Alternatives: (a) A-(i) (b) B-(ii) (c) C-(iii) (d) D-(iv)

   Answer. a) C-(iii)

2. Identify the correct pair from the following Column I and Column II:

Column I	Column II
A. Direct Tax	i. Estate Duty
B. Indirect Tax	ii. Wealth tax
C. Non Tax Revenue Receipt	iii. Recovery of loan
D. Capital Receipt	iv. Disinvestment

Alternatives: (a) A-(i) (b) B-(ii) (c) C-(iii) (d) D-(iv)

Answer: d) D-(iv)

3. Identify the correct pair from the following Column I and Column II:

Column I	Column II
A. Direct Tax	i. Burden can be shifted.
B. Fiscal Year	ii. 1st January-31st December
C. GST	iii. Single Unified Tax
D. Capital Receipt	iv. Gift Tax

Alternatives: (a) A-(i) (b) B-(ii) (c) C-(iii) (d) D-(iv)

Answer: (c) C-(iii)

4. Identify the correct pair from the following Column I and Column II:

Column I	Column II
A. Service Tax	i. Direct Tax
B. Escheat	ii. No legal heir
C. VAT	iii. Value at Tax
D. Subsidies	iv. Reduces welfare

Alternatives: (a) A-(i) (b) B-(ii) (c) C-(iii) (d) D-(iv)

Answer: (b) B-(ii)

5.

Column I	Column II
A. Subsidies	i. Capital Expenditure
B. Profit Tax	ii. Indirect tax
C. Zero Primary deficit	iii. Fiscal deficit = Interest Payment
D. Revenue Expenditure	iv. Creates Assets

Alternatives: (a) A-(i) (b) B-(ii) (c) C-(iii) (d) D-(iv)

Answer: (c) C-(iii)

Assertion-Reason Question

1. Read the following statement -Assertion (A) and Reason (R). Choose one of the correct alternatives given below:

   Assertion (A): Repayment of loan by government is the capital expenditure.

   Reason (R): Repayment of loan creates assets.

   Alternatives:

   a. Both Assertion (A) and Reason (R) are true and Reason (R) is the correct explanation of Assertion (A).

b. Both Assertion (A) and Reason (R) are true and Reason (R) is not the correct explanation of Assertion (A).

c. Assertion (A) is true but Reason (R) is false.

d. Assertion (A) is false but Reason (R) is true.

Answer: (c) Assertion (A) is true but Reason (R) is false.

2. **Assertion (A):** Interest received on loan is revenue receipt.

    Reason (R): Interest received on loan neither creates assets nor reduces liability.

    Answer: (a) Both Assertion (A) and Reason (R) are true and Reason (R) is the correct explanation of Assertion (A).

3. **Assertion (A):** Expenditure on police is capital expenditure.

    Reason (R): Capital Expenditure either creates assets or reduces liability.

    Answer: (d) Assertion (A) is false but Reason (R) is true

4. **Assertion (A):** Revenue expenditure are expenditure done for routine functioning of the government.

    Reason (R): Construction of dam is example of Revenue expenditure.

    Answer: (c) Assertion (A) is true but Reason (R) is false.

5. **Assertion (A):** Indirect taxes are those tax whose burden can be shifted on others.

    Reason (R): Export duty is indirect tax.

    Answer: a) Both Assertion (A) and Reason (R) are true and Reason (R) is the correct explanation of Assertion (A).

6. **Assertion (A):** Non tax revenue is capital receipt.

    Reason (R): Capital receipt either creates liability or reduces assets.

    Answer: (d) Assertion (A) is false but Reason (R) is true

7. **Assertion (A):** Borrowing from general public is one of the best method of financing budget deficit.

    Reason (R): Money supply is not affected if government borrows from general public.

    Answer: (a) Both Assertion (A) and Reason (R) are true and Reason (R) is the correct explanation of Assertion (A)

8. Assertion (A): Fiscal deficit shows better position of the government as compared to budget deficit.

    Reason (R): Fiscal deficit shows borrowing requirement of the government.

    Answer: (a) Both Assertion (A) and Reason (R) are true and Reason (R) is the correct explanation of Assertion (A).

9. Assertion (A): Highways and road work announced in Kerala, Tamil Nadu, West Bengal and Assam in budget 2021.

    Reason (R): Revenue expenditure of the government will increase.

    Answer:(c) Assertion (A) is true but Reason (R) is false.

10. Assertion (A): Government should reduce subsidies to control revenue deficit.

    Reason (R): Providing subsidies on LPG cylinder is a part of government expenditure.

Answer: (a) Both Assertion (A) and Reason (R) are true and Reason (R) is the correct explanation of Assertion (A).

Statement Questions

1. Read the following statements carefully:

   Statement 1: Loan received from foreign government is capital receipt.

   Statement 2: Small savings is a part revenue budget.

   In the light of the given statements, choose the correct alternative from the following:

   a. Statement 1 is true and statement 2 is false

   b. Statement 1 is false and statement 2 is true

   c. Both statements 1 and 2 are true.

   d. Both statements 1 and 2 are false

   Answer:(a) Statement 1 is true and statement 2 is false.

2. **Statement 1:** Revenue Budget contains the details of current receipts and current expenditure.

   Statement 2: Zero Primary Deficit means loan is taken only to pay the interest.

   Answer: (c) Both statements 1 and 2 are true.

3. Statement 1: Tax revenue is also called administrative revenue.

   Statement 2: Passport fees and driving licence fee is administrative revenue.

   Answer: (b) Statement 1 is false and statement 2 is true.

4. Statement 1: Recovery of loan is not a revenue receipt.

   Statement 2: Borrowing is a capital receipt.

   Answer: (c) Both statements 1 and 2 are true.

5. Statement 1: Interest payment is a part of primary deficit.

   Statement 2: Borrowing is fiscal deficit.

   Answer: (b) Statement 1 is false and statement 2 is true.

Numerical Questions:

1. Read the given data and identify the correct value of fiscal deficit.

S. No.	Item	Amount (₹Lakhs)
1	Capital receipt	68
2	Revenue Expenditure	160
3	Interest Payment	20
4	Borrowings	32
5	Tax Revenue	50
6	Non-Tax Revenue	10

Alternatives:

a. ₹ 32 Lakhs

b. ₹ 64 Lakhs

c. ₹ 20 Lakhs

d. ₹ 40 Lakhs

Answer: (a) ₹32 Billion

2. Read the given data and identify the correct value of primary deficit.

S. No.	Item	Amount (₹ lakhs)
1	Tax revenue	47
2	Capital receipts	34
3	Non-Tax Revenue	10
4	Borrowings	30
5	Revenue Expenditure	80
6	Interest Payment	20

Alternatives:

a. ₹ 32 lakhs

b. ₹ 10 lakhs

c. ₹ 20 lakhs

d. ₹ 12 lakhs

Answer: (b)₹ 10 lakhs

Question-Answer (3, 4 and 6 marks)

1. **Explain the concept of fiscal deficit in a government budget. Write the implications of fiscal deficit.**

   Answer: Fiscal Deficit = Total expenditure-total receipt (net of borrowing)

   Fiscal Deficit = Borrowing

   Fiscal Deficit = Total Expenditure (Revenue + Capital)-Revenue Receipt (Tax and Non-Tax Revenue)-Non Debt Capital Receipt (Recovery of loans + Disinvestment.

   Implication of Fiscal deficit:

   1. **Inflation:** To meet fiscal deficit government borrows from RBI or other sources. Sometime government prints one rupee note which is put to circulation. This leads to inflationary pressure in the economy.

   2. **Debt Trap:** As borrowing will lead to interest payment and return of previous loan. Sometimes government takes other loan to return previous loan and to pay interest. This process of taking loan one after other to repay previous loan is called Debt Trap.

   3. **Wasteful Expenditure:** High fiscal deficit is generally due to wasteful and unnecessary expenditure by the government which leads to inflation.

4. **Retards Future Growth and burden on future generation:** Borrowing creates financial burden on future generation which limits economic growth and development of the country.

5. **Partial use of Borrowings**: When the government borrows money, the whole amount is not used for developmental purpose rather a part of it is used for paying interest on theprevious loan. Only primary deficit is used for financial or developmental expenditure. (Primary Deficit = Fiscal Deficit-Interest Payment).

6. **Foreign Dependence**: To overcome fiscal deficit, sometimes government borrows from other countries. Financial dependence leads to political and economic interference in the internal matter of the country.

2. **Explain how government budget can be used to influence distribution of income?**

Answer: Government budget can influence distribution of income as the government budget shows estimated income and expenditure of income. If Estimated expenditure is done for the improvement and betterment of weaker section of the society the distribution of income will be equitable. If expenditure is done for the richer section of the society then the distribution of income will be widening the gap between rich and poor. Even with the help of change in tax rate distribution of income can be influenced. If tax is imposed on the luxurious goods, rich people will pay as they consume luxury goods. If tax is imposed on necessity goods poor will be burdened more as more share of their total income is spent on fulfilling the basic needs.

3. **Does public debt impose a burden? Explain.**

Answer: Yes, public debt can create crisis. When government borrows for meeting its expenditure, it transfers the burden of increased consumption expenditure on future generations to repay it. It borrows by issuing bonds to the people living at present but may decide to pay off the bonds later on by raising taxes. These may be levied on the coming generation, whose disposable income will fall and hence their consumption level will fall. As a result, national savings may decrease.

Government's borrowing from the people also reduces the savings available to the firm sector. This reduces the level of capital formation and future growth in the economy.

If government has borrowed from foreign, then repayment of foreign loans results in drain of wealth.

So, it is in this sense that public debt undoubtedly imposes a burden. But in case public debt increases productivity and income. Then it will not be a burden for future generations.

4. **Are fiscal deficits inflationary?**

Answer: Fiscal deficit turns out to be inflationary if the government finances it by way of "deficit financing", which implies that the government borrows from the Reserve Bank of India. The government issues treasury bills which the RBI buys in return for cash to the government. This will increase the money supply in the economy. The increased money supply leads to increase in the general price level.

A persistent rise in the price level over a period of time will result into a "inflationary spiral" which is wage-price spiral. Wages catching prices and prices catching wages in turn. This certainly affects the process of growth of the economy as it raises the cost push inflation. Fiscal deficit should be managed very carefully. If fiscal deficit is for production purpose or development purpose, then it will not be inflationary.

5. **Explain the relation between government deficit and government debt.**

Answer: Borrowing is done to meet government's deficit, which in turn leads to government debt. Both the concepts of deficit and debt are closely related Deficit is a flow which adds to the stock of debt.

6. **Fiscal deficit is non-inflationary. Do you agree. Justify.**

   Answer: False. Fiscal deficit can be inflationary when we are at full employment level. It is so because large fiscal deficits lead to increased money supply which creates inflation.

7. **Explain the role of the government budget in influencing allocation of resources?**

OR

   Explain the "allocation of resources" objective of government budget?

   Answer: Private sector will use the resources in the production of such commodities from which maximum profit can be earned. Private sector will not bother about the welfare of the society and will not invest in welfare work. They may even produce such things which is not beneficial for the people like cigarette, alcohol, pan masala, etc. Production of such commodities help them to earn high profit.

   Through budgetary policy, government can allocate resources in such a way that resources are utilised for the welfare of the society. High tax should be imposed on production of goods which are injurious for health to discourage its demand. No tax should be taken on the goods which creates welfare and incentives should be given on production of such goods which are beneficial for the society.

   Government should give attractive incentive to start industries in backward areas so that concentration of industries can be checked and it will benefit the people of backward areas as it will generate employment and other opportunities.

8. **How can government budget help in reducing inequalities of income? Explain.**

   Answer: Government budget shows estimated tax and subsidies in a fiscal year. Government uses taxation and subsidies as fiscal measure to reduces inequalities in income and wealth and redistribute it in such a way that divide between rich and poor should reduce. High tax should be imposed on luxuries goods and such goods which are consumed by high income people.

   Expenditure on poverty alleviation programme helps the poor to get minimum basic requirements and better life.

   Public distribution system should be promoted and free food and essential items should be distributed to the needy at subsidised rate.

   Equitable distribution of income and wealth is a sign of social justice and one of the important objective of the government budget.

9. **Explain why public goods must be provided by the government?**

   Answer: Public goods are those goods which are used by all the individuals in general. It is non-rivalrous and non-excluded. No individual can stop others to use it. Use by one individual does not means others cannot use. Example: Roads, Parks, Hospital, bridges, railway station, river, etc.

   General public gets benefits from use of public goods without any payment. These goods are for the benefit of the people, so government should provide it and spend on the development and creation of such goods. Private sector will take no interest in providing such services as it does not generate income or profit for them.

10. **Discuss the issue of deficit reduction.**

    Answer: Government deficit can be reduced by the following ways:

    a. Tax should be increased. Government should increase direct tax and specially tax on luxuries goods so that burden of tax falls on rich and affluent people. Old tax rate should be revised and new tax should be imposed.

b.   Reduction in government expenditure: Unnecessary and wasteful expenditure of the government should be reduced. Proper planning should be done for efficient and judicious uses of resources. Waste of resources should be checked.

c.   Government should generate income and profit from PSUs to reduce its deficit. It can generate income by disinvestment i.e., selling of shares of public sector undertakings.

CASE –BASED QUESTIONS

1. Read the following news report and answer the following questions on the basis of the same.

The Goods and Services Tax (GST) revenue increased in September 2020, snapping a six- month decline caused by the spread of corona virus disease pandemic and the subsequent lockdown, indicating that a recovery is underway in business activity as Asia's third largest economy opens up. GST collection rose to 96,480 crores last month, a 4% year-on-year rise. September marked the first time since March that GST revenue increased, an indicator that business activity is picking up in the economy as lockdown restrictions imposed to curb the spread of pandemic are eased. In the three months ended June, India's economy posted a record 23.9% contraction as the lockdown shut many factories and businesses. GST collections are expected to grow in the coming festival and the government will be hoping to minimizing its deficits/borrowings also.

Hindustan Times; October 2nd, 2020.

a.   Define GST.

b.   Write any two taxes which are subsumed under GST?

c.   Explain how good is a system of GST as compared to the old tax system? State its categories.

Ans. (a)GST-It is a single comprehensive indirect tax on supply of goods and services imposed on manufacturer or service provider to the consumers. It came into effect on 1st July 2017.

(b) Service Tax and Sales Tax.

(c) The system of GST compared to old tax system:

- It has simplified the multiplicity of taxes on goods and services.
- Standardised law, procedures and rate of taxes across the country.
- It has created common market.
- It has facilitated the freedom of movement of goods and services.
- The categories are IGST, CGST, SGST, UTGST

2. Read the following news report and answer the following questions on the basis of the same.

India's fiscal deficit touched a record $ 88.5 billion in the April-June quarter, 83.2% of the target for the whole of the current fiscal year, reflecting the impact of the corona virus pandemic on tax collections and as the government front-loaded its spending. The deficit is predicted by private economists to cross 7.5% of GDP in the 2020-21 fiscal year beginning April, from initial government estimates of 3.5%, due to a sharp economic contraction caused by the COVID-19 outbreak. The economy is forecast to shrink 5.1%in the current fiscal year and 9.1% under a worst-case scenario, according to analysts in a Reuters poll, its weakest performance since 1979. Government data released on Friday showed total net tax receipts in three months through June declined more than 46% year-on-year to 1.35 lakh crore ($18.05 billion), compared with 2.51 lakh crore a year ago, even though taxes on fuel products have been increased. **The Times of India; July 31st, 2020**

a. Explain the concept of fiscal deficit in a government budget. What does it indicate?

b. "Fiscal deficit is necessarily inflationary in nature". Do you agree? Support your answer with valid reasons.

Answer.2:

a. Fiscal deficit is excess of total expenditure over total receipts excluding borrowings during the financial year.

   Fiscal deficit = Total Expenditure-Total receipt excluding borrowings.

   Larger fiscal deficit implies greater borrowings by the government. High fiscal deficit indicates fiscal indiscipline. It is a situation when the growth of GDP is low, unemployment is high and revenue is low. As a result, the economy witnessed stagnation and economic slowdown.

b. Fiscal deficit may not necessarily be inflationary. It is the difference between the government's total expenditure and total receipts other than borrowings.

   Borrowings are generally financed by issuing new currency which may lead to inflation, but if the borrowings are for infrastructural development purposes, it may lead to capacity building in the economy.

3. Read the following news report and answer the following questions on the basis of the same.

Economic costs of COVID-19 are going to be high and widely spread. Even if the world economy is lucky to see a recovery in the second half of the year, the IMF estimates that pandemic will shrink world output by at least 3%. To mitigate the economic costs of the disease rich countries have rolled out huge fiscal and monetary packages. On average the developed economies are looking at fiscal deficits upward of 11% of their gross domestic products (GDP). For this, they are also allocating separate funds in their budgets. In India, a timely executed lockdown has helped in flattening of the COVID curve, saving many lives. The process, however, has put brakes on the economic engine. Rating agencies Fitch and Moody's have slashed growth forecasts for Financial year 2021 to 0.8%, to 0.2%, respectively. To revive, the economy needs a raft of fiscal and monetary measure. **The Economic Times; May 6th, 2020**

(a) Differentiate between monetary and fiscal policy.

(b) Can there be a fiscal deficit in a government budget without a revenue deficit? Explain.

Ans.3: (a) Monetary policy is the policy of central bank to control credit and money supply. It includes control of money supply fixing of interest rate, repo rate, bank rate by Reserve Bank of India. Fiscal Policy is the revenue and expenditure policy of the government.

(b) Yes, there can be a fiscal deficit in government budget without any revenue deficit.

Revenue deficit is a position where total revenue expenditure of the government exceeds its total revenue receipts. Whereas fiscal deficit is a position where total expenditure of the government exceeds sum of its revenue receipts and non-debt capital receipts.

Hence, there can be a fiscal deficit without revenue deficit in following situations:

- When capital budget shows a deficit and revenue deficit in balance.
- When deficit in Capital budget is more than surplus in revenue budget.

4. Read the following and answer the questions on the basis of the same.

Government budget is an annual estimate of income and expected expenditure of the government for a financial year. According to the Article 112 of the constitution, it is mandatory for the government to present their annual budget. Union budget is classified into capital budget, Revenue Budget and Expenditure Budget.

On 18th February 1860 the first union budget was presented by James Wilson. On 26th November 1947 the first finance minister of Independent India R.K. Shanmukham Chetty, presented Union Budget. In the year 2001 when Yashwant Sinha became finance minister of India, he presented the budget at 11am instead of evening which was older practice. In 1970 Indira Gandhi the first women finance minister presented the Union Budget in the parliament.

a.   In which year was the first Union budget presented in India?

   i.   1860

   ii.   1885

   iii.   1890

   iv.   1947

b.   The budget is an estimate of ______________ of the government for a given period.

   i.   Income

   ii.   Expenditure

   iii.   Income and expenditure

   iv.   GDP

c.   Name the first finance minister of India.

d.   According to which article of the Indian constitution, it is mandatory for the government to present Annual budget in the parliament?

   i.   Article122

   ii.   Article112

   iii.   Article132

   iv.   Article 152

Answers:

a.   **(i) 1860**

b.   **(iii) Income and expenditure**

c.   **R. K Shanmukham Chetty**

d.   **Article 112**

X =X

UNIT: 5

BALANCE OF PAYMENT AND FOREIGN EXCHANGE

5.1 Balance of Payment

It is a systematic record of all economic transactions between residents of a country and rest of the world during a given period of time.

5.2 Structure of BOP

BOP has double entry system which have two sides –

Left Side: Credits-the transactions which brings foreign currency is recorded in credit side with positive sign (+). Example: Exports of goods and services, gifts from abroad, Loan from abroad, Investment by the foreigners in the country which brings foreign exchange to the country.

Right Side: Debits- The transactions in which the country has to pay foreign exchange to another country is recorded in debit side with negative (-) sign. Example: Import of goods, services, sending gift, charity, donation abroad. Investment in the foreign countries. These transactions will create outflow of foreign exchange.

STRUCTURE OF BALANCE OF PAYMENT

CREDITS (foreign exchange received)	**DEBITS** (foreign exchange paid)
1-Export of goods. (visible item) 450	5- Import of goods (visible items) 650
2-Exports of services (invisible items) 200	6- Import of services (invisible items) 100
3-Unilateral Receipts (Gifts, donation, remittances received from abroad), Transfer receipt. 100	7.Unilateral payment (Gifts, donation, remittances received to abroad), Transfer Payment 100
4-Capital receipts (borrowing from abroad, investment and selling of domestic assets to the foreigners. 250	8. Capital Payments (Lending to abroad, investment and purchase of assets abroad by the residents of the country. 150
Total Receipts **1,000**	Total Payments **1,000**

5.3 Components of Balance of Payment Accounts

The items which make Balance of Payment Account are as follows:

1. **Export and Import of goods**: Goods are also called merchandise, they are visible items, they can be touched, seen and verified at custom.1st rows show value of export and 5th row shows value of imports. These two rows show Balance of Trade.

2. **Export and import of Services**: Shipping, banking, insurance, IT services, interest, dividends: They are called invisible items.3rd and 6th row shows it. Services are of two types:

   a. Non- Factor services: Income from shipping, banking, insurance, tourism, software services are called non-factor income.

   b. Factor Income (Investment Income): Interest and dividends which people of the country earn on investment abroad or income from shares, bonds, land, factory, shops abroad are called factor income. They are also invisible items.

3. **Unilateral Transfers**: (Gifts, subsidies, donation, charity, remittances sent by the citizens working abroad to their relatives, indemnities to and from abroad): They are called unrequited receipt and payment to or from abroad "for free". These are called transfer receipt or transfer payment. 3rd and 7th row show these transactions.

    NOTE: The sum of above three components (Goods, Services and Transfer income) are called Current Account of Balance of Payment

4. **Capital receipts and payments**: (Borrowings, foreign investments, capital repayments, sale of assets, change in foreign exchange reserve): It records all international transactions which cause change in assets and liabilities of the country. These are shown in the 4th and 8th row of BOP.

5.4 Components of Capital Account of BOP

i.   **Borrowing and lending to and from abroad**: Borrowings from includes borrowings by private individuals, institutions, governments, IMF, World Bank etc. Loan repayments by the foreigner. Lending abroad by Individuals, Institutions etc and repayment of loans.

ii. **Investment to and from abroad:**

   a.   **Foreign Direct Investment**-like purchase of asset abroad and have control on it.eg- shop, factories, houses etc.

   b.   **Portfolio Investment**-Purchase of assets but has no control over it. Example: shares, bonds etc.

iii. **Change in foreign exchange reserve**: Foreign exchange reserves are financial assets of government maintained by the Central Bank (RBI). This reserve keeps on changing due to deficit or surplus in the International transactions.

5.5 Official Reserve Account

It is a separate account which records transactions between RBI and BOP account. The deficit or surplus in current account is equated by Capital account so as to keep Balance of Payment Account in Balance.

Whenever there is deficit in BOP, reserve bank pays the same amount of foreign exchange to make Balance of Payment account in Balance, there will be decrease in the Official Reserve Account of RBI (Negative Balance).

If there is surplus in BOP, the surplus amount is transferred to foreign exchange reserve. It will increase foreign exchange reserve (Positive Balance).

5.6 Difference Between Visible and Invisible Items of BOP

VISIBLE ITEMS	INVISIBLE ITEMS
Export and import of goods /merchandise.	Export and import of services.
The items which can be seen or touched during the process of transaction.	Those items which cannot be seen or touched during transaction.
Example: Machine, tools, clothes, spices, jewellery, food items etc.	Example: Non- factor income: Shipping, banking, tourism. Factor Income: Interest and dividend on investment Unilateral Transfers like donation, charity, remittances.
These items which can be verified at custom.	These items which cannot be verified at custom.

5.7 Current Account of BOP

- It includes Balance of Trade, Balance of services and unilateral transfers.
- Current account transactions are flow in nature.
- These transactions do not affect assets and liabilities of the country.
- It includes both visible and invisible items.

5.8 Capital Account of BOP

- It includes loan to and from foreign countries, investment to or from abroad, foreign exchange reserves.
- Capital account transactions are stock in nature.
- These transaction affects assets and liabilities of the country.

5.9 Difference between Current Account of BOP and Capital Account of BOP

CURRENT ACCOUNT OF BOP	CAPITAL ACCOUNT OF BOP
Current account records transaction of those goods and services between residents of the country and rest of the world which does not changes assets or liabilities of the country.	Capital account records such transactions between residents of the country and rest of the world which changes assets or liabilities of the country.
It is transaction of visible items (BOT), invisible items (BOS) and unrequited transfers.	It includes borrowings from and lending to abroad, investment to and from abroad-Foreign Direct Investment and Portfolio Investment. Change in foreign exchange reserves.
Current account transactions are of flow in nature.	Capital Account transactions are stock in nature.
A deficit in current accounts shows inflow of foreign exchange(receipts) is less than outflow of foreign exchange(payments) due to transaction of goods, services and transfer payments.	A deficit in capital account shows inflow of foreign exchange (receipts) is less than outflow of foreign exchange (payments) due to borrowing, FDI, portfolio investment or change in foreign exchange reserve.
Example: Goods like machine, food items, cloths etc. service: like shipping, insurance, banking and transfer payments.	Example: Purchase of shop, house, factories share, bond etc abroad.

5.10 Difference Between Balance of Current Account and Balance of Trade

Balance of Trade (BOT)	Balance of Payment (BOP)
Export and import of goods are called Balance of Trade.	Current account of BOP includes Export and import of goods and services and unilateral transfer.
Only visible items are included in BOT	Visible and invisible items both are included in it.
It is a narrow concept.	It is a broader concept as compared to BOT

5.11 Distinguish between Balance of Trade and Balance of Payment

BALANCE OF TRADE	BALANCE OF PAYMENT
It records transactions of goods only.	It records transactions relating to both goods and services.
It may be favourable, unfavourable or in balance.	It always remains in Balance.
It does not record transactions of capital nature.	It records transactions of current and capital nature both.
It is a narrow concept as it is a part of BOP.	It is a broad concept as it includes Balance of Trade, Balance of Services and Unilateral Transfers.
Deficit in BOT can be met by BOP	Deficit in BOP cannot be met through BOT.
It is not true indicator of Economic performance of a country.	It is true indicator of Economic performance of a country.

Deficit in BOT: When inflow of Foreign exchange is less than Outflow of Foreign exchange due to less export and more import of goods.

Surplus in BOT: When export of goods is more than import of goods. The inflow of foreign exchange will be more than outflow of foreign exchange.

5.12 Differentiate Between Current Account of BOP and Balance of Payment

Current Account	Balance of Payment
Current account includes Export and import of goods , services and also unilateral transfers.	Balance of payment includes exports and imports of goods, services, unilateral transfer and capital transactions.
Current account of BOP transactions does not alter assets and liabilities of the country.	Balance of Payment includes those transactions also which alter assets and liabilities of the country.
Current account of BOP transactions are a part of Balance of Payment.	Balance of Payment is a broader concept, it includes both Current Account and capital account of BOP.
Current Account can be in deficit, surplus or in equilibrium.	Balance of Payment is always in equilibrium.
Loans, investment, Foreign exchange reserve are not a part of current account.	Loans, investments, foreign exchange reserve are a part of Balance of Payment.

5.13 Difference Between Autonomous Items and Accommodating Items of BOP

Autonomous Items of BOP	Accommodating Items of BOP
Those International Economic Transactions done with the motive to earn money or profit is known as autonomous transactions.	The transaction which is done to adjust the deficit or surplus of autonomous items transactions is known as accommodating Items.

Autonomous item transactions can cause deficit or surplus in BOP account.	Accommodating item transactions are done to make balance in BOP account.
Autonomous transactions can be of current account or capital account.	Accommodating transactions are only from capital account.
Autonomous items are called Above the line items	Accommodating items are called below the line items.

Accommodating items transaction is done only to fill up the deficit or surplus in autonomous transactions

Deficit in BOP Account: When inflow of foreign exchange is less than outflow of foreign currency due to autonomous transaction then there will be deficit in BOP which means there will be decrease in Official Reserve.

Surplus in BOP Account: When inflow of foreign exchange is more than outflow of foreign exchange due to autonomous transaction, then there will be increase in Official Reserve.

The official Reserve: The Official settlement approach is based on the fact that monetary authority is the ultimate financer in case of deficit in BOP and ultimate recipient in case of surplus in BOP.

NOTE: Deficit or Surplus in BOP is due to Deficit or Surplus in autonomous items transaction only.

Overall account of BOP is always in equilibrium. When we say disequilibrium, it means disequilibrium in current account of Balance of Payment. Deficit and surplus are restored with the Capital Account of BOP.

5.14 Causes of Disequilibrium in Balance of Payment

1. **Economic Factors**: When exports and imports are not equal. Imports of machine or raw material are more due to developmental expenditure or due to high domestic prices Fluctuation in the business cycle like recession or depression. Outflow of more foreign exchange due to high import cost.

2. **Social Factors**: If import of goods are more due to change in fashion, taste and preferences of the people of the country. Increase in import can be due to high population and low production in the country.

3. **Political Factors**: Political instability or policies of the government can also lead to large capital outflow. Foreign investors will not invest due to uncertainty in policies and political instability in the country. Domestic investors will not have confidence to invest in the country.

Accommodating items transaction is done only to fill up the deficit or surplus in autonomous transactions.

5.15 Methods to Correct Disequilibrium in BOP

Chronic deficit can be settled by short-term loans or by funding from Official foreign exchange reserve. Other methods are:

1. **Increase in export:** Government should increase export by grants tax rebate, giving subsidies to exporters or making exports licence easy, loan for exports at low interest rate.

2. **Inflation Control**: Government should keep the prices of the commodity in control so as to control imports. High prices make domestic goods costlier for foreigners so export falls.

3. **Import Substitution**: Government should restrict import of such goods which can be produced in the country. High tax should be imposed on imports.

4. **Exchange Control**: Government should keep a control on foreign exchange by forcing the exporters to surrender foreign exchange to central bank and ration them among the importers.

5. **Devaluation of Domestic Currency**: Fall in the value of domestic currency in comparison to foreign currency in fixed exchange rate regime. This will make domestic goods cheaper as compared to foreign goods so export will increase and import will fall.

6. **Depreciation**: Fall in the value of domestic currency in respect to foreign currency in flexible exchange rate regime. This will make domestic goods cheaper in respect to foreign goods hence export will increase and import will fall.

5.16 Relationship between National Income and BOP

Economic activities arise due to two types of transactions involving international payment and receipt. The first is production and sale of current output and the second is sale and purchase of existing assets (real and Financial assets).

1. Total expenditure on production and sale of goods is sum of expenditure done by consumers(households) (C), investors(I), government(G)in domestic market plus expenditure on Exports.

   $$Y = C + G + I + X$$

2. The income is spent (disposed) on purchase of goods and services(G), savings(S), payment of tax(T) and imports of goods(M)

   $$Y = C + S + T + M$$

   As per National Income Accounting, Income generated should be equal to income spent(disposed).

   Thus, **C + G + I + X = C + S + T + M**

I, G, X are injection in the circular flow of income whereas S, T, M are leakages from circular flow of income. An economy will be in equilibrium when planned injection = planned leakage.

FOREIGN EXCHANGE RATE

5.17 Foreign Exchange

Foreign exchange means foreign currency. Currency other than domestic currency is called foreign exchange. For Indians, US Dollars, Japanese Yen, British Pound are foreign exchange.

5.18 Foreign Exchange Rate

The rate at which currency of one country is exchanged with the currency of other countries are called foreign exchange rate. It is the price of domestic currency in terms of foreign currency.

Example: To obtain one Dollar if we have to pay 80 rupees, the exchange rate between US Dollar and Indian Rupees id 1$ = ₹80 it means 80 rupees is equivalent to 1 Dollar.

5.19 Foreign Exchange Market

Foreign Exchange Market is the market in which currencies of various countries are exchanged, converted and traded for one another.

It is a network of communication system in which banks, authorised foreign exchange dealers, brokers and government agencies are the institutions for trading, exchanging and converting foreign currencies.

5.20 Two Types of Foreign Exchange Market

Spot Market: A market in which transactions of foreign exchange is done on spot.

- Here the transaction of currency takes places immediately. Buying and selling of currency takes place on the spot.

- The rate of exchange prevailed here is known as spot market for foreign exchange or spot rate.

Forward Market: A market in which foreign currencies are bought and sold for future delivery is called forward market.

- It deals with future transactions of foreign currency for which contract is made today but implementation takes place in future.

- Exchange rate that prevails in forward market is called forward rate.

- In such transactions, rate of foreign exchange is decided now but actual exchange takes place in future.

- Forward contract or future contract are done for two purpose:

Hedging: to minimise risk loss due to adverse change in exchange rate.

Speculation: to make profit.

5.21 Difference Between Spot Market and Forward Market

SPOT MARKET (CURRENT MARKET)	FORWARD MARKET
It deals with current transactions.	It deals with transactions for future delivery.
Rate of exchange is decided by the market forces of demand and supply.	Rate of exchange decided by mutual consent between two parties.
Hedging is not possible (no risk minimisation)	Hedging is possible

5.22 Nominal and Real Exchange Rate

Nominal Exchange Rate: The price of foreign currency in terms of domestic currency.

Real Exchange rate: The relative price of foreign goods in terms of domestic goods.

5.23 Functions of a Foreign Exchange Market

1. **Transfer function:** It refers to transferring of purchasing power among countries.

2. **Credit Function:** It refers to provision of credit in term of foreign exchange for export and import of goods and services across different countries in the world.

3. **Hedging Function:** It means protecting against foreign exchange risks. Hedging is an activity done to minimise risk of loss.

5.24 Sources of Demand for Foreign Exchange

(Why do people need foreign Exchange?)

The demand for foreign exchange is done by the residents of a country who need to make payment in foreign currencies due to various reasons. It leads to outflow of foreign currency. Foreign currency is demanded by the domestic residents for the following reason.

4. To purchase goods and services from abroad by the domestic residents. (Payment for import of goods and services)

5. To send gifts and grants abroad.

6. To undertake foreign tours.

7. To invest in foreign countries, like purchase of shops, factories, buildings abroad. (Direct Investment)

8. When residents of the country want to purchase foreign shares and bonds. (Portfolio Investment).

9. To study abroad.

10. Repayment of loan or payment of interest on foreign loans.

11. Speculation: Demand for foreign exchange arises when people want to earn gain from appreciation of currencies.

5.25 Reasons or 'Rise in Demand' for Foreign Exchange

The demand for foreign currency rises in the following situations:

1. When foreign currency become cheaper which means price of foreign currency falls, import of foreign goods and services will be cheaper and people will demand more foreign exchange to import. Example: When 1$ = ₹80 falls to 1$ = ₹40, goods of US become cheaper and demand for US dollar increases.

2. When a foreign currency becomes cheaper, it promotes tourism to that country and demand for foreign currency increases.

3. When price for foreign exchange falls, people demand foreign currency for speculative purpose.

5.26 Demand Curve of Foreign Exchange is Downward Sloping

Demand for foreign Exchange is inversely related to Rate of foreign exchange, so demand curve for foreign exchange is downward sloping towards right.

- Demand Curve is downward sloping means when exchange rate is high, less foreign exchange is demanded as foreign currency and foreign goods become costlier for domestic residents (import falls).

- When exchange rate is low, more foreign exchange is demanded as foreign goods and services becomes cheaper for domestic residents (import rises).

In the diagram when 1 Dollar = 70 Rupees, demand for Dollar is1000 units whereas when price of 1Dollar = 40 Rupees, demand for Dollar rises to 3000 units. Thus, higher the rate of exchange lower the demand for foreign exchange and vice versa.

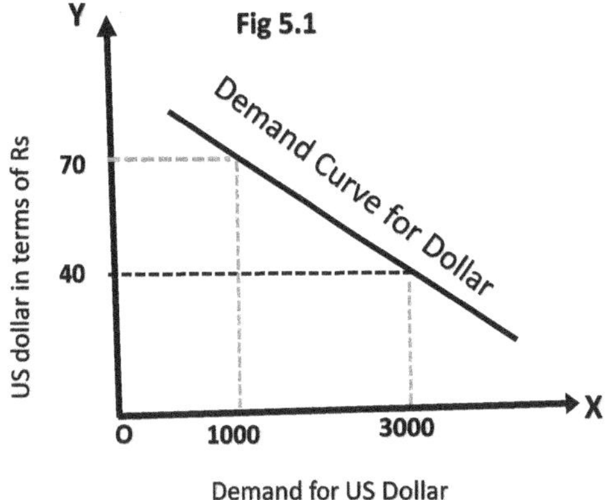

Demand for US Dollar

5.27 Sources of Supply of Foreign Exchange

(How do we get foreign exchange?)

The supply of foreign exchange (inflow)comes from the foreigners to the residents of the country due to following reasons:

1. When foreigners purchase domestic goods and services. (Export of goods and services brings foreign exchange.)

2. When foreigners invest in Indian shares and bonds of the country. (Portfolio Investment by foreigners).

3. When foreigners invest by purchasing home, shop, land, factory in our country. (Direct Investment).

4. When Indian workers working abroad send their savings to families in India. (Remittances from abroad).

5. When foreign tourists come to India.

6. When speculators and currency dealers increase flow of foreign currency speculating to earn gain in future.

5.28 Relationship Between Rate of Foreign Exchange and Supply

There is direct relationship between price of foreign exchange and supply of foreign exchange(currency). When exchange rate rises, supply of foreign exchange also rises and when exchange rate fall, supply of foreign currency falls.

Supply Curve is upward sloping towards right.

5.29 Reason for Increase in Supply When Rate of Foreign Exchange Rises

1. A rise is foreign exchange rate makes home country goods cheaper for the foreigners. Export of domestic goods increases leading to inflow of foreign currency. (Supply Rises).

2. Rise in foreign exchange rate attracts tourist, as a result supply of foreign exchange increases.

3. When foreign exchange rate increases, supply of foreign currency rises as people want to make gain from speculative activities.

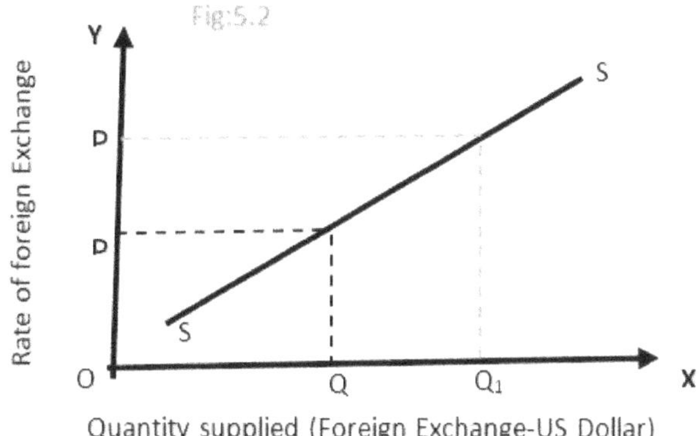

5.30 Determination of Foreign Exchange Rate

In free exchange market, exchange rate of foreign currency is determined with help of demand and supply of foreign exchange. Free exchange rate is also known as market exchange rate or flexible exchange rate or floating exchange rate. Let us take an example of exchange rate between Indian rupees and US Dollars.

X-axis shows quantity of US Dollar demanded. Y axis shows price of Dollar in terms of Indian Rupees or Rate of Exchange between Dollar and Rupees.

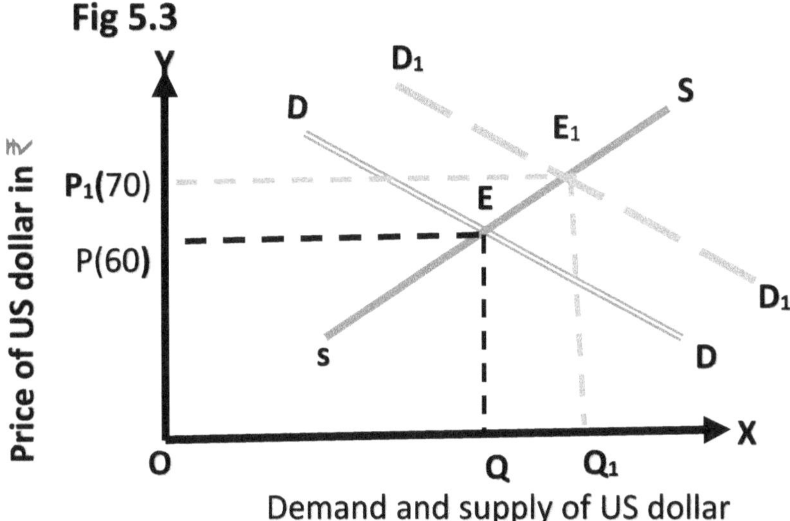

DD is demand Curve for Dollar and SS is supply Curve for Dollar. Demand and Supply Curve intersect at point E, equilibrium point. 1USDollar = ₹60.

If demand for Dollar increases and new demand Curve is D_1D_1. New equilibrium point is E_1 and new exchange rate is 1$ = ₹70.

As demand increases Rate of exchange of US dollar increases.

If supply increases exchange and rate of US Dollar with Indian Rupees falls.

5.31 Fixed and Flexible Exchange Rate

There are two type of exchange rate fixed and floating(market) exchange rate.

FIXED EXCHANGE RATE: (Pegged Exchange Rate System)

When exchange rate between two currencies are officially fixed by the two government. It is called fixed exchange rate. When domestic currency is tied to the value of foreign currency.

Demand and supply foreign exchange do not play any role in fixing the exchange rate.

If there is disequilibrium in BOP creating excess demand or excess supply of foreign exchange, the Central Bank sells or purchase the required amount of foreign exchange to eliminate excess demand or excess supply.

MERIT

1. It ensures stability in exchange rate.

2. It promotes International investment and trade.

3. It prevents speculation in foreign exchange.

DEMERITS:

1. The government has to maintain 100% gold reserve.

2. There is always possibility of undervaluation or overvaluation of currency of one country.

3. In a situation of excess demand, there is fear of devaluation.

FLEXIBLE (floating) EXCHANGE RATE:

When foreign exchange rate is determined by the demand and supply of foreign exchange, it is called flexible exchange rate.

There is no intervention of government in determining the exchange rate.

Central bank does not intervene in the adjustment in excess demand or excess supply.

MERITS:

1. Disequilibrium in BOP is automatically corrected by demand and supply of foreign currency.

2. Central bank of the country does not intervene in any adjustment, it is demand and supply which adjust to equate.

3. The foreign exchange market is busy all the time due to changing exchange rate.

DEMERITS:

1. Instability in International money market.

2. Instability in International trade and capital movement.

3. Encourage speculation due to fluctuation in foreign exchange rate.

4. Creates inflationary pressure import price increases due to depreciation of currency.

5.32 Difference Between Fixed Exchange Rate and Flexible Exchange Rate

FIXED EXCHANGE RATE	FLEXIBLE EXCHANGE RATE
When exchange rate between two currency is fixed by the two government.	When exchange rate between two currency is determined by the demand and supply of foreign exchange.
Demand and supply do not play any role in deciding exchange rate between two currency.	Government do not play any role on determining exchange rate.
Central bank of the country has to maintain foreign exchange reserve.	Central bank of the country need not maintain foreign exchange reserve.
Imbalance in BOP is adjusted by central bank foreign exchange reserve of the country.	Imbalance in BOP is automatically adjusted by demand and supply of foreign exchange.

5.33 Managed Floating Exchange Rate

It is also called Dirty Floating because the exchange rate which is to be settled by the demand and supply of foreign exchange have been intervened by central bank of a country.

Managed floating exchange rate is influenced by buying and selling foreign exchange by Central Bank in the foreign exchange market.

In flexible exchange rate market forces of demand and supply decides exchange rate but sometimes Central Bank influences the rate to reduce fluctuations due to depreciation or appreciation and to stabilize in the exchange rate.

When foreign exchange rate is too high, the Central Bank starts selling foreign currency from its reserve.

When exchange rate is too low, the Central bank starts buying foreign currency in the market.

In this way Central Bank manages floating rate as a bulk buyer or seller of foreign currency to maintain country's currency. This is called managed floating exchange rate.

5.34 Crawling Peg System

In this small but regular adjustment in exchange rate for different currency is done.

±1% is allowed for adjustment.

It can repeat at regular interval.

WIDER BRAND SYSTEM: It is a system which allows wider adjustment in fixed exchange rate system.

It allows ±10% around the parity between two currencies in the foreign exchange market.

5.35 Central Bank and Foreign Exchange Rate

1. **Fixed Exchange Rate**: Central Bank maintains foreign exchange reserve to maintain official exchange rate.

2. **Flexible Exchange Rate**: Central bank does not maintain any foreign exchange reserve as demand and supply of foreign exchange is automatically adjusted.

3. **Managed floating**: To control short term fluctuation or volatility in exchange rate, Central Bank purchase or sells foreign currency. This is called managed floating exchange.

Nominal Exchange Rate: (NER): The amount of domestic currency (₹) needed to buy one unit of foreign currency ($).

Real Exchange Rate (RER): RER is the exchange rate which is calculated after eliminating the effect of price change (based on constant prices).

Real Effective Exchange Rate (REER): Real Effective Exchange Rate is the averages relative strength of one currency with respect to other currencies after removing the effects of price changes.

Nominal Effective Exchange Rate (NEER): Nominal effective exchange rate is average relative strength of one currency in respect of other currency.

5.36 Appreciation and Revaluation of Currency

APPRECIATION OF CURRENCY: It is the increase in the value of domestic currency in respect to the foreign currency in flexible exchange rate regime.

Appreciation take place due to change in demand and supply of foreign exchange.

Example:

1$ = ₹ 70 it means price of 1 dollar is ₹ 70.

1$ = ₹ 60. Which means 1 dollar can be purchased in 60 rupees. Here less rupees are required to buy 1$ as compared to before. It means Indian rupee has become stronger.

REVALUATION OF CURRENCY: It is increase in value of domestic currency in respect to foreign currency **in fixed exchange rate regime**.

Here the government of the two country changes the exchange rate.

5.37 Depreciation and Devaluation

Depreciation of Currency: It is decrease in the value of domestic currency in respect to foreign currency **in floating exchange rate regime.**

Depreciation takes place in flexible exchange rate regime.

Decrease in value of domestic currency occurs due to change in demand and supply of foreign exchange.

Example: 1$ = ₹70 ,1 dollar is purchased in ₹ 70

1$ = ₹80, 1 Dollar can be purchased by paying 80 rupees means more rupees is need to get 1 dollar. It is depreciation of Indian rupees in comparison to US dollar.

Devaluation of Currency: Decrease in the value of domestic currency in respect to foreign currency **in fixed exchange rate regime.**

Demand and supply of foreign exchange do not play any role.

Government of the two countries decides the exchange rate.

5.38 Points to Remember

1. **BALANCE OF PAYMENT**: It is a systematic record of all economic transactions between residents of a country and rest of the world during a given period of time.

2. **BALANCE OF TRADE:** Exports and imports of goods or merchandise between residents of a country and rest of the world is known as balance of trade. Balance of trade is known as trade of visible items. These items can be verified at custom.

3. **BALANCE OF SERVICES**: Exports and imports of services between residents of the country and rest of the world is known as balance of services. Example: Shipping, insurance, IT Services, banking. These are invisible items as it cannot be touched or verified at custom.

4. **CURRENT ACCOUNT**: It records exports and imports of goods and services. It includes unilateral transfer also during a given period of time.

5. **CAPITAL ACCOUNT**: It records all economic transactions between residents of a country and rest of the world which changes assets and liabilities of a country. Example: loans, Borrowings, Direct investment, Portfolio Investment, change in foreign exchange reserve.

6. **FOREIGN DIRECT INVESTMENT:** When investment is done on assets like shop, factory, house purchased abroad and owner has control over his assets.

7. **PORTFOLIO INVESTMENT:** Such investment in foreign country where asset is acquired but the owner has no control over his assets. Example: Purchase of Shares, bonds in foreign country.

8. **AUTONOMOUS ITEMS OF BOP:** The international economic transactions of current account or capital account which is done with the motive to earn profit are called Autonomous Items of Balance of Payment.

9. **ACCOMODATING ITEMS OF BOP:** The international transactions which are done adjust (cover up) deficit or surplus in Autonomous Items of BOP are called accommodating Items of BOP.

10. **STRUCTURE OF BOP:** BOP has double entry system which have two sides –

Left Side: **Credits**-The transactions which brings foreign currency is recorded in credit side with positive sign (+). Example: Exports of goods and services, gifts from abroad, Loan from abroad, Investment by the foreigners in the country which brings foreign exchange to the country.

Right Side: **Debits**- The transactions in which the country has to pay foreign exchange to another country is recorded in debit side with negative (-) sign. Example: Import of goods, services, sending gift, charity, donation abroad. Investment in the foreign countries. These transactions will create outflow of foreign exchange.

Foreign Exchange: Currency of foreign country.

Foreign Exchange rate: The rate at which currency of one country is exchanged with the currency of other country.

The amount of domestic currency paid for buying currency of other countries.

Foreign Exchange market: It the market in which currencies of various countries are exchanged, converted or traded.

Fixed Exchange Rate: The rate of foreign exchange which is officially fixed by the government or monetary authority of two countries is called fixed exchange rate.

Flexible Exchange Rate: The rate of foreign exchange of currencies which is determined by the demand and supply of the foreign exchange is called flexible, floating or market exchange rate.

Spot Rate: It is market of daily nature, in this market foreign exchange rate is decided on the spot at daily basis. It is called spot rate or current rate.

Forward Rate: It is type of foreign exchange rate at which transactions are done in future but exchange rate is decided at present (when contract is done).

Hedging Function: Protection against foreign exchange risk or loss related to variation in foreign exchange rate is known as hedging function. In this foreign exchange rate is fixed for future supplies of foreign exchange.

Pegging: When foreign exchange is fixed with domestic currency to keep the exchange rate stable, it is called Pegging.

Devaluation of Currency: Fall in the value of domestic currency in comparison to foreign currency in fixed exchange rate regime. This will make domestic goods cheaper as compared to foreign goods so export will increase and import will fall.

Depreciation: Fall in the value of domestic currency in respect to foreign currency in flexible exchange rate regime. This will make domestic goods cheaper in respect to foreign goods hence export will increase and import will fall.

Revaluation of currency: Increase in the value of domestic currency in comparison to foreign currency in fixed exchange rate regime is called revaluation of currency.

Appreciation: Increase in the value of domestic currency in comparison to foreign currency in floating exchange rate regime.

Managed Floating exchange rate: It is combination between fixed exchange rate and flexible exchange rate. When central bank of a country intervenes to adjust exchange rate of currency in flexible exchange rate regime.

Crawling Peg system: In fixed exchange rate when ±1% adjustment is allowed, it is called crawling peg system.

Parity Value: It refers to the value of one currency in terms of other currency for a given basket of goods and services.

5.39 Practice Question Answer

Multiple Choice Question-Answers:

1. **Foreign exchange is bought and sold by**
   a. Central Bank

b.   Commercial Banks

c.   Brokers

d.   All of the them

Ans.(d) All of them

2.   **Dirty floating is possible in which type of exchange rate?**

a.   Fixed Exchange Rate

b.   Flexible Exchange Rate

c.   Fixed and flexible both

d.   None of the above

Ans.(b) Flexible Exchange Rate

3.   **Protection against foreign exchange loss is called_____________.**

a.   Credit Function

b.   Hedging Function

c.   Transfer function

d.   All of them

Ans. (b) Hedging Function

4.   **Increase in the value of domestic currency in respect to foreign currency due to market forces:**

a.   Appreciation

b.   Depreciation

c.   Revaluation

d.   Devaluation

Ans.(a) Appreciation

5.   **When one country manipulates the exchange rate against the interest of other country, is known as;**

a.   Parity Value

b.   Dirty floating

c.   Wide Brand

d.   Crawling Peg

Ans. (b) Dirty Floating

6.   **Decrease in exchange rate by the effort of government is known as:**

a.   Depreciation

b.   Devaluation

c.   Appreciation

d.   Revaluation

Ans. (a) Devaluation

7. **Other things remaining unchanged, when in a country price of foreign currency rises, national income is:**

   a. Likely to rise

   b. Likely to fall

   c. Likely to rise or to fall

   d. Not affected

   Ans.(a)Likely to rise

8. **Other things remaining the same, when in a country the market price of foreign currency falls, national income is:**

   a. Likely to rise

   b. Likely to fall

   c. Likely to rise or to fall

   d. Not affected

   Ans.(b) Likely to fall.

9. **The amount of domestic currency needed to purchase one unit of foreign currency:**

   a. Real Exchange Rate

   b. Nominal exchange rate

   c. Real Effective Exchange Rate

   d. Nominal effective exchange Rate

   Ans.(c) Real Effective Exchange Rate

10. **The exchange rate which is calculated after removing the price change (based on constant prices) is called:**

    a. Real Exchange Rate

    b. Nominal exchange rate

    c. Real Effective Exchange Rate

    d. Nominal effective exchange Rate

    Ans. (a) Real Exchange Rate

11. **The average relative strength of one currency in respect to the other is called after eliminating price effect**

    a. Real Exchange Rate

    b. Nominal exchange rate

    c. Real Effective Exchange Rate.

    d. Nominal Effective exchange rate

    Ans. (b)Real Effective Exchange Rate

12. **If 60 rupees is required to purchase one dollar in place of 75 rupees per dollar, rupee value has:**

    a. Appreciated

    b. Depreciated

    c. Neither depreciated nor appreciated

    d. Imports will increase

    Ans.(a) Rupee has appreciated

13. **The rate at which demand for foreign currency is equal to supply of foreign currency is called:**

    a. Parity Rate

    b. Equilibrium Exchange rate

    c. Mint Rate

    d. All the above

    Ans. (b) Equilibrium Exchange rate

14. **When exchange rate of a country falls:**

    a. Import and export both increases

    b. Export and import both falls

    c. Export increases

    d. Export falls

    Ans. (c) Export increases

15. **Balance of Payments is an accounting statement that records monetary transactions between:**

    a. Residents of a country and the rest of the world

    b. Non-residents and the rest of the world

    c. Residents of a country and non-residents

    d. None of the above

    Ans.(a) Residents of a country and the rest of the world

16. **The components of a Balance of Payment account are:**

    a. Capital Account

    b. Current Account

    c. Both (a) and (b)

    d. None of the above

    Ans. (c) Both (a) and (b)

17. **Balance of Payments uses the __________ system of accounting.**

    a. Single-entry

    b. Double-entry

    c. Cash basis

d. Accrual basis

Ans. (b) Double-Entry

18. **The 'resident', whose monetary transactions get recorded under the Balance of Payments system, includes:**

    a. Government agencies

    b. Individuals

    c. Firms

    d. All of the above

    Ans. (d) All the above

19. **In which side of BOP, inflow of foreign exchange is recorded?**

    a. Debit side

    b. Credit side

    c. Both a and b

    d. None of the above

    Ans. **(b) Credit Side**

20. **Balance of trade is:**

    a. Difference between export and import of goods

    b. Total of export and import of services

    c. Difference between export and import of services

    d. Total of export and import of goods

    Ans. (a) Difference between export and import of goods.

21. **Which of the following is not a part of the BOP?**

    a. Capital account

    b. Current account

    c. Real account

    d. None of the above

    Ans. (c) **Real Account**

22. **Import and export of services are called:**

    a. Real trade

    b. Invisible trade

    c. Visible trade

    d. None of the above

    Ans. (b) Invisible Trade

23. **Trading of goods between two countries is:**

a. Nominal trade

b. Invisible trade

c. Visible trade

d. None of the above

Ans. (c) Visible Trade

24. **In which side in the BOP import of raw materials is recorded?**

a. Credit side, current account

b. Debit side, current account

c. Debit side, capital account

d. Credit side, capital account

Ans.(b) Debit side, Current

25. **Donations and charity received from abroad is recorded in the BOP?**

a. Credit side, current account

b. Debit side, capital account

c. Debit side, current account

d. Credit side, capital account

Ans. **(a) Credit side, current account**

26. **Items included in the current account of BOP are:**

a. Imports and exports of goods and services

b. Transfers to and from abroad

c. Income to and from abroad

d. All of the above

Ans.(d) **All the above**

27. **Items included in the Capital account of the Balance of Payments are:**

a. Changes in foreign exchange reserves

b. Investments to and from abroad

c. Borrowings from and lending to abroad

d. All of the above

Ans.(d) All the above

28. **Loan received from abroad will be recorded in which side of balance of payment account of India?**

a. Debit side, current account

b. Credit side, capital account

c.   Debit side, capital account

d.   Credit side, current account

Ans.(b) Credit side, Capital account

29.   **Which one is broader concept:**

a.   Balance of Payment

b.   Balance of current account

c.   Balance of capital account

d.   Balance of trade

Ans.(a) Balance of Payment

30.   **Trade Deficit is a condition when:**

a.   Export of goods is more than imports of goods

b.   Export of goods is less than imports of goods

c.   Export of services is less than imports of services

d.   Export of services is more than imports of services

Ans. (b) Export of goods is less than imports of goods

31.   **The investment done by Tata Motor of India in Spain will be recorded in which side of Balance of Payment Account of India?**

a.   Debit side, capital account

b.   Credit side, current account

c.   Debit side, current account

d.   Credit side, capital account

Ans. (a) Debit side, capital account

32.   **Foreign exchange transactions which are independent of other activities in the Balance of Payments account are:**

a.   Capital account

b.   Current account

c.   Autonomous items

d.   Accommodating items

Ans. (c) Accommodating items

33.   **In BOP account, those foreign exchange transactions which are dependent on other transactions are called:**

a.   Capital account

b.   Current account

c.   Accommodating items

d.   Autonomous items

Ans.(c) Accommodating Items

34. **When payments of foreign exchange are more than receipts, then the Balance of Payments is:**

a. Surplus

b. Deficit

c. Balanced

d. None of the above

Ans. (b) Deficit

35. **The transactions done to cover the deficit or surplus of autonomous transactions are:**

a. Autonomous transactions

b. Capital account transactions

c. Current account transactions

d. Accommodating transactions

Ans. (d) Accommodating transactions

36. **Measures taken to overcome the negative BOP:**

a. Exchange control

b. Currency devaluation

c. Import substitution

d. All of the above

Ans. (d) All the above

37. **Inflow of foreign exchange reserve is recorded on the which side of the Balance of Payments account.**

a. Debit side

b. Credit side

c. Not added to any side

d. It can be added to any side

Ans. (b) credit Side

38. **Which of the following is not included in the Capital account of the Balance of Payments?**

a. Foreign loans

b. Monetary movements

c. Foreign investments

d. Remittances from abroad

Ans. (d) Remittances from abroad

39. **Balance of Payments is an accounting statement for:**

a. Academic year

b. New year

c. Financial year

d. All of the above

Ans. (c) Financial Year

40. **The current account deficit is unfavourable for a country when:**

a. The country has invested abroad.

b. The country has borrowed from abroad.

c. The government does not have sufficient foreign exchange to finance its international payment.

d. Both b and c

Ans.(d) Both b and c

41. **If the value of visible exports is less than the value of invisible imports, the balance relates to:**

a. Trade deficit

b. Capital account

c. Current account

d. Cannot be determined

Ans. (d) Cannot be determined

42. **If the trade deficit is ₹ 2000 crores and the import of goods is ₹3000 crores, then the export of goods will be:**

a. ₹ 2000 crores

b. ₹ 1000 crores

c. ₹ 1500 crores

d. ₹ 500 crores

Ans. (b) ₹1000 crores

True/False Questions

1. Accommodating items of Balance of Payment are independent of other transaction. (True/False)

   Answer: False.

2. Balance of trade is part of Balance of payment. (True/False).

   Answer: True

3. Current account of BOP includes both Visible and invisible transactions. (True/False)

   Answer: True

4. Remittance from abroad is recorded in the debit side of current account of BOP.

   Answer: False.

5. BOP account reflects the growth potential of the economy. (True/False)

   Answer: True

6. Supply of foreign exchange is positively related to the price of foreign exchange. (True/False)

   Answer: True

7. Managed floating exchange rate is decided by the market forces but remains with the specific range decided by the Central Bank. (True/False).

   Answer: True.

8. Capital account of BOP does not alter assets and liabilities of the country. (True/False).

   Answer: False.

9. Devaluation takes place due to change in demand and supply of foreign exchange. (True/False).

   Answer: False

10. Remittances from abroad is a part of capital account of BOP. (True/False).

    Answer: False

Identify the correct Match:

1. **Identify the correct pair from the following Column I and Column II:**

Column I	Column II
A. Balance of Trade	i. Capital Account
B. Capital account of BOP	ii. Portfolio Investment
C. Current account of BOP	iii. Loan from abroad
D. Accommodating items of BOP	iv. Independent of autonomous items transactions.

   Alternatives: (a) A-(i) (b) B-(ii) (c) C-(iii) (d) D-(iv)

   Answer:(b) B-(ii)

3. **Identify the correct pair from the following Column I and Column II:**

Column I	Column II
A. Balance of Payments	i. Records inflow and outflow of foreign exchange.
B. Capital account of BOP.	ii. It records the transactions of visible items.
C. Autonomous transactions	iii. They are called below the line items.
D. Balance of trade	iv. It records transaction of visible and invisible items

   Alternatives: (a) A-(i) (b) B-(ii) (c) C-(iii) (d) D-(iv)

   Answer: (a) A-(i)

1. Read the following statement -Assertion (A) and Reason (R). Choose one of the correct alternatives given below:

    Assertion (A): Imports of goods and services shows demand of foreign currency.

    Reason (R): Import of goods increases inflow of foreign exchange.

    Alternatives:

    a. Both Assertion (A) and Reason (R) are true and Reason (R) is the correct explanation of Assertion (A).

    b. Both Assertion (A) and Reason (R) are true and Reason (R) is not the correct explanation of Assertion (A).

    c. Assertion (A) is true but Reason (R) is false.

    d. Assertion (A) is false but Reason (R) is true.

    Answer: (c) Assertion (A) is true but Reason (R) is false.

2. **Assertion (A):** Current account transactions does not alter assets and liabilities of the country.

    Reason (R): Debts are created or settled by capital account transactions.

    Answer: (b) Both Assertion (A) and Reason (R) are true and Reason (R) is not the correct explanation of Assertion (A).

3. **Assertion (A):** Foreign Exchange Reserve of the country keeps on changing.

    Reason (R): Foreign Exchange Reserve depends upon the net balance of private and official transactions.

    Answer: (a) Both Assertion (A) and Reason (R) are true and Reason (R) is the correct explanation of Assertion (A).

4. **Assertion (A):** Purchase of bond issued by foreign government is portfolio investment.

    Reason (R): There is full control over of the investor on portfolio investment.

    Answer: (c) Assertion (A) is true but Reason (R) is false.

5. **Assertion (A):** Accommodating transactions creates surplus or deficit in BOP.

    Reason (R): When inflow of foreign exchange is more than outflow, there is deficit in BOP.

    Answer: (c) Assertion (A) is true but Reason (R) is false.

6. **Assertion (A):** Appreciation take place in fixed exchange rate regime.

    Reason (R): Appreciation is increase in the value of domestic currency in respect to Foreign currency.

    Answer. (d) Assertion (A) is false but Reason (R) is true.

7. **Assertion (A):** Devaluation of domestic currency is a method to correct disequilibrium in BOP.

    Reason (R): Devaluation increases export and imports.

    Answer: (c) Assertion (A) is true but Reason (R) is false.

8. **Assertion (A):** Balance of current account includes BOT, BOS and unilateral transfers.

    Reason (R): Capital account transactions affects assets and liabilities of the country.

    Answer: (b) Both Assertion (A) and Reason (R) are true and Reason (R) is not the correct explanation of Assertion (A).

9. **Assertion (A):** Portfolio investment is a part of capital account.

    Reason (R): The investor has full control over the asset in direct investment.

    Answer: (b) Both Assertion (A) and Reason (R) are true and Reason (R) is not the correct explanation of Assertion (A).

10. **Assertion (A):** BOT is a part of BOP.

    Reason (R): BOT includes trade of visible items only.

    Answer: (a) Both Assertion (A) and Reason (R) are true and Reason (R) is the correct explanation of Assertion (A).

Statement Questions:

1. Read the following statements carefully:

    Statement 1: Accommodating items of BOP are solely dependent on the outcome of autonomous transactions.

    Statement 2: Accommodating items are the net result of autonomous transactions that are undertaken to correct the disequilibrium in autonomous items of BOP.

    In the light of the given statements, choose the correct alternative from the following:

    a. Statement 1 is true and statement 2 is false

    b. Statement 1 is false and statement 2 is true

    c. Both statements 1 and 2 are true.

    d. Both statements 1 and 2 are false

    Answer: (c) Both statement 1 and 2 are true.

2. **Statement 1**: Increase in the demand for foreign currency leads to currency appreciation of domestic currency.

    Statement 2: Balance of trade is a part of Capital account of BOP.

    Answer: (d) Both statements 1 and 2 are false.

3. **Statement 1:** Other things remaining the same, fall in the value of foreign currency results in fall of national income.

    Statement 2: Appreciation of domestic currency will reduce exports.

    Answer: (c) Both statements 1 and 2 are true.

4. **Statement 1:** Price of one currency in respect to other currency is called fixed exchange rate.

    Statement 2: Exchange rate of currency fluctuates when demand and supply of currency changes.

    Answers: (b) Statement 1 is false and statement 2 is true.

5. **Statement 1:** Supply of foreign exchange is inversely related to the foreign exchange rate.

6. **Statement 2:** Borrowing from abroad is recorded in the credit side of capital account.

    Answers: (b) Statement 1 is false and statement 2 is true.

7. **Statement 1:** Demand of foreign exchange is inversely related to the foreign exchange rate.

Statement 2: Foreign Direct Investment is recorded on the credit side of capital account.

Answer: (c) Both statements 1 and 2 are true.

Question-Answers (3 marks, 4 marks ,6 marks):

1. Distinguish between the followings:

   a. **Autonomous items of BOP and accommodating items of BOP.**

   b. **Fixed and flexible exchange rate.**

   c. **Current Account of BOP and Capital Account of BOP.**

   Answer: (a) **Autonomous Items of BOP:**

1. Those International Economic Transactions done with the motive to earn money or profit is known as autonomous transactions.

2. Autonomous item transactions can cause deficit or surplus in BOP account.

3. Autonomous transactions can be of current account or capital account.

4. Autonomous items are called Above the line items.

Accommodating Items of BOP:

1. The transaction which is done to adjust the deficit or surplus of autonomous item transactions are known as accommodating Items.

2. Accommodating item transactions are done to make balance in BOP account.

3. Accommodating transactions are only from capital account.

4. Accommodating items are called below the line items.

(b) FIXED EXCHANGE RATE:

1. When exchange rate between two currencies is fixed by the two government.

2. Demand and supply do not play any role in deciding exchange rate between two currencies.

3. Central bank of the country has to maintain foreign exchange reserve.

4. Imbalance in BOP is adjusted by central bank foreign exchange reserve of the country.

FLEXIBLE EXCHANGE RATE:

1. When exchange rate between two currencies is determined by the demand and supply of foreign exchange.

2. Government does not play any role on determining exchange rate.

3. Central bank of the country need not maintain foreign exchange reserve.

4. Imbalance in BOP is automatically adjusted by demand and supply of foreign exchange

(c) CURRENT ACCOUNT OF BOP:

1. Current account records transaction of those goods and services between residents of the country and rest of the world which does not changes assets or liabilities of the country.

2. It is transaction of visible items (BOT), invisible items (BOS) and unrequited transfers.

3. Current account transactions are of flow in nature.

4. A deficit in current accounts shows inflow of foreign exchange(receipts) is less than outflow of foreign exchange(payments) due to transaction of goods, services and transfer payments.

5. Example: Goods like machine, food items, cloths etc. service: like shipping, insurance, banking and transfer payments.

CAPITAL ACCOUNT OF BOP:

1. Capital account records such transactions between residents of the country and rest of the world which changes assets or liabilities of the country.

2. It includes borrowings from and lending to abroad, investment to and from abroad. Foreign Direct Investment and Portfolio Investment.

3. Capital Account transactions are stock in nature.

4. A deficit in capital account shows inflow of foreign exchange (receipts) is less than outflow of foreign exchange (payments) due to borrowing, FDI, portfolio investment or change in foreign exchange reserve.

5. Example: Purchase of shop, house, factories share, bond etc. abroad

2. Is the concept of 'demand for domestic goods' and 'domestic demand for goods' the same? [NCERT]

Answer: No, both the concepts are not same. Demand for domestic goods is a broader concept it is the demand of indigenous product in domestic market as well as international market.

Whereas domestic demand for goods means only demand of goods within the country not by the foreign countries.

3. Explain the term managed floating.

Answer: When the central bank of a country intervenes to restore the value of domestic currency in respect of the foreign currency within the desired limits in floating exchange rate regime, it is called managed floating. Managed floating is also called Dirty Floating because the exchange rate which is to be settled by the demand and supply have been intervened by central bank.

Managed floating exchange rate is influenced by buying and selling foreign exchange by Central Bank in the foreign exchange market.

4. Recently the Government of India has doubled the import duty on gold. What impact is there on the foreign exchange and how? (D2014)

Answer: As the Government of India has doubled the import duty on gold, importing gold has become costlier for the Indians. Demand to import gold will fall and demand for foreign exchange also falls. Supply of foreign exchange remains same. As a result, price of foreign exchange will fall or we can say that foreign exchange rate falls.

5. Explain the effect of appreciation of the domestic currency on exports?

Answer: When domestic currency price rises in respect to foreign currency, less amount of foreign currency is need to import or buy assets abroad. Foreign goods will become cheaper so import will rise. Domestic goods will become costlier so export will fall.

6. Balance of payments always remains balanced. Explain.

Answer: Balance of payments is always balanced in the accounting sense. In operating sense also, BOP is always in equilibrium because if current account is in deficit, the same is restored (compensated) with capital account. The provision of 'balancing item' is also there in the BOP that intends to eliminate errors in measurement. The deficit in Balance of Payment can be financed by borrowing from abroad or by absorbing foreign currency reserves. Hence, BOP is always remains in balance.

Case –Study Questions:

1. Read the following news report and answer the following questions on the basis of the same.

India's trade with China last year fell to the lowest since 2017, with the trade imbalance declining to a five-year low on the back of a slump in India's imports from China.

Two-way trade in 2020 reached $87.6 billion, down by 5.6%, according to new figures from China's General Administration of Customs (GAC). India's imports from China accounted for $66.7 billion, declining by 10.8% year-on-year and the lowest figure since 2016. India's exports to China, however, rose to the highest figure on record, for the first time crossing the $20 billion-mark and growing 16% last year to $20.86 billion. The trade deficit, a source of friction between India and China, declined to a five year-low of $45.8 billion, the lowest since 2015.

(a) What does "trade deficit" mean?

    i.   The value of exports of goods and services is less than the value of imports of goods and services.

    ii.   The value of imports of merchandise is less than the value of exports of merchandise.

    iii.   Negative balance on account of trade in goods, services and transfers.

    iv.   Foreign exchange payments on account of visible items are in excess over the receipts of visible items.

1. "The trade deficit, between India and China, declined to a five year-low of $45.8 billion." The (increase/decrease) in imports from China has caused this.

2. Increase in foreign exchange reserve is due to________ in imports from China. (Boom/Slump)

    Answer:

a. (iv)Foreign exchange payments on account of visible items are in excess over the receipts of visible items.

b. Increase

c. Slump

2. Read the following and answer the questions on the basis of the same:

Forex rate is the price of one currency in terms of other. It is also called foreign exchange rate. There are two types of exchange rate, fixed exchange rate and flexible exchange rate. In fixed exchange rate the government of two countries or the monetary authorities of two country fixed the exchange rate of their currency which remains unaffected by the change in demand and supply of the currency in the international market. Whereas in in flexible exchange rate the currency rate of two countries are determined by the market forces of demand and supply. It is continuously changing based on change in market forces. If 80 rupees is to be paid to buy one dollar, the exchange rate is ₹80 per dollar. People demand foreign exchange because for different reason like: to purchase goods and services from abroad, to send gifts abroad, to purchase financial assets abroad etc. A rise in the price of foreign exchange means increase in the price of foreign goods in respect to domestic goods. Imports declines and export rises as domestic goods become cheaper for foreigners.

a. A rise in foreign exchange __________ the cost of purchasing a foreign goods.

    i.   Decreases

    ii.   Increases

    iii.   Remains constant

    iv.   Fluctuate

b. Forex rate is kwon as:

    i.   Foreign Direct Investment

ii. Foreign Exchange rate

iii. Foreign Market Rate

iv. Foreign Direct Exchange

c. A rise in the foreign exchange rate will decrease:

i. Exports

ii. Imports

iii. Money cost

iv. None

d. Flexible exchange rate is also called market exchange rate. (True/ False).

Answers: a) (ii) increases

b) (ii) Foreign Exchange Rate

c) (ii) Imports

d) True

3. Read the following and answer the questions on the basis of the same:

The country should reduce its dependence on those commodities which can be produced indigenously, when there is situation of disequilibrium in BOP. The country should try to increase the production of food-grains, edible oils, sugar, medicine and completely stop import of these commodities. The country should also increase the production of coal, paper, iron and steel, fertilizers etc. Export promotion and import substitution can help to tackle the problem of disequilibrium in BOP. Non-traditional items like engineering goods, processed foods (fish and meat preparation), fruits and handicrafts etc. should be exported in higher quantity. The country should diversify its export markets into some non-traditional areas to generate export surplus by limiting home consumption of non-traditional commodities.

a. In the situation of disequilibrium in BOP country should try to reduce the production of:

i. Food grains

ii. Edible Oil

iii. Medicine

iv. None

b. Read the following statements carefully and choose the correct alternatives given below:

Statement 1: Country should reduce import of those commodities which it can produce at home.

Statement 2: The country should completely stop the import of traditional items like food-grains, edible oil, paper etc.

In the light of the given statements, choose the correct alternative from the following:

i. Statement 1 is true and statement 2 is false.

ii. Statement 1 is false and statement 2 is true.

iii. Both statements 1 and 2 are true.

iv. Both statements 1 and 2 are false

c. In the light of the given text and common knowledge, identify the correct statement:

    i. Problem of BOP disequilibrium can be handled through import of manufacturing goods.

    ii. Country should promote exports of non-traditional items like engineering goods.

    iii. The government should not give rise to import substitution.

    iv. The country should try to diversify its import markets.

d. The government should derive sufficient export surplus by containing home consumption of commodities.

    i. Non-traditional

    ii. Traditional

    iii. Manufacturing

    iv. Agricultural

Answers:

a. (iv)None

b. (iii) Both statements 1 and 2 are true.

c. (ii) Country should promote exports of non-traditional items like engineering goods.

d. (i) Non-Traditional

X--X

MACROECONOMICS

PRACTICE PAPER – 1

ECONOMICS (030) CLASS XII

GENERAL INSTRUCTIONS:

Section A – Macro Economics

1. This paper contains 10 Multiple Choice Questions of 1 mark each.

2. This paper contains 2 Short Answer Questions of 3 marks each to be answered in 60 to 80 words.

3. This paper contains 3 Short Answer Questions of 4 marks each to be answered in 80 to 100 words.

4. This paper contains 2 Long Answer Questions of 6 marks each to be answered in 100 to 150 words.

Q. No	Section-A : Introductory Macroeconomics	Marks
1.	Observe the given figure carefully and choose the correct option from the alternatives given. These are the objectives of_____________. a. Fiscal Policy b. Monetary Policy c. Foreign policy d. All of the above.	1
2	Consider the following statement about 'Portfolio Investment in India' and choose the correct alternative: a. Investments by a foreign company to start its subsidiary company in India. b. Investment by a foreign company to acquire an Indian company in India. c. A foreign investor buying shares in Indian markets. d. A foreign investor buying raw material from Indian market.	1

3	For a closed economy, which one of the following is correct? a. GDP = GNP b. GDP > GNP c. GDP < GNP d. GDP + GNP = 0	1
4	Identify the correct pair from the following Column I and Column II:	1

	Column I		Column II
A.	RBI	i.	Accepts deposits from the public
B.	Money Supply	ii.	Quantitative measure to control credit.
C.	CRR	iii.	Currency held by public and demand deposits.
D.	High powered money	iv.	Monetary authority of the country.

Alternatives: (a) A-(i) (b) B-(ii) (c) C-(iii) (d) D-(iv)

5	**Assertion (A):** Size of multiplier is given by the inverse of LRR. **Reason(R):** There is direct relationship between LRR and value of money multiplier. **Alternatives:** a. Both assertion (A) and Reason (R) are true and Reason (R) is the correct explanation of Assertion (A). b. Both assertion (A) and Reason (R) are true and Reason (R) is not the correct explanation of Assertion (A). c. Assertion (A) is true but reason (R) is false. d. Assertion (A) is false but reason (R) is true.	1
6.	Primary deficit is the borrowing requirements of government for making __________. a. Interest Payments b. Other than Interest payments c. All type of payment d. Some specific payments	1
7	In the light of the given statements, choose the correct alternative from the following: **Statement1**: No interest is paid to current account holders. **Statement 2**: M4 measure of money has maximum liquidity. **Alternatives:** a. Statement 1 is true and statement 2 is false b. Statement 1 is false and statement 2 is true c. Both statements 1 and 2 are true. d. Both statements 1 and 2 are false	1

| 8 | **In India, supplier of money is:** | 1 |

a. Government

b. Banking system in the country

c. Both (a) and (b)

d. Central Bank of the country.

OR

Quantitative instrument of RBI can be:

a. Bank Rate

b. Cash Reserve Ratio

c. Statutory liquidity Ratio

d. All of the above

| 9 | Observe the given image carefully and identify the depicted economic issue for Indian rupees. | 1 |

a. Currency Appreciation

b. Currency Depreciation

c. Currency Revaluation

d. Currency Exchange

| 10 | **Assertion (A): At break-even point consumption is equal to National Income.** | 1 |

Reason(R): APC falls continuously with the increase in income as the proportion spent on consumption goes on decreasing.

Alternatives:

a. Both assertion (A) and Reason (R) are true and Reason (R) is the correct explanation of Assertion (A).

b. Both assertion (A) and Reason (R) are true and Reason (R) is not the correct explanation of Assertion (A).

c. Assertion (A) is true but reason (R) is false.

d. Assertion (A) is false but reason (R) is true.

11	Keeping in the view the continuing hardship faced by the banks in terms of social distancing of staff and consequent strain on reporting requirements, the reserve bank of India has extended relaxation of the minimum daily maintenance of the CRR of 80% for up to 25th September 2020. Currently CRR is 3% and SLR is 18.5%.
	
	An announcement in the statement of development and regulatory policies of 27th March 2020, the minimum daily maintenance of CRR was reduced from 90% to the prescribed CRR of 80% effective from the fortnight beginning from 28th March 2020 till 26th June 2020, that was now extended up to 25th September 2020, said RBI.
	
	a. **What will be the value of money multiplier?**
	  i. 3.33
	  ii. 5.4
	  iii. 4.65
	  iv. None of these.
	
	b. **Decrease in CRR will lead to:**
	  i. A fall in aggregate demand
	  ii. A rise in aggregate demand
	  iii. No change in aggregate demand
	  iv. A fall in general price level
	
	c. **SLR implies:**
	  i. Certain percentage of total bank deposit to be kept with current account of RBI.
	  ii. The minimum percentage of deposits that a commercial bank has to maintain in the form of liquid cash, gold or other securities.
	  iii. Certain percentage of net demand deposit to be kept with the RBI.
	  iv. None of the above.
		3

12	Do you agree that an increase in Real GDP always leads to an increase in the welfare of the people? Explain. **OR** Give reason and state whether the following statement is true or false. a. Net investment is a stock variable. b. Real GDP reflects the level of economic growth but Nominal GDP does not. c. Remittances by the NRIs are included in the calculation of national income	3
13	Complete the following table:	4

Income	MPC	Savings	APC
100	____	____	0.60
200	____	90	____
____	____	125	0.50

14	Explain the concept of fiscal deficit in a government budget. Write the implications of fiscal deficit. OR Identify the following as Revenue receipt or capital receipt Give reason for your answer. a. Recovery of loan b. VAT c. Escheat d. Provident Funds	4
15	**Distinguish between the followings:** a. Autonomous items of BOP and accommodating items of BOP b. Fixed and Flexible Exchange Rate.	4
16	**Calculate National Income by (a) GDP at FC (b) Factor Income to Abroad.**	

S. No	Particulars	Amount (₹ cores)
1	Compensation of employees	800
2	Profits	200
3	Dividends	50
4	GNP at MP	1400
5	Rent	150
6	Interest	100
7	Gross Domestic Capital formation	300
8	Net Fixed Capital formation	200
9	Change in Stock	50
10	Factor income from abroad	60
11	Net Indirect Tax	120

OR

a. If the Nominal GDP is ₹600 and Price Index is 120, Calculate the Real GDP. (Base = 100)

b. Calculate National Income:

		S. No	Particulars	Amount (₹ cores)	3 + 3
		1	Compensation of employees	2000	
		2	Profits	800	
		3	Consumption of fixed capital	120	
		4	Rent	300	
		5	Interest	250	
		6	Mixed Income of self-employed	7000	
		7	Net current transfer to abroad	200	
		8	Net exports	-(100)	
		9	Net Factor income to abroad	60	
		10	Net Indirect Tax	1500	

17	Discuss the working of adjustment mechanism in the following situations(with diagram).
	
	  a. Aggregate demand is greater than aggregate supply.
	
	  b. Ex-ante investment is lesser than Ex-ante savings.
					3 + 3

MACRO ECONOMICS
ANSWERS OF PRACTICE PAPER – 1

ECONOMICS (030) ------------CLASS XII

Q.No	EXPECTED ANSWERS	MARKS
1	(a) Fiscal Policy	1
2	(c) A foreign investor buying shares in Indian markets.	1
3	(a) GDP = GNP	1
4	(d) D-(iv)	1
5	(c) Assertion (A) is true but reason (R) is false.	1
6	**(b)** Other than Interest payments.	1
7	(a) Statement 1 is true and statement 2 is false.	1
8	**(c)** Both (a) and (b) OR (d) All of the above	1
9	**(b)** Currency Depreciation	1
10	(b) Both assertion (A) and Reason (R) are true and Reason (R) is not the correct explanation of Assertion (A).	1
11	a. (iii) 4.65 b. (ii) A rise in aggregate demand c. (ii) The minimum percentage of deposits that a commercial bank has to maintain in the form of liquid cash, gold or other securities.	3
12	Normally it is considered that higher level of GDP is higher index of well-being. But this is not correct due to following limitation: i. **Unequal distribution of GDP**: An increase in the GDP or GNP may not increase economic welfare if distribution of income is unequal or wealth is concentrated in few hands or households. Unequal distribution will result in making rich richer and poor poorer. ii. **Production of harmful material**: If GDP increases because of production of war material, liquor, weapons, cigarette, tobacco (pan masala and gutka), etc. It will not increase economic welfare. iii. **Non**-Monetary Work: Many activities are not paid, it is done due to love and care which are not evaluated in terms of money. Services of housewife, Mother teaching her own children, barter exchange, social work etc. increases welfare (rejuvenate, energies and recreates, refresh, increase Knowledge) but not included in measurement of GDP. Thus GDP under estimates welfare by not including non-monetary exchange.	3 **Any three points.**

| 12 | iv. **High Population Growth Rate:** If population growth rate is higher than growth of GDP or GNP than welfare will decrease. | |
| | v. **Externalities:** Any benefit or harm done by an individual or firm for which they are neither paid nor penalised is known as externalities. It can be of two types: Positive and Negative. | |

OR

a. False, Net investment is a flow variable as it is measured over a period of time.

b. True, because nominal GDP is affected by change in price whereas real GDP is not affected by change in price.

c. False, Remittances by the NRIs are transfer payments so it is not included in calculation of National Income.

13	Income	MPC	Savings	APC	C = Y-S	4
	100	____	40	0.60	60	
	200	0.5	90	0.55	110	
	250	0.3	125	0.50	125	

| 14 | Fiscal Deficit = Total expenditure-total receipt (net of borrowing) | 4 |

Fiscal Deficit = Borrowing

Implication of Fiscal deficit:

1. Inflation:

2. Debt Trap:

3. Wasteful Expenditure:

4. Retards Future Growth:

5. Partial use of Borrowings

6. Foreign Dependence (Explain any Three points)

OR

a. Capital Receipt-Reduces Assets

b. Revenue Receipt-Neither creates liability nor reduces assets.

c. Revenue Receipt-Neither creates liability nor reduces assets.

d. Capital Receipt-Creates Liability

15	a.	**Autonomous Items of BOP:** Those International Economic Transactions done with the motive to earn money or profit is known as autonomous transactions. -Autonomous transactions can be of current account or capital account. **Accommodating items of BOP:** The transaction which is done to adjust the deficit or surplus of autonomous items transactions is known as accommodating Items.	2 + 2
	b.	**FIXED EXCHANGE RATE:** When exchange rate between two currencies is fixed by the two government. Demand and supply do not play any role in deciding exchange rate between two currencies. **FLEXIBLE EXCHANGE RATE:** When exchange rate between two currencies is determined by the demand and supply of foreign exchange Government do not play any role on determining exchange.	
16	a.	GDP at FC = NDP at FC + Depreciation [Dep = GDCF-(NFCF + Δ Stock) = 300-250] or, [Dep = 50] GDP at FC = (800 + 200 + 150 + 100) + 50 = ₹1300 crores	3 + 3v
	b.	NFIA = GNPmp-GDPmp = 1400- (1300 + 120) NFIA = -20 NFIA = FIFA-FITA = -20 = 60- FITA FITA = ₹80 crores **OR**	
	a.	**Nominal GDP** = Current Year Price X Current Year Production(Quantity) 600 = 120 X Current Year Quantity Current Year Quantity = $\dfrac{600}{120}$ = 5 **Real GDP** = Base Year Price X Current Year Production Real GDP = 100 X 5 **Real GDP = 500**	
	b.	National Income = COE + OS + MISE + NFIA = 2000 + {800 + 300 + 250} + 7000-60 = 2000 + 1350 + 7000-60 = **₹10,290 crores**	
17	a.	When Aggregate demand is greater than aggregate supply, the buyers are planning to buy more goods and services than what producers are planning to produce. This leads to fall in planned inventories below the desired level. The producers will get abnormal profit because of high demand and they will be induced to produce more. So they will employ more people, income, employment and output will increase. This process of increase will continue till Aggregate Demand is equal to Aggregate Supply.	3 + 3

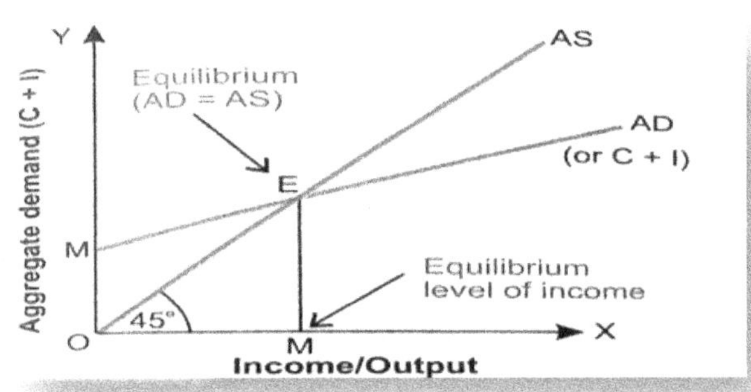

b. When Ex-ante investment are lesser than Ex-ante savings i.e., (I<S) means planned aggregate demand is less than planned aggregate supply. This will lead to rise in unplanned inventories above the desired level. Producers will incur loss as a result they will cut down production, remove people from job, income, employment output all will fall. This process of fall will continue till Ex-ante investment is equal to Ex-ante savings.

(Draw Diagram to explain)

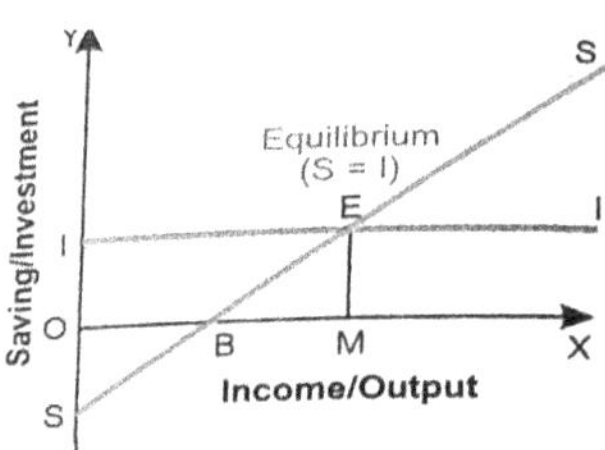

MACROECONOMICS

PRACTICE PAPER – 2

GENERAL INSTRUCTIONS:

1. Section A –Macro Economics

2. This paper contains 10 Multiple Choice Questions type questions of 1 mark each.

3. This paper contains 2 Short Answer Questions type questions of 3 marks each to be answered in 60 to 80 words.

4. This paper contains 3 Short Answer Questions type questions of 4 marks each to be answered in 80 to 100 words.

5. This paper contains 2 Long Answer Questions type questions of 6 marks each to be answered in 100 to 150 words.

Q.No	SECTION A – MACRO ECONOMICS	MARKS

1	Read the following statements carefully:
	
	Statement 1: The saving curve is an upward sloping straight line curve due to the direct relationship between income and savings and the assumption of constant Marginal Propensity to save.
	
	Statement 2: Saving is negative when consumption is more than income
	
	In the light of the given statements, choose the correct alternative from the following:
	
	    a. Statement 1 is true and statement 2 is false
	
	    b. Statement 1 is false and statement 2 is true
	
	    c. Both statements 1 and 2 are true
	
	    d. Both statements 1 and 2 are false
		1

2	If government increase tariff on import of goods, how it will impact the balance of payment of the country?
	
	    a. This will lead to inflow of foreign exchange.
	
	    b. This will lead to outflow of foreign exchange.
	
	    c. There will be no impact on the state of BOP.
	
	    d. None of these
		1

3	Money supply in India is:
	
	(Fill up the blank with correct alternative)
	
	    a. Currency with Public
	
	    b. Demand Deposits with banks
	
	    c. Demand deposits with banks + Currency with public
	
	    d. None of the above
		1

<table>
<tr><td>4</td><td>

Identify the correct pair from the following Column I and Column II:

Column I	Column II
A. Balance of Payment	i. It records inflow and outflow of goods and services.
B. Capital Account	ii. It records transaction related to income and expenditure.
C. Autonomous Transaction	iii. They are also known as above the line items.
D. Balance of Trade	iv. It records sum of exports and imports of visible items during a given year.

Alternatives:

    a. A-(i)

    b. B-(ii)

    c. C-(iii)

    d. D-(iv)

</td><td>1</td></tr>
<tr><td>5</td><td>

Read the following statements carefully:

Statement 1 – Balance in a bank account is a stock concept.

Statement 2 - Capital is a flow concept.

In the light of the given statements, choose the correct alternative from the following:

    a. Statement 1 is true and statement 2 is false

    b. Statement 1 is false and statement 2 is true

    c. Both statements 1 and 2 are true

    d. Both statements 1 and 2 are false

OR

Read the following statement -Assertion (A) and Reason (R). Choose one of the correct alternatives given below:

Assertion (A): Machine purchase is always a final good.

Reason (R): Final goods directly satisfy the needs of consumers or investment on fixed assets.

Alternatives:

    a. Both Assertion (A) and Reason (R) are true and Reason (R) is the correct explanation of Assertion (A).

    b. Both Assertion (A) and Reason (R) are true and Reason (R) is not the correct explanation of Assertion (A).

    c. Assertion (A) is true but Reason (R) is false.

    d. Assertion (A) is false but Reason (R) is true.

</td><td>1</td></tr>
</table>

6	If in an economy, the value of investment multiplier is 4 and Autonomous Consumption is ₹ 50 Crore, the relevant consumption function would be: a. C = 50 + 0.80 Y b. C = (-)50 + 0.25Y c. C = 50 + 0.75Y d. C = 50 + 0.20Y OR If increase in National Income is equal to increase in consumption, identity the value of Marginal Propensity to Save: a. Equal to unity b. Greater than one c. Less than one d. Equal to zero	1
7.	Money supply in India may increase if, _________________(Choose the correct alternative) 1. Reserve Bank of India(RBI) injects more money in circulation 2. The commercial banks expand their credit operation 3. Tax rates are increased by the Central Government. 4. Reserve Bank of India decreases the Bank Rate. **Alternatives:** a. 1,2 and 3 are correct b. 2,3 and 4 are correct c. 1,3 and 4 are correct d. 1,2 and 4 are correct	1
8	Giving reasons explain where charity to foreign countries is recorded in the Balance of Payment Accounts. **OR** The following information is given for an imaginary country: <table><tr><td>Current account</td><td>Amount in (₹'000 crores)</td></tr><tr><td>Visible imports</td><td>200</td></tr><tr><td>Invisible imports</td><td>150</td></tr><tr><td>Visible Exports</td><td>180</td></tr><tr><td>Invisible exports</td><td>160</td></tr><tr><td>Net current transfer payment</td><td>50</td></tr></table> Balance on current account will be _____________ of ₹ ______ thousand Crore. a. Deficit, 60 b. Surplus,60 c. Deficit, 40 d. Surplus, 40	1

| 9. | Assertion (A): Government Budget is the statement showing actual receipts and expenditure of the government in the coming financial year.

Reason (R): Government budget is presented by the finance minister of India.

Alternatives:

  a. Both Assertion (A) and Reason (R) are true and Reason (R) is the correct explanation of Assertion (A).

  b. Both Assertion (A) and Reason (R) are true and Reason (R) is not the correct explanation of Assertion (A).

  c. Assertion (A) is true but Reason (R) is false.

  d. Assertion (A) is false but Reason (R) is true. | 1 |
| 10. | **Read the following statement -Assertion (A) and Reason (R). Choose one of the correct alternatives given below:**

Assertion (A): Public goods and services are non- excludable and non- rivalrous.

Reason (R): Public goods and services are provided through market mechanism.

Alternatives:

  a. Both Assertion (A) and Reason (R) are true and Reason (R) is the correct explanation of Assertion (A).

  b. Both Assertion (A) and Reason (R) are true and Reason (R) is not the correct explanation of Assertion (A).

  c. Assertion (A) is true but Reason (R) is false.

  d. Assertion (A) is false but Reason (R) is true. | 1 |

11	**Giving reason explain how are the following treated estimation of National Income?**
	
	  a. Payment of interest by an individual to a bank on a loan to buy a car.
	
	  b. Expenditure on purchase of machine installed in a factory.
	
	OR
	
	Calculate value of output from the following data:
	
			Particulars	₹ in lakhs

i	Net Value added at factor cost	100
ii	Intermediate Consumption	75
iii	Excise Duty	20
iv	Subsidy	5
v	Depreciation	10		3
12	Distinguish between Balance of trade and in Balance of Payments Accounts. **OR** What is foreign exchange rate? What is the relationship between demand for foreign exchange and rate of foreign exchange?	3

13	If an economy plans to increase its income by ₹ 4,000 crores and the Marginal Propensity to Consume is 75%. Estimate the increase in investment required to achieve the targeted increase in income.	4
14	What is fiscal deficit? Explain implications of fiscal deficit.	4
15	'Reserve Ratio and Credit Creation are inversely related.' Do you agree with the given statement? Justify your answer with a suitable numerical example.	4

OR

Read the following news report and answer the following questions on the basis of the same.

The RBI announced a host of measures today aimed at increasing liquidity in the liquidity in the economy. As a consequence, individuals may see bank reducing their margins on interest rates charged on loans. However, fixed income earner should be aware of these steps might exert downward pressure on interest rate offered to the fixed deposits by banks, as per some experts. However, the impact of these announcements will not be immediate and may be marginal.

   a. Reduction in the interest rates charged on loans will lead to ____________(decrease/ increase/no change) in the overall demand in the economy.

   b. Deceasing interest rate on fixed deposits by banks will(increase/decrease) the purchasing power of the people in general.

   c. Increasing liquidity in the economy is generally done when there is:

      i. Excess aggregate demand ii) Deficient aggregate demand

      ii. Excess aggregate supply iv) neither(i) nor (ii)

   d. Which of the qualitative measures taken by the Central Banks to ease liquidity in the market?

      i. Increase Margin Requirement

      ii. Decrease Margin Requirement

      iii. Increase in Repo Rate

      iv. Decrease in Repo Rate

| 16 | Given the following data, find the missing value of 'Private Final Consumption Expenditure' and 'Operating Surplus'. | 6 |

S. No	Particulars	Amount (in ₹ cores)
1	National Income	50,000
2	Gross Domestic Capital Formation	17,000
3	Government Final Consumption Expenditure	12,500
4	Mixed Income of self-employed	13,000
5	Net factor Income from Abroad	500
6	Net Indirect Tax	1,000
7	Profits	1,000
8	Wages and Salaries	20,000
9	Net exports	2,000
10	Private Final Consumption Expenditure	?
11	Consumption of Fixed Capital	700
12	Operating Surplus	?

| 17 | Discuss the working of adjustment mechanism in the following situations with diagram: | 6 |

a. Aggregate Demand is greater than Aggregate Supply.

b. Ex-Ante Investment is lesser than Ex-Ante Savings.

OR

Given consumption function is $C = 80 + 0.75\ Y$ (C = consumption function, Y = National Income) and investment expenditure is ₹ 200.

a. What will be equilibrium level of income.

b. What will be new equilibrium level of income if investment increases by ₹25 crores?

PRACTICE PAPER – 2

ANSWERS OF PRACTICE PAPER – 2

Q.No	Expected Answers	Marks
1	c) Both statements 1 and 2 are true	1
2	b) This will lead to outflow of foreign exchange.	1
3	c) Demand deposits with banks + Currency with public	1
4	c) C-(iii)	1
5	a) Statement 1 is true and statement 2 is false. **OR** d) Assertion (A) is false but Reason (R) is true.	1
6	c) C = 50 + 0.75Y **OR** d) Equal to zero	1
7	d) 1,2 and 4 are correct.	1
8	Charity to foreign countries is recorded in the debit side of current account of Balance of Payment as it is transfer payment. Any transaction which is not affecting assets or liabilities will be recorded in the current account. It is outflow so it will be recorded in the debit side. **OR** a) Deficit, 60	1
9	d) Assertion (A) is false but Reason (R) is true.	1
10	c) Assertion (A) is true but Reason (R) is false..	1
11	a. No, it will not be included in estimation of National Income because loan is taken for consumption purpose not for production purpose. b. Yes, it will be included in estimation of National Income because it is investment which will be used for production. **OR** Value of Output = NVAfc + Dep + NIT + IC = 100 + 10 + 20-5 + 75 = ₹ 200 Lakhs	3

12	BALANCE OF TRADE	BALANCE OF PAYMENT	3
	It records transactions of goods only.	It records transactions relating to both goods and services.	
	It may be favourable, unfavourable or in balance.	It always remains in Balance.	
	It does not record transactions of capital nature.	It records transactions of current and capital nature both.	
	It is a narrow concept as it is a part of BOP.	It is a broad concept as it includes Balance of Trade, Balance of Services and Unilateral Transfers.	
	Deficit in BOT can be met by BOP	Deficit in BOP cannot be met through BOT.	
	It is not true indicator of Economic performance of a country.	It is true indicator of Economic performance of a country.	

13	$K = 1/1\text{-}MPC$, $K = 4$, $K = \Delta Y/\Delta I$, $\Delta I = 4000/4 = 1000$, $\Delta I = ₹1000$	4

14	Fiscal deficit is excess of all expenditure over revenue receipt and non-debt capital receipt.	4

Implications:

1. Inflationary Pressure
2. Debt Trap
3. Wasteful Expenditure
4. Partial use

(Explain any three points)

15	Credit creation function	4

Yes, there exists an inverse relation between Reserve Ratio and Credit Creation in the economy.

We know that: Money Multiplier = 1/reserve ratio

Credit Creation = Initial Deposit x 1/Money Multiplier

Money Multiplier = Initial Deposit x 1/RR

OR

i. increase

ii. increase

iii. Deficient aggregate demand

iv. Decrease in Margin Requirement

16	**Operating Surplus** = 50,000-(20,000 + 13,000 + 500) = ₹ 16,500 crores **Private Final Consumption Expenditure** = 50,000-(17,000 + 12,500 + 2,000 + 500) + 700 + 1,000 = ₹19,700 Crores	$\frac{1}{2}$ $+1\frac{1}{2}$ $+\frac{1}{2}$ and $\frac{1}{2}$ $+1\frac{1}{2}$ $+\frac{1}{2}$
17	a) When AD>AS, buyers are demanding more goods and services then what the producers planned to produce. It will lead to decrease in planned inventories. Producers will be induced to produce more goods and services which will increase employment, income and output(AS). This process will continue till AD becomes equal to AS. b) When Ex-Ante Investment is less than Ex-Ante Savings(I<S), buyers are planning to buy less than what the producers are intended to produce. It will lead to rise in unplanned inventories, producers will incur lose so they will cut down production. Income, employment, output will fall. This process will continue till Saving becomes equal to Investment. OR a. $Y = 80 + 0.75Y + 200$ $Y = \dfrac{280}{0.25}$ $Y = ₹1120$ b. $Y = 80 + 0.75Y + 225$ $Y = \dfrac{305}{0.25}$ $Y = ₹1220$	3 + 3

MACROECONOMICS

PRACTICE PAPER – 3

GENERAL INSTRUCTIONS:

1. This paper contains 10 Multiple Choice Questions type questions of 1 mark each.

2. This paper contains 2 Short Answer Questions type questions of 3 marks each to be answered in 60 to 80 words.

3. This paper contains 3 Short Answer Questions type questions of 4 marks each to be answered in 80 to 100 words.

4. This paper contains 2 Long Answer Questions type questions of 6 marks each to be answered in 100 to 150 words.

Q.No	SECTION A – MACRO ECONOMICS	MARKS

1	Read the following statements carefully:
	
	Statement 1: The value of MPS lies between 0 to 1.
	
	Statement 2: Consumption curve starts from the origin.
	
	In the light of the given statements, choose the correct alternative from the following:
	
	    a. Statement 1 is true and statement 2 is false
	    b. Statement 1 is false and statement 2 is true
	    c. Both statements 1 and 2 are true
	    d. Both statements 1 and 2 are false
		1

2	Foreign Exchange Transactions which depends other foreign exchange transactions are called:
	
	    a. Current account transaction.
	    b. Capital account transaction.
	    c. Autonomous Transactions
	    d. Accommodating Transactions.
		1

3	The part of LRR which kept by the banks with themselves is known as:
	
	(Fill up the blank with correct alternative)
	
	    a. CRR
	    b. Bank Rate
	    c. SLR
	    d. Repo rate
		1

| 4 | Identify the correct pair from the following Column I and Column II: | 1 |

Column I	Column II
A. Depreciation	i. Decrease in the currency value due to market forces.
B. Appreciation	ii. Increase in currency value by the government.
C. Unilateral Transfer	iii. Capital Account
D. Borrowing and lending	iv. Current Account

Alternatives:

a. A-(i)

b. B-(ii)

c. C-(iii)

d. D-(iv)

| 5 | Read the following statement -Assertion (A) and Reason (R). Choose one of the correct alternatives given below: | 1 |

Assertion (A): Wealth is stock concept.

Reason (R): Wealth is measured over a period of time.

Alternatives:

a. Both Assertion (A) and Reason (R) are true and Reason (R) is the correct explanation of Assertion (A).

b. Both Assertion (A) and Reason (R) are true and Reason (R) is not the correct explanation of Assertion (A).

c. Assertion (A) is true but Reason (R) is false.

d. Assertion (A) is false but Reason (R) is true.

| 6 | If increase in National Income is equal to increase in consumption, identity the value of Marginal Propensity to Consume: | 1 |

a. Equal to one   b. Greater than one

c. Less than one   d. Equal to zero

| 7. | The central bank can increase credit facility: | 1 |

a. Increasing repo rate

b. Increasing reverse repo rate

c. Buying Government securities

d. Selling Government securities.

| 8 | Giving reasons explain where remittance foreign countries is recorded in the Balance of Payment Accounts. | 1 |

| 9. | Assertion (A): Dividend received on investment is revenue receipt of the Government. | 1 |
| | Reason (R): Revenue receipts neither reduce liabilities nor create assets. | |

Alternatives:

   a. Both Assertion (A) and Reason (R) are true and Reason (R) is the correct explanation of Assertion (A).

   b. Both Assertion (A) and Reason (R) are true and Reason (R) is not the correct explanation of Assertion (A).

   c. Assertion (A) is true but Reason (R) is false.

   d. Assertion (A) is false but Reason (R) is true.

---

10. Read the following statement -Assertion (A) and Reason (R). Choose one of the correct alternatives given below: **[1]**

Assertion (A): Stationary purchased by a school is an intermediate good.

Reason (R): Intermediate goods once used in production lose their utility.

Alternatives:

   a. Both Assertion (A) and Reason (R) are true and Reason (R) is the correct explanation of Assertion (A).

   b. Both Assertion (A) and Reason (R) are true and Reason (R) is not the correct explanation of Assertion (A).

   c. Assertion (A) is true but Reason (R) is false.

   d. Assertion (A) is false but Reason (R) is true.

---

11 Give reason and explain which among the following are capital goods and which are consumer goods. **[3]**

   a. A car used in Taxi.

   b. Refrigerator in a hotel.

   c. Air conditioner in a house.

OR

   1. **Calculate:** Net Value Added at factor cost

Items	₹ in lakhs
Purchase of machinery	100
Sales	200
Intermediate costs	90
Indirect taxes	12
Change in Stock	10
Excise Duty	6
Stock of raw material	5

12	Distinguish between Autonomous items and accommodating items of balance Payments Accounts. **OR** Differentiate between floating and fixed exchange rate.	3

13	An increase of ₹250 crores in investment in an economy, resulted in total increase in income of ₹1000 crore. Calculate the following:
	
	   a. Value of investment multiplier
	
	   b. Change in savings
	
	   c. Change in consumption expenditure
	
	   d. Marginal propensity to consume
		4

14	Explain how the Government can use the budgetary policy in reducing inequalities in incomes.	4

15	Answer the following questions on the basis of the following information:
	
	The Commercial Banks are considered as the leading financial intermediaries in our country as these banks channelize huge amount of savings into investment. In the financial framework of India these banks occupy the second position after Reserve bank of India. RBI was nationalised in 1949 while 14 major commercial banks were nationalised in 1969 in first phase and 6 banks in the second phase in 1980. RBI produces money while commercial banks increase the money supply by creating credit. Credit creation is determined by two factors namely primary deposits and Legal Reserve Ratio (LRR) i.e., minimum ratio of deposits which is legally compulsory for the commercial banks to keep as cash in liquid form. Broadly when a bank receives cash deposits from the public, it keeps a fraction of deposits as cash reserve (LRR) and uses the remaining amount for giving loans. In the process of lending money, banks are able to create credit through secondary deposits many times more than initial deposits (primary deposits). Money multiplier = 1/LRR, Total deposit creation = Initial deposit × 1/LRR.
	
	   i. According to the given information, _________ is at the first place in the financial framework of the country.
	
	   ii. Choose the correct
	
	   Statement 1: The credit creation process of commercial banks is largely determined by the Primary deposits and Legal Reserve Ratio.
	
	   Statement 2: Money multiplier is directly proportional to Legal Reserve Ratio (LRR).
	
	   Alternatives:
	
	   (a) Both the statements are true.
	
	   (b) Both the statements are false.
	
	   (c) Statement 1 is true and Statement 2 is false
	
	   (d) Statement 2 is true and Statement 1 is false.
		4

	iii.	In the light of the given text and common knowledge, identify the incorrect statement.	
		a. Savings are converted into investment with the help of commercial banks.	
		b. RBI is the apex financial authority while commercial banks intermediaries are financial.	
		c. RBI was nationalized in 1939 while commercial banks were nationalized in 1969.	
		d. Credit creation is by lending initial deposits of the customers in the form of loans.	

iii. In the light of the given text and common knowledge, identify the incorrect statement.

    a. Savings are converted into investment with the help of commercial banks.

    b. RBI is the apex financial authority while commercial banks intermediaries are financial.

    c. RBI was nationalized in 1939 while commercial banks were nationalized in 1969.

    d. Credit creation is by lending initial deposits of the customers in the form of loans.

iv. Number of commercial banks that were nationalized under first phase_____ are in second phase_____ are:

    a. 14,6

    b. 12,6

    c. 14,8

    d. 6,12

16. Calculate NNP_{fc} with Income and Expenditure method: **6**

ComponentsC	₹ in Crores
Interest	150
Rent	250
Government Final Consumption Expenditure	600
Private Final Consumption Expenditure	1200
Profits	640
Compensation of employees	1000
Net Factor Income to Abroad	30
Net Indirect Taxes	60
Net Exports	(-)40
Consumption of Fixed	50
Net Domestic Capital Formation	340

17. (a) Derive Consumption Function from Saving Function.   **6**

(b) Distinguish between induced investment and autonomous investment.

OR

Explain underemployment equilibrium with diagram and remedies to control it.

ANSWERS OF PRACTICE PAPER – 3

Q.No	Expected Answers	Marks
1	(a) Statement 1 is true and statement 2 is false.	1
2	(d) Accommodating Transactions	1
3	(c) SLR	1
4	(a) A-(i)	1
5	(c) Assertion (A) is true but Reason (R) is false.	1
6	(a) Equal to one	1
7	(c) Buying Government securities	1
8	Remittances from foreign countries are recorded in the credit side of current account under transfer receipt. As it is transfer income.	1
9	(c) Assertion (A) is true but Reason (R) is false.	1
10	a) Both Assertion (A) and Reason (R) are true and Reason (R) is the correct explanation of Assertion (A).	1
11	a. A car used in taxi is a capital good because it is investment to generate service and earn income. b. Refrigerator in a hotel is a capital good because it is investment to generate service over a period of time. c. Air condition in a house is a consumer good as it is used to satisfy human wants. **OR** **NVAfc** = Sales + Change in stock –IC –Dep –NIT = 200 + 10 -90-(12-0) NVAfc = 210-102 **NVAfc = ₹ 108 lakhs**	3

| 12 | **Difference Between Autonomous Items and Accommodating Items of BOP** | | 3 |

Autonomous Items of BOP	Accommodating Items of BOP
Those International Economic Transactions done with the motive to earn money or profit is known as autonomous transactions.	The transaction which is done to adjust the deficit or surplus of autonomous items transactions is known as accommodating Items.
Autonomous item transactions can cause deficit or surplus in BOP account.	Accommodating item transactions are done to make balance in BOP account.
Autonomous transactions can be of current account or capital account.	Accommodating transactions are only from capital account.
Autonomous items are called Above the line items	Accommodating items are called below the line items.

OR

FIXED EXCHANGE RATE	FLEXIBLE EXCHANGE RATE
When exchange rate between two currency is fixed by the two government.	When exchange rate between two currency is determined by the demand and supply of foreign exchange.
Demand and supply do not play any role in deciding exchange rate between two currency.	Government do not play any role on determining exchange rate.
Central bank of the country has to maintain foreign exchange reserve.	Central bank of the country need not maintain foreign exchange reserve.
Imbalance in BOP is adjusted by central bank foreign exchange reserve of the country.	Imbalance in BOP is automatically adjusted by demand and supply of foreign exchange.

| 13 | | 4 |

(a) $K = \dfrac{\ddot{A}Y}{\ddot{A}I} = \dfrac{1000}{250} = 4$

(b) $\Delta S = MPS \, X \, \Delta Y = 0.25 \, X 1000 = ₹ \, 250$

(c) $\Delta C = MPC \, X \, \Delta Y = 0.75 \, x \, 1000 = ₹750$

(d) MPC = 1-MPS = 1-0.25 = 0.75

| 14 | The government budget is helpful in equitable distribution of income. | 4 |

Taxes should be made progressive and stern steps should be taken to check tax evasion.

Tax base should be broadened and more services should be incorporated in the tax instead of indirect taxes. This will help in reducing disposable income of rich.

- Expenditure on social sector such as education, health care and housing for the poor should be raised.

- Expenditure on poverty alleviation and employment generation schemes so as to bring more people above the poverty line.

- Subsidies to small scale industries, which adopt labour intensive techniques should be provided so that a large number of employment opportunities are generated.

- It will lead to an increase in disposable income of the poor.

15	i. (b) Reserve Bank of India	4
	ii. (c) Statement 1 is true and statement 2 is false.	
	iii. (c) RBI was nationalised in 1939 while commercial banks were nationalised in 1969.	
	iv. (a) 14, 6	

16	*Income Method: NNPfc = COE + OS + MISE + NFIA*	6
	$= 1000 + (150 + 250 + 640) + (-)\ 30$	
	$= ₹\ 2010\ Crores$	
	Expenditure Method: NDPmp = C + G + NDCF + (X-M)	
	$NDPmp = 1200 + 600 + 340 + (-)\ 40$	
	$NDP_{mp} = 2100$	
	$NNP_{fc} = NDPmp + NFIA - NIT = 2100 - 30 - 60$	
	$NNP_{fc} = ₹\ 2010\ Crores$	

(a) Derivation of Consumption Function from Saving Function

Straight line consumption curve can be derived from saving curve. Consumption and saving curve are complementary curves. Income = consumption + savings.

Saving curve SS' start from a point from negative side below origin, it shows at 0 level of income or low level of income there is some dissaving.

Point B' is on X-axis showing zero savings it is break-even point.

Saving curve is upward sloping because as income increases saving also increases.

17	(b)		3 + 3

Induced Investment	Autonomous Investment
Investment which is done with the motive to earn profit.	Investment which is done with the motive of social welfare.
Induced investment is income elastic.	Autonomous investment is income inelastic.
Induced Investment is directly related to the level of income.	Autonomous investment is unrelated to the level of income.
Induced investment curve is positively sloped towards right.	Autonomous investment curve is parallel to X-axis.
Induced investment is normally done by private entrepreneurs.	Autonomous investment is normally done by the government.

OR

When aggregate demand is less than aggregate supply at full employment, the demand is said to be deficient demand and the gap is called deflationary gap.

This situation is caused not by low level of output but by lack demand.

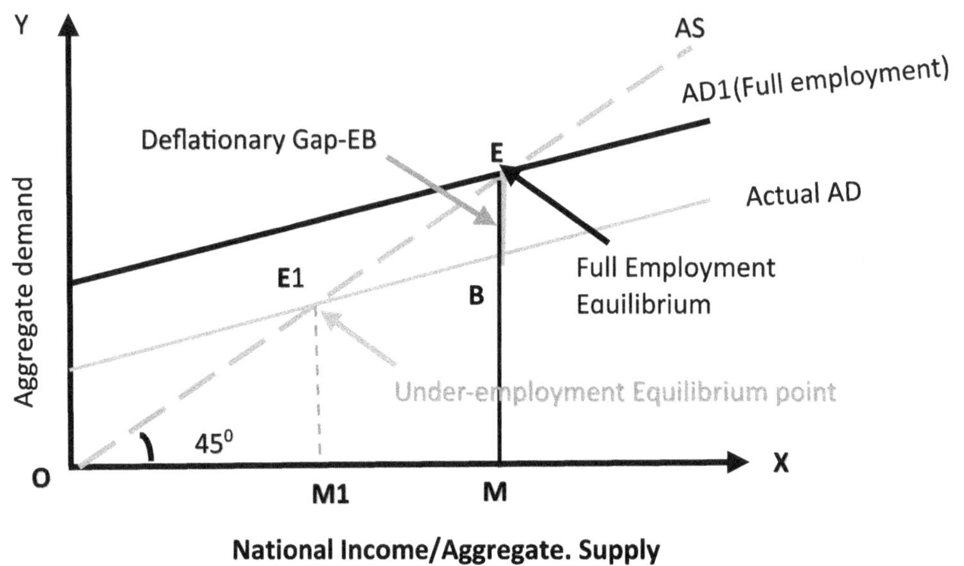

This gap between actual aggregate Demand and full employment aggregate demand is Known as deficient Demand and the gap is known as deflationary gap. This situation is known as deficient Demand and deflationary gap or underemployment equilibrium.

In the figure point E shows full employment equilibrium. E_1 shows under employment equilibrium.

AD_1 is actual aggregate Demand which is less than full employment demand. At E_1 actual AD intersect with AS, so it is point of underemployment equilibrium, OM_1 is underemployment equilibrium. OM is full employment equilibrium whereas EB shows amount of deficient Demand or Deflationary Gap.

To reach full employment, additional investment equal to EB is required.

Measures to control the situation of underemployment equilibrium

Fiscal policy: Revenue and Expenditure policy of the government is known as Fiscal Policy.

    a. Public Expenditure (Increase): Government should make huge investment in public work like construction of roads, railways, bridges, buildings canals, and provide free health and education facilities. It will pump money in the economy. People will get income and they will increase their demand. Keynes advocates deficit Budget to increase aggregate Demand.

    b. Revenue Policy (Reduce): Taxes on personal income and Corporate income should be reduced to encourage consumption and investment as when more money is left with people demand and investment will increase leading to increase in Aggregate Demand.

Monetary Measures: It is the policy of Central Bank of a country to control credit and money supply.

    1. Repo Rate (Reduce): Repo rate is the rate of interest at which central bank lends to commercial bank for short period. At the time of deficient demand, the central bank reduces lending rate (Bank rate and repo rate) to the commercial banks. Commercial bank reduces rate of interest which make credit cheap and people can take loan at low interest and investment.

    2. Open Market Operation (Buy Security): The Central bank should buy government bonds and security from commercial banks by paying them cash to increase their cash stock and lending capacity. The commercial banks lend money at low interest rate which increases borrowing capacity of the people. This will help to increase aggregate demand and reduce deflation.

www.ingramcontent.com/pod-product-compliance
Lightning Source LLC
Chambersburg PA
CBHW040140110726
48005CB00018B/2595